HER HONOR

HER HONOR

My Life on the Bench . . .
What Works, What's Broken,
and How to Change It

LaDORIS HAZZARD CORDELL

CELADON
BOOKS
—
NEW YORK

Library of Congress Cataloging-in-Publication Data

Names: Cordell, LaDoris H., author.
Title: Her honor : my life on the bench . . . what works, what's broken, and how to change it / LaDoris Hazzard Cordell.
Description: First edition. | New York, NY : Celadon Books, 2021. | Includes index.
Identifiers: LCCN 2021016082 | ISBN 9781250269607 (hardcover) | ISBN 9781250269584 (ebook)
Subjects: LCSH: Criminal justice, Administration of—United States. | Cordell, LaDoris H. | Judges—California—Biography.
Classification: LCC KF9223 .C675 2021 | DDC 347.794/0234 [B]—dc23
LC record available at https://lccn.loc.gov/2021016082

First Edition: 2021

10 9 8 7 6 5 4 3 2 1

In loving memory of my parents

When my brothers try to draw a circle to exclude me, I shall draw a larger circle to include them. Where they speak out for the privileges of a puny group, I shall shout for the rights of all mankind.

—Pauli Murray, "An American Credo"

Contents

Juries and Judges

Hot-Button Issues

Conclusion

A Note on Sources

To ensure that the appendices ("Links to Judicial Discipline Information by State" and "Juror Compensation by State") and endnotes for *Her Honor* are both link enabled and searchable, they have been published online rather than in the pages of this book. You can find them, as well as the legal cartoons mentioned in the "Bad Judges" chapter, at judgecordell .com/her-honor/.

Introduction

Bitten by the Judge Bug

We'll probably never save our souls—but hell,
at least we'll get our hair sorted.

—SIDDHARTH DHANVANT SHANGHVI, *THE LAST SONG OF DUSK*

t was after I received a phone call from a stranger in the summer of 1980 that I began to think about becoming a judge. I was working at Stanford Law School as an assistant dean and practicing law, part-time, in my private law practice in East Palo Alto. Judging was nowhere on my radar and for good reason. The only judges that I had ever appeared before were White males—no women, no people of color. There was certainly not today's plethora of Black judges, so many of whom now populate court shows on television. Nothing of the sort existed back then, so my image of a judge excluded anyone who looked like me.

The caller introduced himself as municipal court judge Mark Thomas. He asked if I would consider volunteering as a judge pro tem, meaning presiding as a judge for a day in small-claims court where people sue each other for monetary damages up to $5,000. (Today, the monetary limit has been raised to $10,000. Corporations, however, are limited to $5,000.) The most wonderful feature about small-claims trials is that no lawyers are allowed—no lawyers, no jury, just the litigants going at one another, leaving it to a judge to sort it all out. I later learned that Judge Thomas's call to me was motivated by his desire to bring at least a hint of diversity to a bench with no African Americans and only a handful of women. I was flattered and happily accepted his invitation. I didn't think much more about it until several weeks later when I received my assignment to preside over a small-claims case. One case and no lawyers—how hard could it be? It was a Friday afternoon when I eagerly drove to the Sunnyvale courthouse, a few miles to the south of Stanford.

Upon my arrival, I went to the clerk's office, where a friendly female staffer handed me a black robe and the court file in a thin manila folder. Then she directed me to a small courtroom. My private law practice had taken me into lots of courtrooms—some large, some small, some cavernous; I knew where everyone was supposed to sit, and I knew that the judge's seat was at the center and on high. I mean, who of us hasn't seen a courtroom in a movie or on television?

I stood in the hallway and took a quick peek into the courtroom. Upon seeing the judge's bench, I was a little excited and a little scared. With no judicial experience or training, the closest I'd come to the judge world was in courtrooms, appearing in front of judges when litigating my own cases. Since my college major had been drama and speech, I went into acting mode, telling myself: that's your seat; you're the judge; you can do this. I slipped on the robe, closed it with the snaps that ran down the front, clutched the file folder, straightened my posture, assumed an actor's air of confidence, and stepped into the courtroom, determined to sit down and get through the hearing without looking like a complete fraud.

When I walked in and took my seat at the bench, two Black women in their late twenties were sitting at the pair of counsel tables facing the bench. I looked around and saw that there was no one else in the courtroom but us—three Black women.

Sunnyvale is a city in Santa Clara County—the sixth-largest of California's fifty-eight counties. During the time that I was on the bench, Black folks constituted only about 5 percent of the county's population, so the odds of both litigants and the judge being Black were slim to none. The women appeared as stunned as I. I'm sure that we were all thinking, *Can you believe this?* We cautiously nodded at one another.

I had observed enough judges to have some notion of what to say; the judicial script is not terribly difficult to recite: "All rise. Please stand and be sworn in. Be seated. State your names." We've all heard these phrases spoken by the bailiff followed by the courtroom clerk who administers the oath to witnesses. But none of that happened in this case. There was no bailiff or clerk, and there were no spectators. I understood why. This was, after all, a run-of-the-mill small-claims case with no jury and no witnesses other than the two litigants.

After telling the women to stand and raise their right hands, I asked, "Do you solemnly swear to tell the truth, the whole truth, and nothing but the truth?" They answered yes. So far, so good. I told them that they could sit, and then I opened the file folder. Inside was just one thin piece of paper with the names of the two women, a case number, and nothing else. I panicked. Now what do I do? I asked the plaintiff, the woman who had filed the complaint, what the case was about.

"Well, Your Honor, I'm a hairdresser and I'm really good at what I do. I braided her hair"—she nodded at the other woman—"and she won't pay me. That's not right. I spent hours doing her hair. I can't do this work for free, you know." I couldn't believe it. My first case as a judge, albeit a pro tem judge, not only had two Black women as plaintiff and defendant, but was also about hair, *our* hair, a subject I knew from the roots on up.

Hair for Black folks, especially Black women, is as important as the air we breathe. It is critical to our very existence. It is what we talk about endlessly and on which we spend inordinate amounts of money. When my sisters and I were in elementary school, we wore two long braids, one on either side of the parts down the center of our heads. There was an unspoken competition among us for who had the longest braids. (I won!) My hair was the thickest and kinkiest of the three of us. My siblings' hair was of a finer texture, something of which I was quietly jealous. Once a week my mother washed our hair at the kitchen sink and then straightened it with a hot comb. God help us if we fidgeted when she wielded that hot comb.

My shoulders relaxed. I turned to the defendant and asked, "Why didn't you pay her?" "Judge, I did not get what I asked for." She removed a colorful scarf from her head and continued, "These cornrows, as you can see, are a mess. I can't be wearing my hair like this. She rushed, and it seemed like she was in a hurry to go somewhere. Anyway, I'm not going to pay for a bad hair job." *Got it. The issue is the quality of the cornrows that she braided. If they were done well, the plaintiff wins. If they weren't, verdict for the defendant.* So, I needed to examine the evidence; I needed to see her hair up close.

When we were kids, my sisters and I lined up awaiting our turns to get our hair braided before going off to school. At the appointed hour, we would sit down in front of our mother, wedged securely between her knees. After rubbing some oil (usually Alberto VO5) on our hair and scalps, she'd brush our hair and then comb through the tangles (the worst part) to get it as straight as possible. Next, she'd grab a section of our hair and twist it hard—tear-generating hard—to fit into tiny barrettes. Our mother had the grip from hell. And she could braid at the speed of light. Next, she tied freshly washed and ironed ribbons, with colors matching our outfits, on the ends of our braids. When she finished, our hair was pulled so tight that we looked as if we had undergone face-lifts. My mother was determined that her daughters would always look good. We did.

I asked the defendant to approach the bench. She walked up, put her hands on the bench, and leaned forward, bending her head in my direction. I leaned over and peered at her hair. Now I needed to touch the evidence to get a better view.

"Is it okay if I touch your hair?"

"Yes. Go ahead."

I gently parted her hair with my fingers and observed that the roots of her hair were matted and not pulled up tightly and cleanly into the cornrows, as they should have been. I had seen enough and told her: "You can return to your seat at the table." I turned back to the plaintiff. "The braiding looks a little sloppy. They aren't tight and neat. Do you have anything to say about that?"

"Your Honor, I have a reputation as an excellent hairstylist. I can give you the names of some of my customers; you can ask them. I would have brought them to court as my witnesses if I had known that she was going to attack my reputation. I really don't appreciate that. There is nothing wrong with my work. What you're seeing, Judge, is a little wear and tear. I mean, I did her hair a few weeks ago." *Good point.*

The defendant retorted, "Your Honor, cornrows are supposed to last a couple of months, at least. What's this 'wear and tear' crap? That's ridiculous. The only reason that I went to her was because the better hairdressers were booked up. I can't go to work looking like this. I've had to wear a scarf ever since she did my hair." *Another good point.*

A few years later, my own hair catastrophe would force me to delay the start of the morning's court proceedings. Upon my arrival at work, Benita, my bailiff (a quietly authoritative and lovely Black woman who would work with me for nineteen years), pulled me aside to let me know that I should seriously consider not going into the courtroom with my hair looking the way it did. This was in the mid-1980s, when I was wearing my hair long and straightened. Turns out that the weather that morning was very foggy and damp. From the time that I exited my car in the courthouse parking lot and walked the short distance into the courthouse, the dampness in the air had caused my long and straightened locks to kink up.

Benita was right. I was a mess. So, I called Rabiah, the one person to whom I had ever entrusted my locks (to this very day). The woman had put up with all manner of my hair craziness over the years. I told her of the emergency, and she agreed to meet me at her nearby salon. I was out the door! Rabiah quickly administered her hot-comb and curling-iron magic on my locks, and voila!—no more kink. I drove back to the court and, this time, before exiting my car, I covered my hair with a scarf to keep the dreaded morning moisture at bay. Court started a little late that morning.

It was time for me to rule. I had heard enough. The legal principle quantum meruit popped into my head. A basic tenet of contract law, it means "as much as it deserves, as much as she has earned." In other words, if you provide a service to someone, then you must be paid the reasonable value of the service. So, I ordered that the defendant, the braidee, had to pay the plaintiff, the braider, but an amount less than what they had originally agreed upon; the hairdresser should have done a better job pulling up those roots into the cornrows. After I ruled, I held my breath, fearing their reaction. Would they be outraged? Would they storm out of the courtroom? None of that happened. The women looked at each other, nodded, said, "Thank you, Your Honor," and off they went.

I sat in the empty courtroom and thought about what had just happened and how remarkable it was that I had been assigned this particular case. Maybe this was some sort of a sign. I am not a religious person, but three Black women in a Sunnyvale courtroom litigating over hair was remarkable. If this case had been assigned to one of the judges on the court, it would inevitably have landed in the courtroom of a White male clueless about roots, braids, cornrows, and matted hair. Would such a judge have performed the scalp examination that was critical to the fact-finding process? No way.

I reluctantly handed in the robe. As I drove home from the Sunnyvale courthouse on that summer day in 1980, I couldn't stop smiling. I had pulled it off. I had been a judge for a day. I liked the decision-making process. I liked telling people what to do. I felt comfortable. I liked being in charge. I liked the control. Sitting on high, listening to the litigants tell me their stories, conducting the hair inspection—I loved all of it. The robe fit, and I wanted more. I wanted one of my own.

Three months later, armed with my hairy small-claims court experience, I applied to Governor Jerry Brown for a position on the municipal court. Judges in California can either be appointed by the governor or elected to a seat on the bench when the governor is, by law, not permitted to fill it. At the time, the only prerequisite was that one must have been an attorney for a minimum of five years. (In the mid-1990s, municipal courts and superior courts merged, so that now California has just one trial court—the superior court. Today, one must practice law for a minimum of ten years to be eligible to serve on the superior court.) Since judicial campaigns are expensive, costing hundreds of thousands, if not millions, of dollars (more on this later), it's far easier to go the gubernatorial appointment route, which is all about politics—*who* you know and who you can enlist to convince the governor to pick you. In 1980, I did not have political connections; what I did have was Stanford Law School on my résumé and faculty members who had access to the governor. I told them that I had applied for a judgeship and they stepped up for me. The appointment process required that I interview with a variety of local lawyers' groups, community organizations, and state bar committees. While my law school job as an administrator kept me busy, it did little to diminish my desire to wear the black robe.

I continued to recruit students of color to apply to Stanford, and I traveled around the country to encourage those students who had the good fortune to be admitted to the law school to enroll. My now part-time law practice kept me in the courtroom, where I represented defendants charged with a variety of crimes. Each time that I appeared in court before a judge, I not only wanted his job, but I also truly believed that I could do it better. But after months and months had passed with no word about the status of my application, I figured that it was a lost cause. I wasn't going to be a judge. It was time to move on.

Cut to Thursday, April 12, 1982, at 4:00 P.M.; I was working in my office at the law school when the phone rang. I answered, and the gentleman on the line told me that he was calling on behalf of Governor Jerry Brown. My heart was pounding. "I'm the governor's appointments secretary and am calling to let you know that the governor has appointed you to the Municipal Court of Santa Clara County." I was stunned. It had been two whole years since I had applied for a judgeship and now, after all of this time, I had been appointed to the municipal court. I was going to be named the first African American woman judge in all Northern California. He told me not to reveal my appointment to anyone until Governor Brown made his formal announcement the following day. I hung up, called my parents and my husband, and then I placed a call to the most important person of all—Rabiah. I needed to get my hair done.

I also needed a judicial robe. One buys such a thing at the robe store. Really. Among the items in the packet that the municipal court's administrator mailed to me was a brochure with pictures of different styles of judges' robes. I had always thought that robes were, well, robes. Wrong. There is much to consider when choosing a robe. For one thing, *The California Rules of Court* provide that judicial robes "must be black, must extend in front and back from the collar and shoulders to below the knees, and must have sleeves to the wrists."

I wanted a robe with reinforced elbows because judges before whom I had appeared frequently leaned forward on their elbows, rubbed their chins, and massaged their temples as they pondered their decisions. I was going to do that, so my robe had to have padded elbows. I also learned from the brochure that robes come in sexes—boy robes and girl robes. Manly robes had wide, flowing sleeves and rectangular and commanding necklines. These robes were definitely regal. The robes for women had lacy-edged collars and scalloped cuffs—heavy on the frilly and light on the regal. Both genders of robes came in silk or polyester. Silk was a bit too upscale for me, so I ordered a polyester robe with scalloped cuffs sans the frilly collar. When it arrived a few weeks later, I tried it on and was disappointed to find it rather skimpy and thin. Actually, it resembled a dress more than it did a robe. But girly robe or not, I was now a judge.

Before I could start my work, it was necessary for me to be sworn into office. With most jobs, people simply show up, attend brief orientations, and go to work. Judging, however, is not most jobs. A judge "ascends" to the bench with great pomp and circumstance. This rite of passage is called an investiture, a very public event attended by family members, politicians, judges, lawyers, and former law professors. And, if you are the first Black woman judge to preside on the court, members of the local press make it a point to be there.

I decided to hold my investiture at Stanford Law School, my alma mater.

For the occasion, my parents flew in from Philadelphia; I wanted this judgeship as much for them as I did for myself. Lewis and Clara Hazzard had worked hard to provide for us and to ensure that my two sisters and I went to college. Their mothers had been "the help," domestic workers who toiled, for next to nothing, serving wealthy White families who resided in Philadelphia's prestigious Main Line suburbs. When my mother, a high school graduate, and my father, a graduate of North Carolina Agricultural and Technical College, married in 1943, they had neither an inheritance nor a nest egg to get them started. What they did inherit, though, was a terrific work ethic and a powerful drive to succeed. My parents would come to own a home and operate Spring Cleaners, a dry-cleaning business that supported our family for forty years.

Surrounded by my parents, my husband, our two young daughters, and my soon-to-be colleagues from the court, on June 11, 1982, I took the oath of office, administered to me by the Honorable Thelton Henderson, a highly respected federal judge who had been the assistant dean of Stanford Law School when I was admitted in 1971. The auditorium was full of well-wishers, a few of whom I recognized as former clients from my law practice, two of whom still hadn't paid me.

Judge Henderson raised his right hand and, facing him, I did the same. "Repeat after me, I do solemnly swear . . ."

"I do solemnly swear . . ."

". . . to support and defend the Constitution of the United States and the Constitution of the State of California . . ."

". . . to support and defend the Constitution of the United States and the Constitution of the State of California . . ."

And so it went, ending with "and that I will well and faithfully discharge the duties upon which I am about to enter."

Thelton smiled and said, "Welcome to the judiciary, LaDoris." We hugged, and the attendees gave me a standing ovation. I was now officially the Honorable LaDoris H. Cordell.

Everything about judging was new to me. Even though I had regularly appeared before judges as an attorney, it quickly dawned on me that I knew next to nothing about this job. One thing that I did know, however, was that I should expect the unexpected.

There is no apprenticeship for a new judge. Judging is learned by doing; it is on-the-job training. One day you're a lawyer who may have never set foot in a courtroom, and the next day you are a judge in charge of a courtroom, making life-altering decisions. While today orientation courses for newly appointed judges are offered at the B. E. Witkin Judicial College (formerly the California Judicial College) in Berkeley, when I was sworn in, those courses were not available. So, in May of 1982, I set forth to mete out justice—untrained, untutored, and unnerved.

In the judging world, first names are a no-no. It is always "Your Honor" or "Judge Cordell" or simply "Judge," but it is never "LaDoris." I learned this when walking down the hallway, scouting out my assigned courtroom on my first day at the municipal courthouse in San Jose. "Judge!" someone yelled. I kept walking. "Your Honor!" I continued walking, thinking, *Wonder where the judge is?* "Hey, Judge Cordell!" I stopped, turned, and felt a little silly when it dawned on me that "Your Honor" was I. Responding to my new name was one hurdle; an even bigger one was how to enter the courtroom and make it safely to my seat.

On Monday, May 24, 1982, Deputy Benita Jones sounded the buzzer in my chambers to let me know that it was showtime—9:05 A.M. I donned my robe, took a deep breath, and walked out into the courtroom. Benita stood up and announced, "All rise! Court is now in session. The Honorable LaDoris Hazzard Cordell presiding." A courtroom full of people stood up—for me! I smiled, sat down, leaned in to the microphone, and called my very first case.

Every California trial judge gets to choose her own court staff—one courtroom clerk, one court reporter, and one bailiff. The courtroom clerk keeps track of the cases, writes the court minutes (notes about what transpired in each case), hands the court files to the judge, and swears in witnesses and jurors. The court reporter has the impossible job of typing on a transcription machine every word that is uttered in court by witnesses, jurors, lawyers, and the judge. The bailiff's job is to protect everyone. My bailiff, my protector, was Benita Jones, a beautiful woman, 5'10", with a quiet and commanding presence. She was a deputy sheriff—an experienced law enforcement officer—who had broken the racial and gender glass ceilings as one of the first African American women hired by the Santa Clara County Sheriff's Office. Lucky for me, after years of patrolling the streets of San Jose and working in the county's jails, Benita had opted for the less hectic world of the courts. We immediately hit it off. The first-ever Black female duo to grace the courthouse, Deputy Jones and Judge Cordell were a unique twosome. With the lawyers, litigants, and spectators standing in response to Benita's call to "All rise!" I'd walk the few steps from my chambers to the bench, look around the courtroom, make eye contact with Benita, and then take my seat. But just before uttering the words "Be seated," Benita would wait just a second or two—time enough for us to exchange a quick *can-you-believe-that-all-of-these-White-folks-are-standing-up-for-us* look. For the twenty years that we worked together, we never tired of our private ritual.

My parents raised their three daughters to be polite, to listen respectfully to others, and, above all, to never interrupt. Interrupting, we were taught, is just plain rude. The Hazzard sisters did not interrupt. So, it took a while for me to learn that when a judge interrupts, it isn't rude. It's essential. Initially, I listened to the lawyers as they argued their cases before me and took great pleasure in considering the legal issues that they presented. When I heard a lawyer make the same point over and over, or when the argument had absolutely no relevance to the subject matter at hand, I'd hang in there with them—smiling, nodding, listening politely, never interrupting. My parents taught me well.

However, a judge can take only so much repetition and irrelevancy. One attorney, a tall White man in his fifties with a booming voice and a reputation for getting his way, succeeded in pushing me to my limit. He had been in the trenches far longer than I, and he was a man—a big, loud man. I, on the other hand, was a baby female judge in her early thirties with less than a year under my judicial belt. Yes, I was the judge, and yes, this was my courtroom. Even so, the thought of interrupting this man was unthinkable. I was thoroughly intimidated. At this hearing, he stood and began, "Judge, opposing counsel can't have it both ways. She can't object to the evidence I'm offering and at the same time, claim that my client committed the crime." *Good point,* I thought. "What I'm saying, Judge, is that her objection has no merit. The evidence should be admitted. My client's defense needs this evidence." *Okay, I get it.* "As I've said, Judge, you should overrule her objection. There is no basis for her objection. There is no merit to her argument." *Enough, already. I'm not stupid. I understand the issue.* "Once again, it couldn't be clearer, Judge. Her objection is—" Then I did it: "Counsel, I've heard enough. Please stop. I understand your position. You can sit down now." It worked! He stopped talking, sat down, and, most amazing of all, apologized for going on so long. My parents were wrong. Interrupting is good, very good.

I learned quickly that one of the measures of a successful trial judge is her ability to get through each day's volume of cases in a timely fashion. In our trial courts, judicial caseloads tend to be so voluminous that unless a judge is fast, she can end up in the courtroom well into the lunch hour and past the 5:00 P.M. closing time. Run overtime too often and you wind up with hostile court staff, impatient lawyers, angry litigants, and a less-than-stellar reputation. So, it is imperative to move the cases along as quickly as possible.

My approach was to let everyone in the courtroom know that I was not one to dillydally. I gave them the rule of the three *B*s: Be clear. Be brief. Be seated. And then I dispensed the majority of my cases with maximum efficiency. Whether they were dispensed with justice, I can't be sure. I like to think that they were.

Some judges like to stay put. They become accustomed to one assignment and there they remain throughout their entire judicial careers, developing an expertise in one area of the law. While there is much to be said for that approach, I chose the more scenic route, rotating every two or three years through a variety of assignments, making me a judge-of-all-trades, albeit master of none.

There are judges who are just plain slow; it's in their genes. They read slowly, speak slowly, and think slowly. They can't help themselves. Other judges are slow because they find decision-making to be a painstaking and arduous process. While it is true that the essence of judging is deciding things, the ability to do so isn't among the judicial selection criteria. There is no guarantee that an arbiter of justice will be decisive.

But among the slowest of the slow are those judges possessed of a desperate need to please and be thought of well by everyone. For she who would be loved, judging is a frustrating line of work; whenever a judge renders a decision, she is bound to make someone unhappy. The side in whose favor she has ruled will promise to name their firstborn after Her Honor, while the side she has ruled against will announce to all that at best, the judge has made a serious error, and at worst, she is the scum of the earth. The very nature of judicial decision-making is that someone wins and someone loses. A successful salesperson propitiates; a judge who propitiates, alas, is rarely successful. When I ascended to the bench on my first official day as a judge, these considerations were not yet known to me.

As I sat and nervously looked out across the courtroom full of people, I saw a sea of faces: some with frowns and others with perplexed looks. I quietly vowed, *Go ahead and frown. I'm here and I'm in charge. You'd think that my wearing this robe would be enough. Does it matter to you that I have a Stanford law degree and passed the bar exam? Probably not. But you know what? I'm not going to let you all get to me. I'm not.*

I knew that I was an oddity in the courtroom. For more than two decades, the Santa Clara County bench had few women and was devoid of African American judges, save one. Appointed to the bench in February 1964, Maurice Hardeman was the first African American jurist in the county and the only to precede me. His tenure on the bench was short-lived. On Thanksgiving Day in 1963, a barn on the judge's ranch property burned to the ground, after which the judge collected an insurance payment. In October 1964, he was indicted for conspiracy to commit arson and conspiracy to obstruct justice. After twenty-three days of trial and nineteen hours of deliberation, Judge Hardeman was convicted of both crimes. In 1971, his appeal of the convictions was finally denied. What followed was a twenty-year drought of Blackness on our bench. When I entered the courtroom in 1982, I was not what anyone expected.

Among the frowns and puzzled looks that first day, there were a few smiling faces in the spectator seats. In the back row sat five or six young Latinx males. When I took my seat, they nodded to one another, smiled, and raised their fists, and one of them said, "Right on!" I glanced at Benita, who smiled and then turned to my cheerleaders in the back row and gave them her *okay-that's-enough-even-though-I-really-liked-what-you-all-just-did* look. I should have savored that moment far more than I did, for some of my future courtroom entrances would be far less welcoming. Over the next two decades, I would preside over thousands of cases and come to learn that judging is not for the faint of heart.

TRIALS AND TRIBULATIONS
IN JUVENILE COURT

Les Enfants Terribles

Criminal Cases

Train up a child in the way he should go, and when
he is old, he will not depart from it.

—PROVERBS 22:6

What does a judge do with a child who has murdered his brother? That was the question confronting me after the five-day trial of fifteen-year-old Leopoldo (Leo) M. Because there are no juries in the juvenile system, I was both judge and jury.

We've come a long way since the first juvenile court was established in 1899 in Chicago. The idea of a separate juvenile justice system was predicated on the theory that children are developmentally different from adults and, therefore, more amenable to treatment and rehabilitation. Punishment, the primary goal of our adult criminal courts, was, until fairly recently, nowhere to be found in the juvenile courts. I use the word "was" because over time, the juvenile justice system has become increasingly punitive. The notion that juvenile offenders are children in need of rehabilitation and guidance is fading fast, in part because of the public's perception that violent juvenile crime has been on the rise. It hasn't. But that fact has not deterred opportunistic politicians, legislators, and the media from promoting laws that increasingly blur the lines between the treatment of juveniles and that of their adult counterparts.

In this country, 365 adults have been executed for murders they committed as juveniles. No doubt, there would have been more executions had the U.S. Supreme Court not stepped in, in 2005, when it ruled in *Roper v. Simmons* that it is unconstitutional to execute anyone who was a juvenile when he or she committed the crime.

Currently, there are over twenty-six hundred inmates who were seventeen years of age and younger (some as young as thirteen) at the time of their crimes, who are serving life sentences without the possibility of parole. Of those child lifers who were fourteen years and younger when they committed their crimes, 70 percent are children of color.

In 2010, in *Graham v. Florida,* the U.S. Supreme Court banned sentences of life without parole for juveniles who were convicted of non-homicide offenses, and in 2012, in *Miller v. Alabama,* the court banned *mandatory* life-without-parole sentences for juveniles convicted of homicide. This means that while a convicted juvenile killer can still receive a sentence of life without parole, it is the sentencing judge who makes that call. Today, as many as twenty-five hundred men and women who are currently serving mandatory life sentences as a result of offenses they committed as children are now eligible to be resentenced. When fifteen-year-old Leo M. was accused of murdering his brother, Julio, it was 1997, well before the U.S. Supreme Court had issued any of these rulings.

The events leading up to Julio's murder began at 4:30 A.M., when Reyna, Julio's girlfriend, awoke and insisted that he drive her home. The two had been sleeping in Julio's bedroom in the San Jose home of the boys' mother. Julio awakened his mother and demanded the keys to the family's van. When she refused, the two argued, awakening Leo, Julio's younger brother. It was later determined that Julio's blood-alcohol level that morning was .06 percent. (A person is presumed to be legally under the influence with a .08 percent blood-alcohol level.)

When their mother continued to refuse to give her keys to Julio, he grabbed an exercise bicycle and threw it at her. Bouncing off the floor, the bike hit her knee. Julio picked up the bicycle again—this time, in a rage—throwing it against his mother's bedroom wall. Hearing the thud of the bicycle and the cries of his mother, a sleeping Leo awoke and ran to his mother's bedroom, insisting that Julio leave their mother alone. Julio reacted as he usually did, by starting a fistfight with Leo.

The brothers had a long history of fighting. Since he was two years younger and slightly smaller in stature, Leo bore the brunt of their battles. The early-morning fistfight went on for about fifteen minutes, during which time Leo continuously implored his brother to stop. Ultimately, their mother grabbed the kitchen telephone to call 911. But before she could complete the call, Julio pulled the telephone cord from the wall, whereupon his mother ran next door to use a neighbor's telephone.

Undaunted, Julio chased after her, ordering her back into the house. Terrified, she complied and returned inside; then Julio resumed fighting with Leo, knocking him to the floor and pummeling him. Reyna, Julio's girlfriend, somehow managed to pull Julio off Leo, at which point Leo got up, only to have his brother come at him again. By this time, the brothers were at the front doorway where Julio shoved his brother out of the house.

At this point, Leo pulled a folding knife from his back pocket, opened it, and waved it at his brother. Undeterred, Julio advanced on Leo, threatening to take the knife and kill Leo. As Leo continued to brandish the knife, he jabbed it at Julio, inflicting a superficial wound on the underside of Julio's right arm. Now, completely out of control, Julio ran toward Leo, who reacted by quickly thrusting the knife in Julio's direction, stabbing him in the abdomen. Julio backed up, staggered to the driveway, sat down, and then, unbeknownst to Leo, quickly bled to death.

Immediately after stabbing Julio, Leo ran into the house, sat on his bed, and screamed, "I shanked him! I shanked him!" Then he ran back outside and, with his mother at his side, administered mouth-to-mouth resuscitation to his brother. His mother frantically called 911. The operator eventually spoke to Leo who, as he screamed and cried, admitted to stabbing his brother. Shortly thereafter, Leo was arrested and once in police custody, he gave a taped confession to the police.

At the trial, the tape recording of Leo's interview with the police was played in court. Throughout his hour-long interrogation, Leo could be heard sobbing and tearfully asking to see his mother and brother. He co-operated and told the police what happened, all the while insisting that he had not meant to hurt his brother. The interview was excruciating for all of us in the courtroom to hear. At no point during the questioning did the police officer tell Leo that his brother was dead. At the conclusion of the interrogation, when the officer finally broke the news of Julio's death to him, Leo went berserk, sobbing and screaming for his mother. Amid the screams, the police interrogator could be heard on the tape yelling: "You fucked up, Leo! You killed your brother! He's dead! You killed him!"

It only got worse. After the county coroner, three police officers, and Leo's mother testified, it was Leo's turn. He didn't have to testify because children, just as adults, have the Fifth Amendment right against self-incrimination; they cannot be forced to testify against their own inter-ests. Since it was the prosecutor's responsibility to prove his guilt beyond a reasonable doubt, Leo could choose to remain silent throughout the entire trial; he was presumed innocent and therefore not obligated to prove anything.

Nevertheless, on his attorney's advice, Leo chose to testify. Sitting in the witness stand, he described what happened. While he was nervous, he was clear and seemed to me to be speaking truthfully. However, when, during cross-examination, the prosecutor held up graphic color photographs of Julio's lifeless body covered in blood, Leo buried his head in his hands and sobbed uncontrollably. I called a recess. We all needed a break.

The district attorney's office had charged Leo with second-degree murder, the unlawful killing of a human being with "implied malice aforethought." There are two kinds of malice aforethought—express and implied. Had Leo planned the murder of his brother, he would have acted with express malice, which meant that he would have faced a charge of first-degree murder. But early on, both the prosecutor and Leo's de-fense attorney had agreed that Leo did not deliberately set out to kill his brother. There was no premeditation and, therefore, no express malice.

For Leo to be found guilty of second-degree murder, as the prosecutor alleged, he would have had to stab his brother with implied malice, meaning he deliberately endangered his brother's life and did so with "conscious disregard for life." I had no problem concluding that when Leo waved his knife at his brother, he had deliberately endangered his brother's life. The more difficult question was whether the evidence demonstrated that he acted with "conscious disregard for life."

This is where Leo's taped confession describing the moment of the stabbing was critical:

Leo: But then I was trying to go back inside and ignoring him, like he come and pushed me out. And then that's when I stabbed him back. I don't know why . . . Like he was still four feet away . . . he still had his hands up, like me, like boxing . . . [I was] telling him to stay away.

Police: You actually swung the knife more than one time, right? To keep him away?

Leo: Twice. I didn't even use it on him, man.

Police: Do you remember actually stabbing him though?

Leo: No.

After considering Leo's taped confession, along with his testimony and that of his mother and Reyna, who were the only eyewitnesses to the stabbing, I didn't feel the need to prepare a written decision and ruled right then, saying,

At the trial, Leo testified on cross-examination that he knew that if he were to stab someone, he could hurt the person badly or even kill the person. He was aware of the dangerousness of wielding a knife at another person. However, the evidence does not support the conclusion that he acted with conscious disregard for human life when confronting his brother. Rather the evidence is that Leo brandished the knife, waving it back and forth, to keep his brother at bay, that he made an effort to keep a distance from Julio and that, while brandishing the weapon, he continued to plead with his brother to stop the fighting.

By expressing fear of Julio, by warning Julio to stay away from him, and by showing a reluctance to use the knife against Julio, Leo evinced a concern for his brother's welfare. This was not the conduct of one who treats his victim as unworthy of regard or notice. When Leo stabbed his brother, he did not act with a conscious disregard for his brother's life. He stabbed his brother without malice aforethought. Therefore, he is not guilty of second-degree murder, so that charge in the petition is not sustained.

But that wasn't the end of the matter.

The prosecutor now wanted me to find that the evidence supported the charge of manslaughter. Manslaughter is the unlawful killing of a person *without malice aforethought*. There are three types of manslaughter—voluntary, involuntary, and vehicular.

Voluntary manslaughter occurs when someone is killed "during a sudden quarrel, in the heat of passion, or based on an honest but unreasonable belief in the need to defend oneself." In 2014, a California jury properly convicted thirty-six-year-old Tom Franks of voluntary manslaughter when, during a heated argument, he shot and killed his domestic partner, forty-eight-year-old Jacqueline Millan. He intended to kill but hadn't planned to; the killing had been a spur-of-the-moment decision.

Involuntary manslaughter is the *unintentional* killing of another that can occur when someone is killed as the result of someone committing an *unlawful* act that isn't a felony. For example, when someone steals a bicycle (a misdemeanor) and while riding it collides with a pedestrian, killing her, that's involuntary manslaughter. Or, the crime is committed when a person commits a *lawful* act that results in death because the person failed to take appropriate precautions. That happened when Michael Jackson's personal physician, Conrad Murray, *lawfully* prescribed and administered doses of propofol to Michael but failed to maintain proper oversight of the treatments. Dr. Murray was convicted of involuntary manslaughter in the resulting death of Michael Jackson and received the maximum sentence of four years in prison.

Finally, there is vehicular manslaughter, where a death results from the gross negligence of a person operating a motor vehicle. Intoxi-cated drivers who have multiple drunk driving convictions are typically charged with vehicular manslaughter when their drunk driving results in the deaths of others. In California, the maximum punishment for voluntary manslaughter is eleven years in prison; for involuntary man-slaughter, it is four years; and for vehicular manslaughter, it is six years.

After quickly ruling out vehicular manslaughter, I was left to consider whether Leo's conduct constituted voluntary or involuntary manslaugh-ter. My analysis was short and direct: Since both the prosecutor and the defense attorney agreed that Leo never intended to stab his brother, he could not have committed voluntary manslaughter. What he *did* commit was involuntary manslaughter. Why? When Leo brandished a knife, he committed an unlawful act (brandishing is a misdemeanor) that resulted in Julio's death—the textbook definition of involuntary manslaughter.

But Leo's public defender wasn't satisfied. She contended that when Leo unintentionally stabbed Julio, he did so in self-defense, which would mean that the killing was justified and, therefore, not a crime at all. The prosecutor could not have disagreed more; he vehemently argued that Leo's stabbing of his brother was definitely not a case of self-defense.

In law school, students are taught to "think like lawyers" by analyzing legal issues in four steps: (1) identify the issue, (2) identify the rule, (3) apply the rule to the facts, and (4) make your conclusion—longhand for the acronym IRAC. So, thinking like a lawyer, I resorted to the IRAC analysis to determine if self-defense was applicable to Leo's situation:

(1) The issue: Did Leo act in self-defense?

(2) The rule: For self-defense to apply, the force used must be propor-tionate to the assault. If, for example, someone threw a small rock at you and you reacted by shooting the assailant with a gun, your claim of self-defense would not be justified because your use of deadly force—firing a gun in response to a thrown rock—is unreasonable and unwarranted.

(3) Apply the rule to the facts: The evidence adduced at the trial was that Julio and Leo had a long history of fighting that never escalated beyond the use of fists. At no time, before this incident, had they ever used weapons of any sort.

(4) Conclusion: It was unreasonable for Leo to believe that Julio would inflict sufficient force upon him to warrant Leo introducing a knife into the fight.

So, I agreed with the prosecution and ruled that this was not a case of self-defense. Leo, I announced, had committed involuntary manslaughter.

Now, I was faced with the difficult question of what to do with this devastated fifteen-year-old who, for the rest of his life, would live with the knowledge that he had killed his brother. From the time of his arrest and throughout his trial, Leo had been detained on a suicide watch at the juvenile hall and was prescribed antidepressant medications.

I had two options: send Leo to one of three youth prisons operated by the California Youth Authority (CYA) for four years or place him in a residential- or community-based treatment program, where he would remain for two years. Juvenile prisons are locked facilities, the last stop for minors before they enter the adult prison system. Located in remote areas of the state, the focus of these institutions is punishment and control. Far less punitive are local residential and community treatment programs, whose primary goal is rehabilitation. (In September 2020, California's governor signed Senate Bill 823, which eliminated youth prisons and replaced them with local facilities where juvenile offenders are provided rehabilitative services.)

The probation officer's report recommended that Leo be committed to CYA, exactly what the prosecutor had requested. Leo's attorney objected; she wanted me to consider an alternative placement. Since the probation officer had not included any alternatives in his report, I asked him for information about placements that might be appropriate for Leo. Grudgingly, he nodded and said that he would provide me the information.

True to his word, the probation officer prepared a supplemental report in which he listed seven alternative placements, ranging from an out-of-state boys' treatment program to six residential programs located throughout the state. However, he noted five of these placements had rejected Leo based solely on the seriousness of his crime. The other two—one based in San Jose and the other in San Francisco—agreed to accept him. I had just four days until the next court date to decide.

On February 27, 1998, the hearing resumed. The prosecutor argued forcefully that placing Leo in CYA was appropriate because of the violent nature of the crime and, as importantly, the public would be protected for the next four years from this "aggressive, impulsive, and angry" young man. Leo's public defender countered that he was not impulsive or aggressive or angry. Rather, she said, he was "depressed, guilt ridden," and in dire need of treatment. Given that I had found that the killing was unintentional, Leo's lawyer insisted that her client wasn't a cold-blooded murderer; he needed treatment, she pleaded, not punishment.

I decided that Leo would go to the program in San Francisco and remain until his seventeenth birthday. The highly structured program with a focus on intensive psychiatric care housed sixty juveniles ages thirteen to seventeen, but it was, by law, *unlocked.* I knew that Leo could walk away, but I also knew that Leo understood that if he were to leave, the California Youth Authority was next. A handcuffed and visibly relieved Leo walked out of the courtroom, Benita at his side.

A few months later, Leo was back, having failed the placement in San Francisco. Still reluctant to send him to CYA, I decided to try another placement. Leo didn't make it there either. He broke the rules, started fights, and attacked the counselors. None of this was surprising to me. Leo had killed his brother, and no amount of therapy was likely to diminish his overwhelming sense of guilt. At his trial, fifteen-year-old Leo was thin and forlorn. Now, at age seventeen, he was bloated, likely a reaction to medications, and suicidal. Our juvenile justice system left me no further options; I ordered Leo to the California Youth Authority, where he served his time and was released.

Ten years later, in July 2009, Leo was sentenced to two years in a California state prison, convicted of multiple drunk driving offenses. The juvenile justice system failed Leo and so had I.

I presided over a variety of cases in juvenile court—thefts, vandalism, drunk driving, robbery, drug possession. But those cases involving acts of violence, like Leo's story, stay with me. To this day, I am haunted by the case of Kristyn K. On October 5, 1995, thirteen-year-old Kristyn K. was the victim of a gang rape. Her accused rapists—five of them—ranged in age from fifteen to seventeen. All were African American; Kristyn was Caucasian. Nearly two years later, in April 1997, I presided over the juvenile court trial of two of the juveniles, fifteen-year-olds Edward B. and Lemar C. The other three defendants—sixteen- and seventeen-year-olds—faced trial in adult court. (In California, juveniles must be at least sixteen years of age to be tried as adults.) Why had it taken this long for their cases to get to trial? There were lots of reasons: pretrial motions, investigations, busy lawyers, overcrowded court dockets.

I quietly wondered what Kristyn and her mother would think when I entered the courtroom to preside over this trial. Would they worry that a Black judge would be biased in favor of the two Black juveniles? Conversely, what would the two accused rapists think when seeing me for the first time? Would they breathe a sigh of relief, thinking that with a "sister" on the bench, they would surely get a break? I hated the optics— Black males accused of raping a White female—a stereotype that for more than four hundred years has dogged African American men.

While the testimony of the investigating police officer was important, the key prosecution witness was Kristyn. From the witness stand, she described in excruciating detail what her attackers did to her, adding that she had been on her menstrual cycle and had a tampon inside of her when she was raped.

On cross-examination, Kristyn had to face not one but two defense attorneys. Amazingly, she held up remarkably well under their intense questioning. She was clear, and I found her to be credible. Still, I withheld my judgment; the accused had a right, if they chose, to tell their side of the story.

The physician who examined Kristyn testified that as a result of the gang rape, her tampon had been shoved into her vaginal canal; testing of the tampon revealed the presence of Edward's DNA. With such damning testimony, Edward's lawyer must have figured that his client had no choice but to testify. And what a witness he was.

Edward testified that he didn't rape anyone and that even though she was on her period, they had consensual sex in Kristyn's bathroom. He arrogantly boasted that Kristyn "wanted it." After listening to Edward's fourth version of the incident, I lost count, and I lost my patience. The evidence was clear that Edward had orchestrated this entire affair, left Kristyn to be raped by his buddies, and then returned to rape her. Sitting stoically in the front row of the spectator seats, Kristyn never took her eyes off of him.

Then there was the matter of Lemar, the other accused juvenile. Kristyn was unable to say with any certainty that he was among her attackers. While there was some evidence that placed Lemar at the scene, without Kristyn's testimony identifying him as taking part in the rape, there likely wasn't sufficient evidence to establish beyond a reasonable doubt that Lemar assaulted her. As a result, Lemar's attorney wisely chose not to put his client on the witness stand.

When the trial testimony concluded, I ruled that the prosecution had proven beyond a reasonable doubt that Edward B. had raped Kristyn. I looked right at Edward and told him that he was a liar, that he had not helped himself by testifying falsely, and that what he had done to Kristyn was heinous and despicable. I usually refrain from lecturing defendants, but this little thug warranted a lecture. He sat next to his attorney, glaring at me. I would see him again at his dispositional hearing.

With respect to Lemar C., I ruled that the prosecution had failed to prove that he had participated in the rape and found him not guilty. I later learned that Lemar had earlier been convicted and sentenced in an unrelated case of strong-armed robbery (forcibly taking the property of another, without the use of a weapon). So, he wasn't going anywhere anytime soon.

The dispositional hearing for Edward B. was set for the week after the Memorial Day weekend. I had read the probation report and knew that both the deputy district attorney and Edward's public defender would be in full attack mode. I needed the weekend to contemplate my decision. Wouldn't you know, that weekend was Memorial Day, and I was the duty judge.

At least once a year, every judge on our court is required to be on call for a week (Monday to Friday), starting at 5:00 P.M. and ending at 8:00 A.M., and for a full forty-eight hours on the weekend (Saturday and Sunday). When the court is not in session, the duty judge responds to requests from law enforcement throughout the county for search warrants, arrest warrants, and emergency restraining orders.

I never mastered the trick of getting back to sleep after being awakened by a phone call at 2:00 or 3:00 A.M. from a police officer who politely and cheerfully says, "Good morning, Your Honor!" or "How are you, Your Honor?" Throughout that week and particularly on that weekend, there was no shortage of requests from law enforcement officers for emergency protective orders (EPROs) for victims of domestic violence, whose abusers were frequently intoxicated. Alcohol is typically consumed in greater quantities than usual on holidays; that Memorial Day weekend was no exception. As requests for emergency protective orders poured in, my phone rang incessantly throughout the night and early morning. Here's a sampling of the more than twenty phone calls I answered that weekend:

(1) A thirty-three-year-old woman, holding their eight-month-old baby, was punched by her husband. When her seventy-six-year-old father attempted to intervene, the husband picked him up and threw the man over a sofa, whereupon the husband grabbed the baby and ran out of

the house. When I issued the EPRO, neither the husband nor the baby had been located. In the background, I could hear the screams of the mother, so I asked the officer to let me speak with her. "I just want my baby back!" I tried to calm her down but without much success. How does a mother calm down when her child has been kidnapped?

(2) A couple, both fifteen years old, one of whom was five months pregnant with the other's baby, argued. The baby's father punched his expectant partner several times, threatened to kill her, and throughout the day left messages reading "187" on her pager. California Penal Code Section 187 defines the crime of murder.

(3) A husband (6'1", 240 pounds, thirty-three years old) pushed his wife, held her down on the ground, and punched her in the arms and chin in the presence of their ten-month-old child.

(4) A man became angry with his female friend and punched her in the face with so much force that he fractured her eye socket.

(5) An eighteen-year-old, upset that his wealthy parents wouldn't allow him to drive one of their cars, threw both of them against a wall and spit in their faces.

At the end of this action-packed weekend and with little sleep, I dragged myself back to work to bring the juvenile gang rape case to a close. But first, I had a full docket of cases awaiting me. It was going to be a long day.

People v. Esparza, a jury trial assigned to me that morning, started things off. This was a felony drunk driving case in which forty-year-old Mr. Esparza was charged with his *eighth* DUI. *How in the world would someone be out and about driving the freeways after amassing seven drunk driving convictions?* I wondered. Why wasn't this man behind bars? Clearly, someone had dropped the ball. I met with the attorneys and briefly discussed a few pretrial matters. When settlement discussions went nowhere, I scheduled jury selection to begin the following morning.

Next was the sentencing of twenty-eight-year-old Mr. Castillo who, a few weeks earlier, had pled guilty in my court to assaulting his woman friend. The two had been drinking heavily when they argued. He punched her repeatedly, dragged her by her hair, and choked her into unconsciousness. Mr. Castillo had been down this road before. After being released from the California Youth Authority (the juvenile prison), at the age of nineteen, he assaulted the first person he saw—a twenty-three-year-old woman, a complete stranger, whom he attempted to rape. In the process, he beat her so severely that she required twenty stitches in her head. For that attack, he was sentenced to eight years in state prison. It was following his release from prison for that crime that he committed the assault on his female companion.

Between Mr. Castillo and his mother, I don't know who sobbed more as he begged me not to sentence him to life in prison. While I could certainly hand down such a sentence, I opted not to; I agreed with his attorney's contention that his twenty-eight-year-old client, after serving substantial time behind bars, might be rehabilitated. Mr. Castillo would serve twenty-seven years, eligible to be released after serving twenty-three, when he would be a fifty-year-old man.

Then I had to deal with Vernon C., a fourteen-year-old African American boy whose mentally disturbed and drug-addled mother had subjected him and his three brothers to horrific physical abuse. Of her four sons, Vernon, a sweet and gentle soul, received the harshest treatment. After he had acted out at school and at the home of his aunt, where he now resided, I had placed Vernon in a residential program for troubled adolescents. But when his destructive behaviors continued, I had to remove him from the program and send him to the county's children's shelter. Now, his lawyer wanted some judicial guidance about what to do with Vernon.

In the courtroom, Vernon sat mute, eyes cast downward. I explained to him that I was not going to give up on him. I told him that until he was able to change his behavior, I was placing him in a group home where he would undergo a psychological evaluation. At that point he yelled, "This is a bunch of crap!" I welcomed the outburst since I had been told that this was more than anyone had been able to get out of this kid for weeks.

I went ahead and made the order, adjourned for a brief recess, and stepped into the public hallway just outside of the doors to my chamber. There was Vernon, sitting on a bench with his child advocate. She was a middle-aged White woman who belonged to a group of volunteers, appointed by the court, who were trained to provide support and guidance to abused and neglected children. As tears streamed down Vernon's face, she held his hand and quietly spoke to him. I walked over and sat on the other side of him, put my arm around him, and again explained that this was going to take time and that he had plenty of people, including me, in his corner. Then I stood and returned to my chambers. The gang rape sentencing was up next—my last case of the day. I knew that this was going to be a long day; I'd had days like this before. Still, the distress and anger in the courtroom engendered by my decision-making always left me emotionally exhausted, my poker face and stoic demeanor notwithstanding. So, when it was time to head back into the courtroom that afternoon, I took a deep breath and with trepidation entered the courtroom.

Seated on my right, behind the defense attorneys, were several anxious Black folks—the family and friends of Edward B. On the other side, seated behind the deputy district attorney were anxious White folks—the family and friends of Kristyn, including her mother. The maximum sentence that I could impose on Edward was four years at the California Youth Authority. Had this been in adult court, Edward's maximum sentence for raping Kristyn would have been close to thirty-nine years. Recall Mr. Castillo from earlier in the day, the man who *tried* to rape a woman and to whom I gave a twenty-seven-year prison sentence? Here I had a young man who not only had raped a girl, but had also facilitated her gang rape, and his maximum punishment was *four years*. What's wrong with this picture? Because I believed (and still do) that most young people, when given the proper counseling and treatment, can be redeemed, I was inclined to err on the side of leniency when sentencing juvenile offenders. But this crime was so callous, so cruel, and Edward was so lacking in remorse, I was actually left wishing that I could send him away for a long, long time.

When I asked Edward if he had anything to say, his response was: "I'm sorry it happened." *It* happened? I told him: "No, *it* didn't happen. *You* did this." I then sent him to the California Youth Authority for the maximum of four years.

After I adjourned for the day and retreated to my chambers, I sat in my chair and exhaled. I was exhausted. Then Benita opened the door and told me that Kristyn wanted to speak to me. I got up and returned to the courtroom where Kristyn stood next to her mother. She thanked me and then stepped forward and gave me a hug. When I hugged her back, she began sobbing. When her mother said that this was the first time that Kristyn had cried since the gang rape, a group hug was in order. I knew that while this child had been through so much, there was still more to come. She would soon have to testify in adult court at the trial of the other three defendants.

Edward B. served his time at the California Youth Authority and eventually left California. Lemar C. was released from prison when he reached the age of twenty-four and resides in Southern California. After Kristyn testified against them in a preliminary hearing, the three adult defendants pled guilty, making a trial unnecessary. All three were sentenced to state prison. One of them, William B., a cousin of Edward B., was subsequently arrested in Michigan and convicted of raping three thirteen-year-old girls. In 2009, Kristyn traveled to Michigan and testified at William's sentencing hearing about his participation in her rape. The judge sentenced him to life in prison.

Last I heard, Kristyn was doing amazingly well.

Making a Murderer

The Felony Murder Rule

Each of us is more than the worst thing we've ever done.
—BRYAN STEVENSON, *JUST MERCY*

n 1992, I was assigned the juvenile court trial of Jessica T., a fifteen-year-old Latina charged with the murder of eighteen-year-old Mark Berkey. At the time, juveniles accounted for 15 percent of murder arrests; 6 percent of those arrestees were teenage girls.

Juvenile courts have traditionally been closed to the public. According to the Reporters Committee for Freedom of the Press, "As a policy matter, it was believed that youthful offenders should not be stigmatized forever because of one mistake. Another justification for secrecy was promoting rehabilitation of the youthful offender." However, some states, including California, open juvenile proceedings to the public when a minor is charged with a serious crime such as robbery, rape, arson, or murder. Members of the public were permitted to observe Jessica T.'s murder trial, although they were not allowed to know her full name. Steven Bitz (eighteen years), Jeffrey Douglas Hall (nineteen years), Joseph Allen Franklin (twenty years), and Jessica Richie (eighteen years), also charged with Mark's murder, were tried in adult court.

As provided in the Sixth Amendment, adults who are charged with crimes have a constitutional right to jury trials; juveniles do not. Their cases are tried before judges alone, who hear the evidence, determine the facts, and deliver the verdicts. Why is that? Why do adults have access to jury trials, while juveniles don't? Because the United States Supreme Court said so in the case of *McKeiver v. Pennsylvania.*

In separate cases, Joseph McKeiver, age sixteen, and Edward Terry, age fifteen, were tried in a Pennsylvania juvenile court. According to the U.S. Supreme Court's decision, "McKeiver's offense was his participating with 20 or 30 youths who pursued three young teenagers and took 25 cents from them. Terry's offense consisted of hitting a police officer with his fists and with a stick when the officer broke up a boys' fight Terry and others were watching."

In a third case, forty-five Black children, ranging in age from eleven to fifteen years, were convicted of "willfully impeding traffic," a misdemeanor in a North Carolina juvenile court. They were charged for "walking along Highway 64 singing, shouting, clapping, and playing basketball," as they protested school assignments and a school consolidation plan. The forty-five cases were combined into one juvenile court trial. In each of the three cases, the lawyers' requests for jury trials were denied; in all three cases, the lawyers appealed to the U.S. Supreme Court.

Appearing before the Supreme Court in 1971, the juveniles' lawyers argued that their clients were entitled to jury trials because juveniles are tried in proceedings "substantially similar to a criminal trial" and subject to incarceration for lengthy periods. The majority of the Supreme Court's nine justices disagreed, citing four reasons: (1) a jury trial would make juvenile proceedings "fully adversary" and destroy "the idealistic prospect of an intimate, informal protective proceeding"; (2) a jury would fail to significantly improve the ability of courts to determine the facts; (3) jury trials would undermine the confidentiality of juvenile court proceedings; and (4) a jury trial would bring with it "the traditional delay, the formality, and the clamor of the adversary system, and possibly, the public trial."

Seriously? When juveniles are arrested, they are confined in locked juvenile detention centers just like adult arrestees; their cases are frequently resolved by plea bargains just like adult cases; the rules of evidence apply to their trials just like adult trials; and they may be confined in locked institutions for years just like adults—sometimes even longer than adults.

The "idealistic prospect of an intimate, informal protective proceeding" is just that: idealistic. It couldn't be further from the truth. Juvenile court criminal proceedings are just as adversarial as adult criminal trials. And there is absolutely no support for the court's assertion that jurors would do no better as fact finders than would judges. The six Supreme Court justices who voted to deny jury trials to juveniles in the *McKeiver* case (Blackmun, Burger, Stewart, White, Harlan, and Brennan) had never practiced juvenile law, nor had they ever presided over a juvenile court trial.

There's more. Four years before the *McKeiver* decision, in 1967, President Lyndon Johnson's Commission on Law Enforcement and Administration of Justice issued a report entitled *The Challenge of Crime in a Free Society*. The commission began its work in 1965 and evaluated "every facet of crime and law enforcement in America," including the juvenile justice system. About juvenile court judges, the report pulled no punches, noting that as of 1964, half of the nation's juvenile judges had no undergraduate degrees, a fifth had no college education at all, and a fifth were not even members of the bar! It concluded that the informality of juvenile proceedings was no longer acceptable. The commission recommended that "the system should operate with all the procedural formality necessary to safeguard adequately the rights that any person has when he is subject to the application of coercive power."

But just because the U.S. Supreme Court put the kibosh on jury trials for juveniles doesn't mean that individual states are so restricted. Yes, the court ruled that the U.S. Constitution's Sixth Amendment right to a jury trial does not apply to juveniles, but the states remain free to require jury trials under their own constitutions and legislatures. Today there is a growing trend among the states to do just that. Eighteen states either require or allow jury trials for juveniles. I believe that it is time for the U.S. Supreme Court to reconsider the

McKeiver decision and declare that juveniles in all fifty states have a constitutional right to jury trials under the Sixth Amendment. But twenty years after the *McKeiver* decision, when I presided over the trial of Jessica T., the idea of considering a jury trial for her never crossed my mind. Juveniles charged with crimes in California's juvenile courts were tried before judges, not juries; that was the law, end of story. Jessica T.'s fate was in my hands alone.

The testimony of police officers and witnesses at her trial established that Jessica T. and her four adult friends, all of who were white, called themselves the Krew. They had no history of violence. Two days before the murder, they had decided to relocate from San Jose to Los Angeles. To get there, they planned to steal a 1987 Jeep Cherokee from Chris Sturdevant, an acquaintance of theirs.

Just after midnight, Jessica T. telephoned Chris and asked him for a ride to her brother's house. She lied; Jessica T. did not have a brother. When Chris arrived at their agreed-upon meeting place in a parking lot at a high school in San Jose, Jessica was there along with her fellow Krew members. To their dismay, Chris had brought along his buddy Mark Berkey, which complicated the Krew's plan to simply jump Chris and take his car. After hanging out together for an hour, Chris and Jessica T. went on a fast-food run in Chris's Jeep; his buddy Mark elected to stay behind with the Krew. On the drive back to the park, Jessica T. asked Chris to make a quick stop at her home. While Chris waited in the Jeep, she ran in and quickly packed her clothing in two bags, then returned to the Jeep.

They returned to the park. As soon as Jessica T. stepped out of the Jeep, Jessica Richie ran up and whispered that the plan to steal the vehicle was happening. Suddenly, the three male Krew members jumped Chris, wrestled him to the ground, and grabbed his car keys, whereupon the entire Krew jumped into the Jeep and sped off.

Chris struggled to his feet and discovered the body of Mark Berkey lying on the grass a few yards away. Mark had been stabbed and slashed ten times in his neck and chest. Frantic, Chris ran to a nearby pay phone to call 911, only to find that the phone had been vandalized and left inoperable. By the time Chris was able to get help, the medics determined that Mark was dead. Within thirteen hours, the Krew was apprehended in Port Hueneme, in Southern California. In the Jeep, officers found the part they had removed from the pay phone.

Even though Jessica T. was somewhere else when Mark was killed, took no part in planning his murder, and had no idea that the Krew was going to kill him, the prosecution charged Jessica with the murder. They could do so under the felony murder rule.

The rule's purpose is to hold perpetrators and their accomplices liable for killings that result from the commission of dangerous felonies, such as robbery and arson. Felony murder works like this: Let's say that you conspire with two of your friends to rob the neighborhood 7-Eleven and that you are the getaway driver. You drive your friends to the store and wait in the car while they commit the robbery. Suddenly, you hear gunshots and as your friends run outside and jump into the car, they tell you that the cashier refused to give them the money, so one of your friends shot her. When all of you are apprehended, the police tell you that the cashier is dead. Even though you never entered the store, did not kill the cashier, had no idea that anyone would be shot, let alone killed, and did not know that anyone had a gun, you are deemed just as guilty as your friend who pulled the trigger. Why? You participated in an "inherently dangerous" felony: an armed robbery that left someone dead. Yes, you were bad, and you should be punished for your getaway driving. But does punishing you as a murderer fit the crime? I think not. And I'm not alone.

Unlike the Sixth Amendment, the felony murder rule applies equally to juveniles. It was first enacted in America in the early 1800s, and by the time of the Civil War, half of the states had felony murder statutes. Today, forty-four states and the District of Columbia have such a law. Forty years ago, the Michigan Supreme Court abolished the rule, calling it "a historic survivor for which there is no logical or practical basis for existence in modern law." Legislatures in Hawaii, Ohio, and Kentucky similarly ended it. The Massachusetts Supreme Judicial Court abolished it in 2018. As far back as 1983, the California Supreme Court called the felony murder rule a "barbaric rule of dubious origins from a bygone age" but left it to legislators to end it. In 2018, they finally did. (As a general rule, when criminal laws are changed, they are applied prospectively, not retroactively. The abolition of the felony murder law wasn't retroactive, which means that those defendants who were convicted of felony murder and sentenced *before* the abolition in the law were not affected by the change. Their convictions and sentences as felony murderers remain.) In 1957, England abolished its version of the felony murder rule. Thereafter, India, Canada, and other countries that followed the British legal system followed suit. Today, the only country in which the felony murder rule continues to be utilized is the United States.

In 1992, when I presided over the Jessica T. trial, the felony murder rule was alive and well in California. Jessica was fortunate to be represented by Tony Christiansen, an attorney in private practice whose reputation as a criminal defense attorney was stellar. He had appeared in my court on previous occasions but never before on a homicide. Tony is White, tall, and soft-spoken, and was in his early forties. I knew that he was a savvy and smart litigator. Kurt Kumli was the prosecutor. Kurt, also White, was smart, good-looking, and ambitious. He was a young deputy DA just starting his legal career. A decade later, Kurt would be appointed to the bench, where he would serve as a compassionate jurist in juvenile court.

Since I was the judge *and* jury, I had to pay close attention to everything—no drifting off, no half listening. At jury trials, I would occasionally go into cruise control. Once I had made all of the preliminary rulings, such as what evidence could be admitted or what witnesses could testify, I could just sit back and let the jury do the listening. After all, jurors are the ones who have to carefully scrutinize the witnesses to determine the facts and whom to believe. When, in the midst of a jury trial, I had to rule on an objection, if I missed something, I'd simply ask the court reporter to read the objection back to me so that I could rule on it.

Jurors constantly watch judges, which is why, during especially mind-numbing trials, I appeared to be taking copious notes. What I was really doing was doodling. I drew the paper clips and clamps on my desk, the witness stand, my microphone, even the faces of the jurors and witnesses—anything to stay awake. Don't get me wrong. I presided over dozens of jury trials and paid close attention—most of the time. But when, for example, it's your umpteenth drunk driving jury trial, a sameness sets in. In drunk driving cases, with rare exception, it's the same pattern—the police officer testifies about the defendant's performance on the field sobriety tests, the prosecution expert testifies about the defendant's Breathalyzer results, and the defense expert refutes the testimony of the prosecution expert with her own Breathalyzer expert. Imagine your tenth or twentieth or thirtieth such jury trial. It can drive you to doodling.

The Jessica T. case was an entirely different animal. This was a murder trial and I alone was the decider. No doodling. I needed to be present at all times. Turns out, nothing about this trial was boring or predictable.

First, I had to determine if Jessica was part of the plan to commit a robbery of Chris's Jeep. If she was, then she would be guilty of the felony murder of Mark. Mr. Christiansen argued that the Krew's plan was not to commit the inherently dangerous crime of robbery (defined as theft by force) but was, instead, to commit simple theft of a car (without use of force). Were I to find Jessica guilty of theft as opposed to robbery, the felony murder would not apply to her. Mr. Christiansen had my attention.

The testimony of Chris Sturdevant and that of the investigating police officers was powerful. They established that Jessica T. convinced Chris and Mark to get out of the Jeep at the park, lied about the need to go to her nonexistent brother's house, retrieved her clothing in preparation to leave with the Krew, and, importantly, voluntarily got into the Jeep after Chris was attacked and knocked to the ground.

Common sense told me that the Krew did not expect Chris to simply hand his vehicle over to them. So, I ruled that the Krew had committed a robbery and not a simple theft; the felony murder rule applied to Jessica T. In juvenile courts, the words "guilty" and "not guilty" are never used. Instead, judges either "sustain" or "deny" the charges that are listed in documents called petitions. (Criminal charges filed against adults are listed in "complaints" or "indictments.") This is because juvenile courts are based on the legal doctrine of parens patriae (literally, "parent of the fatherland"), a principle that views the courts as the protector of children. Juveniles who break the law are "delinquents," not "criminals," whose best interests, welfare, and rehabilitation are, at least in principle, the courts' only concerns.

I sustained the petition that the DA's office had filed against Jessica T. She cried, her attorney sighed, and the prosecutor smiled. With the word "sustained," I had just labeled this fifteen-year-old a killer—for the rest of her life. Did I make the right call? Had I blown it? I tried not to second-guess myself. *You made your ruling; time to move on.* Now, I had to decide what to do with this murderer who had murdered no one at all.

In juvenile court, judges don't impose "sentences." Instead, they issue "dispositional orders." But it's a distinction without a difference: prosecutors want to lock juveniles up; defense attorneys want to let them go. At Jessica T.'s dispositional (sentencing) hearing in March 1993, twenty witnesses testified. I received thirty-five letters from the family and friends of Mark Berkey, a letter written by Jessica T., and two pre-sentencing reports. The battle lines were drawn, the local media was on high alert, and I was feeling the pressure.

The prosecutor, along with Mark's family members, wanted me to send Jessica T. to the California Youth Authority (CYA), the state's juvenile prison, for the maximum term of seven years. Her attorney wanted me to send her to a ranch program, a far less punitive placement that emphasized therapeutic treatment. The maximum stay at the ranch was only a year. Since her arrest, Jessica T. had been held at the county's juvenile detention hall, a facility meant to temporarily house juveniles for thirty to ninety days. By the time of her dispositional hearing, Jessica T. had been held at the juvenile hall for more than a year. This provided the lawyers the time they needed to collect and analyze evidence, line up expert witnesses, review police reports, and develop their trial strategies. Justice moves slowly in a murder case.

In preparation for the dispositional hearing, I read a predispositional report authored by the probation officer assigned to the case. Each of California's fifty-eight counties has a probation department with a chief probation officer who supervises several deputy probation officers. One of their responsibilities is to prepare written predispositional reports with the purpose of helping judges determine the appropriate placements for juveniles.

John Augustus, a crusading Boston shoemaker, pioneered presentencing reports in the 1800s. He firmly believed that the "object of the law is to reform criminals and to prevent crime, and not to punish maliciously or from a spirit of revenge." According to the Center on Juvenile and Criminal Justice:

> *Mr. Augustus gathered background information about the offender's life and criminal history. If he determined that the person was worthy, Augustus provided bail money out of his own pocket. If he succeeded in winning the person's release, he helped her or him find employment and housing. He also appeared at the sentencing hearing and provided the judge with a detailed report of the person's performance. If the report was a good one, Augustus would recommend that the judge suspend the sentence and release the person to his custody.*

Known as the Father of Probation, in 1878 Augustus persuaded the Massachusetts legislature to enact the country's first probation law.

Back then, the purpose of presentence probation reports was to promote individualized sentencing with a focus on the particular offender's potential for rehabilitation and integration back into the community. Over the years, the focus of presentencing reports has shifted dramatically from rehabilitation to punishment. Today, these reports dwell on the nature of the crime, the culpability of the offender, the mitigating and aggravating circumstances, if any there be, and the impact of the crime on the victim. Most simply regurgitate what is written in the police reports, provide cursory statements from the offenders, include extensive victim impact statements, and conclude with sentencing recommendations that are, with rare exception, consistent with the sentences or dispositions requested by prosecutors.

In the 1960s, to counter the prosecution-oriented bent of probation reports, defense attorneys began to utilize privately commissioned pre-sentencing reports that provide in-depth analyses of their clients' back-grounds and describe the circumstances that motivated the criminal conduct—information generally not available in reports authored by pro-bation officers. Today, private presentencing and predispositional reports, along with a new tool—sentencing mitigation videos—are frequently employed by defense attorneys in juvenile and adult courts. The videos are mini-documentaries about the defendants' lives, designed to persuade judges to impose lenient sentences, and according to their proponents, they do. Mr. Christiansen had retained the services of a nonprofit orga-nization in San Francisco to prepare a private predispositional report for Jessica T.

Jessica T.'s female probation officer recommended that Jessica serve a maximum of seven years at the California Youth Authority, identical to the disposition requested by the prosecutor. I noted that her probation report failed to include any mention of possible alternative placements to CYA. Further, there was no information about Jessica's psychological status; I had no idea who this fifteen-year-old girl was. The dispositional report was merely a rehash of the facts disclosed at trial. The report concluded: "Seven years is short compared to one whole lifetime gone for Mark Berkey." *That's really helpful,* I thought. Her predispositional report was little more than a victim impact statement.

Too often there is an informal partnership between probation officers and prosecutors. During adult and juvenile trials, they sit side by side at the counsel table, operating as one entity with two goals—get the conviction and the maximum punishment. True to form, during the trial and dispositional hearing for Jessica, the prosecutor and the probation officer sat together and frequently conferred with one another. Not once did I see the probation officer speak to Jessica T.'s lawyer.

And no one, certainly not judges, ever says anything about this cozy and, in my view, improper arrangement. Never mind that the law clearly states that the probation officer is there to represent the interests of the juvenile; never mind that it is the role of the probation officer to furnish to the judge any assistance and information that Her Honor may require to make an informed decision. The close relationship between prosecutors and probation officers troubled me when I was a defense attorney in private practice in the late 1970s. I said nothing then because I didn't think it would help my client and might actually be held against him, me, or both of us. But now, as a judge, maybe I could or should say something.

At the dispositional hearing, I listened to the heart-wrenching testimony of Mark's family and friends and was deeply touched by their grief. And yet, as much as I felt for them, I had to consider more than their hurt and their understandable desire for retribution. I had to consider the perpetrator. I had to think about Jessica T.

Judges get lots of letters. I have certainly received my share— correspondence from defendants, from inmates, from litigants, and from jurors. Defendants implored me to give them a break, inmates begged me to shorten their sentences now that they had found God, litigants berated me for ruling against them or thanked me for ruling in their favor, and jurors gave me their frank opinions of my courtroom demeanor. In a letter likely written at the behest of her attorney, Jessica T. expressed remorse, writing, in part: "With the time that has passed, at night I lie in bed crying. I pray that somehow I could have stopped what happened." She added that she was now a changed person and that she had found God. "He has helped me to see the evil of my actions and I have asked for his forgiveness." While I did not question her sincerity, the letter did little to assist me in deciding her fate.

And I read letters from Mark's friends attesting to his good character and demanding justice for him. I listened to the cogent and impassioned arguments of Mr. Christiansen and Mr. Kumli. Still, I wondered, *Who is this fifteen-year-old?* Was Jessica's involvement in this crime an aberration or proof of her bad character? How could I fashion the appropriate disposition without knowing the answer to this fundamental question?

Most trial judges announce their rulings from the bench right after the conclusion of the case. Given our substantial caseloads, we have neither the time nor, in some instances, the inclination to reduce our decisions to the written word. In Jessica T.'s case, I believed that a thorough and detailed written decision would ensure that my decision would not be misinterpreted or misconstrued by the attorneys, by Jessica, and especially by the local media. I didn't yet know how I was going to rule; there was much for me to consider.

At home over the weekend, I sat in my living room and penned the decision. A few days later, I read it from the bench, starting off with this:

> *I should note that the prosecutorial bias exhibited in this case is not unusual. Indeed, I have observed this bias, with dismay, from probation officers in every juvenile delinquency case that has come before me. Such an attitude is of no help to the court and flies in the face of the spirit and letter of the law. The probation officer's responsibility is to provide information and assistance to the court so that the judge may carry out the mandate of protecting society and of furnishing care, treatment, and guidance to the minor. Of equal importance is the probation officer's statutory duty to represent the interests of the minor. The probation officer should not be the extension of the office of the district attorney. She should not play a prosecutorial role.*

The prosecutor and the probation officer, sitting together, shifted uncomfortably in their seats. I then announced that I needed a psychological evaluation of Jessica to assist me in understanding who she was. Our court maintained a list of psychologists from which judges could choose to undertake an evaluation of a juvenile or an adult defendant. If the person to be evaluated is indigent, as was Jessica T., the cost of the evaluation is paid by the county, aka the taxpayers. For those who can afford to pay for these evaluations, the juvenile's parents or guardians must foot the bill. I appointed a psychologist from the list and directed him to provide a written evaluation of Jessica at the county's expense. I could see that neither the probation officer nor the prosecutor was pleased about where this was headed. *I* had no idea where this was headed.

A few weeks later, I received the psychological evaluation. As I read it, I began to get a picture of this teen felony murderer. I learned that Jessica T. was an only child whose parents divorced when she was three years old. She resided primarily with her mother, who remarried and divorced a second time when Jessica T. was seven. The stepfather physically abused her mother and was psychologically abusive to Jessica T. Her biological father was a recovering alcoholic. Jessica T.'s acting-out behaviors began when she was twelve years old. She was defiant and came and went as she pleased, sometimes sneaking out of the house at night. She ran away from home several times. Her attendance at school was sporadic and her grades were poor. Still, throughout those years, she was never involved in any criminal activity.

In his assessment, the psychologist concluded:

About the most remarkable thing about Jessica is how basically unremarkable she is. She is reasonably intelligent. She manifests no discernible underlying anger or hostility. She is not prone to act-out in an aggressive fashion. She does show signs of some underlying depression. . . . I think Jessica's involvement with the co-parts [co-defendants] was based primarily on two factors. First of all, in a sense they offered to take care of her. Thus, her dependency needs could be met and at the same time she didn't have to get too close to them emotionally. Second, they offered to take her away to a world of excitement, providing her the opportunity to escape from her despondency over a breakup with her boyfriend . . . I am inclined to believe that Jessica did not realize that anyone was going to be seriously hurt.

A few weeks later, after I had given copies of the psychological report to the attorneys and the probation officer, I reconvened the dispositional hearing. Now, I was ready to rule.

When making dispositional orders, juvenile court judges are required to consider the juvenile's background, her age, her criminal history, if any, and the circumstances and gravity of the crime that she has committed. This is not what victims and their families want to hear. Indeed, if Mark Berkey had been my child, I would not have wanted to hear any of this, either. Reading from my decision, I explained it this way:

> *While retribution may never be a factor in fashioning a dispositional order, punishment and accountability by the minor must be considerations. I have read thirty-five letters from the family and friends of Mark Berkey. The consistent theme throughout is the demand for punishment. All of the writers have asked that I incarcerate Jessica for the longest period of time possible. I respond by telling you that if by locking up Jessica for the rest of her life, I could bring Mark Berkey back, I would do it. But nothing I do will bring Mark back to his family. What I can do, however, is pay attention to Mark's family's and friends' need for punishment, as long as that punishment is consistent with rehabilitation, as required by the law.*

While the law had legally branded Jessica a murderer, in fact, she wasn't. Yes, she had helped set in motion the events that culminated in the taking of Mark Berkey's life; but her conduct, as deceitful as it was, amounted to aiding and abetting a robbery of Mark's friend's Jeep. I believed that placement at CYA—the place of last resort in the juvenile system and the last stop before adult prison—would serve no useful purpose in this case. I told everyone that I had decided to place Jessica in a ranch program, a less punitive environment than the California Youth Authority, where rehabilitation and treatment were emphasized. But there was a problem.

Santa Clara County had no ranch program for girls. Due to budget cuts, the county's only girls' ranch had been eliminated. The two boys' ranches remained. That wasn't going to fly, so I continued the hearing for five days and began making phone calls around the state. I learned that there were eight girls' ranches throughout California. I telephoned every one of them and found that six of the ranches were coed, two were female only, and placement in each program was limited to a maximum of one year. Four of the ranch programs were willing to consider Jessica T. for placement. I chose Kuiper Youth Center in San Bernardino County, in Southern California. Its program had twenty girls, ranging from twelve to eighteen years of age. There was a school on the grounds that provided individual and group therapy.

Back in court, I made it final. I ordered our county to pay San Bernardino County for Jessica T.'s placement at the Kuiper Youth Center where she would serve the maximum term of one year. I quietly hoped that the expense of paying for an out-of-county placement would motivate the reinstatement of the girls' ranch in our county; it eventually did. I further ordered that upon her release, Jessica T. was to be placed on probation for three years, during which time she was to perform one hundred hours of community service.

The next day I was blasted in the headlines of the local newspaper: JUDGE GIVES MURDERER A YEAR. The prosecutor was all over me in the press. Since the *California Code of Judicial Ethics* prohibited judges from responding to public criticism about their decisions, I could say nothing. I was unable to explain my reasoning, even though I had fully explained it in my written decision. The not-so-subtle allegations that I was soft on crime would go unrebutted. It was at times like these that I found some solace in that old judicial adage: "Be long of fuse and thick of skin." I held my tongue, went back to work, and tried not to take it personally.

A judge's worst nightmare is handing down a lenient sentence to a defendant who then reoffends. I certainly had that thought when I chose to send Jessica T. to a ranch program rather than to the California Youth Authority. If she were to mess up, I'd be back in the headlines. But that's the risk of the job. After being locked up in the juvenile hall for more than two years—at the time the longest stay in the history of our county—Jessica was transferred to the Kuiper Youth Center, where she successfully served out her time. After her release, she eventually graduated from college and has remained crime-free.

Steven Jon Bitz, Jeffrey Douglas Hall, Jessica Rene Richie, and Joseph Allen Franklin were convicted of the murder of Mark Berkey. Mr. Bitz is serving a life sentence. Mr. Hall's life-without-parole sentence was commuted by Governor Jerry Brown in 2019, making him eligible for a parole hearing and possible release from prison. Ms. Richie is still incarcerated at the California Institution for Women. As for Joseph Allen Franklin, whether or not he remains incarcerated is unclear.

DOMESTICITY AND
ITS DISCONTENTS

Family Matters

Marriage and Divorce

Marriage has no guarantees. If that's what you're looking for, go live with a car battery.

—ERMA BOMBECK, AMERICAN HUMORIST

I. For Better

It was 1989, a warm Saturday in San Francisco, when I walked into a small hotel room. I was there to solemnize a wedding. John Preiskel, a friend and fellow Stanford Law grad, had asked me to perform the ceremony for the bride and groom, acquaintances of his. I thought, *Why not?* Plus, spending a sunny day in San Francisco would be a treat. With my robe and ceremony script in tow, I was set to perform a weekend wedding, one of the many over which I presided during my time on the bench.

John and the couple were all smiles. The bride was lovely and looked strangely familiar to me. I knew that I had seen her before, but where? Then it hit me. She was the film and television actress Marg Helgenberger, who played K. C. Koloski in the popular ABC drama *China Beach*. (Years later, we would know her as Catherine Willows in the hit show *CSI: Crime Scene Investigation*.) I maintained my cool, smiled, and introduced myself to her and to the groom, Alan Rosenberg, a talented actor in his own right. In a matter of minutes, the ceremony was over, the appropriate papers signed, and the ritual kiss planted. My first (and only) celebrity wedding! And it stuck—for twenty years, until 2009, when she filed for divorce.

Because marriages are regulated by the states, Marg Helgenberger, Alan Rosenberg, and anyone else who wants to marry must first come to someone who, like me, can officiate. In 1639, Massachusetts was the first state to regulate marriage by requiring marriage licenses. By 1929, marriage license laws were mandatory in all of the states. There are no federal marriage laws, although when constitutional issues arise, federal courts will weigh in, such as when the United States Supreme Court lifted the ban on interracial marriage in 1967.

"Common law" marriages—when unmarried couples live together and hold themselves out to the public as married—are exempt from the license requirement. However, only a handful of states recognize common law marriages.

The states give couples permission to tie the knot by issuing them marriage licenses, a task usually assigned to county clerks, with one exception. In response to their displeasure with the U.S. Supreme Court's decision legalizing same-sex marriage, in 2019 the Alabama legislature and its governor abolished marriage licenses entirely. Alabama judges and clergy who oppose the unions of same-sex couples are now off the hook. Newlyweds merely sign marriage contracts. In the Cotton State, governmental approval is no longer needed to wed.

But those couples who seek to marry in the rest of the country must obtain marriage licenses and be quick about it. In California and Mississippi, marriage licenses expire ninety days from their issuance; in Ohio and Vermont, it's sixty days; in Tennessee, it's thirty days; in South Dakota, it's just twenty. But Oklahoma tops them all—just *ten days,* after which the marriage license isn't worth the paper it's printed on. If a couple fails to marry before the license's expiration date—and assuming the wedding is still on—it's back to the county clerk's office to purchase yet another license. The exceptions are Georgia, Idaho, Mississippi, New Mexico, South Carolina, and the District of Columbia, where marriage licenses have no expiration dates.

A marriage is "solemnized" by an "officiant" and witnessed by two adults, all three of whom must sign the marriage license. Once the document is filed with the county clerk, the marriage is legally recognized—everywhere. Because they are public documents, anyone can look at them and learn a boatload of personal information: date and place of the marriage, the newlyweds' full names, their occupations, home addresses, birthdates, birthplaces, their parents' names, and their former names, if they take the last names of their spouses. Understandably, celebrities and other high-profile individuals have concerns about revealing that kind of information to the public—think paparazzi and stalkers, for starters. If, however, they reside in California or Michigan, the problem is solved with the "confidential" marriage license. In Michigan, the confidential license, also called a marriage license without publicity, is permanently sealed by the judge who solemnizes the marriage in a courtroom closed to the public and cannot be accessed without a court order.

In 2012, one-fifth of all marriage licenses in the Golden State were confidential, which means that unless a judge issues a court order allowing the license to be viewed by someone other than the married couple, for all intents and purposes it's as if the marriage never happened.

And then there's the person who figures out a way to use the confidential marriage to her advantage. Janet Manser-LaMont married confidentially in California and in the wake of her spouse's death received Social Security survivor benefits. However, in 1991, when she turned sixty-six, she applied for and received the Social Security benefits she had legitimately earned under her former (aka maiden) name, benefits that totaled more than $130,000 over a period of fifteen years. She received these payments in addition to the survivor benefits payments that resulted from her deceased husband. In 2006, Ms. Manser-LaMont was indicted for the double-dipping, pled guilty in federal court to theft of government property, was placed on five years' probation, and was ordered to pay back the feloniously obtained $130,000.

The majority of wedding officiants are clergy (priests, rabbis, ministers, imams), who solemnize marriages in the name of God. State court judges also preside over weddings and do so in the name of the law.

What if the couple wants their yoga instructor or their best friend to marry them? In most states, including California, anyone eighteen years or older can perform weddings if she becomes an "authorized person of *any* religious denomination." (Emphasis added.) Translation: get ordained. Online churches with names such as the Church of Spiritual Humanism, Rose Ministries, the Temple of Earth, and the Universal Life Church offer quickie ordinations to any adult with boasts such as: "Get Ordained Instantly at the Universal Life Church. Utilizing the ULC's instant online ordination platform, anyone who feels so called can become a minister within seconds"; "First Nation Church and Ministry offers free minister ordination, which permits you to perform marriage ceremonies and other basic rites throughout the United States"; and "United National Ministry does not require any courses or classes to become an ordained minister and you can do it online. Our Minister's Ordination License is Valid in all 50 States and Washington D.C."

The last decade saw a dramatic rise in the number of private citizens who performed weddings. In 2016, 43 percent of couples wed in the United States had friends or family members officiate. The Universal Life Church boasts ordinations of twenty million people worldwide on its website. With minister "ordination kits" commonly selling for $45 and deluxe packages going for more than $95, online ordination is a lucrative cottage industry.

Still, some states frown upon online ordinations. Connecticut requires ministers who solemnize marriages to be "settled in the work of the ministry," meaning if you don't have a congregation or a track record of religious activities, forget it. In July 2019, Tennessee lawmakers, in an effort to block LGBTQ marriages, imposed an outright ban on online ordinations. (Although, in response to litigation initiated by four ordained ministers, a federal court judge has placed a temporary hold on the ban.) In Pennsylvania, while the law permits solemnization by "a minister, priest or rabbi of any regularly established church or congregation," two courts have concluded that an online-ordained minister fits the definition, while another court disagreed. So, in the Keystone State, a couple married by their online-ordained yogi risks a do-over.

When judges perform weddings at courthouses during business hours, they must do so without charging a fee, since weddings are presumed to be all in a day's judicial work. Weekend weddings, however, are an entirely different matter. Judges are free to charge with abandon. In the 1980s when I presided over weddings, the going rate was $50 to $75 per wedding. I am sure the rate has gone up substantially in subsequent years, but there is still no rule for how much to charge; it all depends on for whom the nuptials are performed. If it's the wedding, for example, of one of Mark Zuckerberg's children, go high. On the other hand, if it's your dentist's child who is getting married and you've got lots of cavities, go low or not at all.

Weekend weddings aren't for everyone. Some judges have no desire to spend their Saturdays and Sundays driving around, robes in tow, visiting random homes. But for those judges who can use a bit more compensation, giving up the occasional weekend at home is worth the sacrifice. For me, a divorced single parent with two college-bound children, the extra money was a godsend.

In one instance, I presided over a wedding *twice*—on a Saturday and again the following Monday at the courthouse. The couple, in their thirties, held the first ceremony at their lovely home in a well-to-do community near the city of San Jose on a beautiful Saturday afternoon. Wearing my robe and standing in their handsomely decorated living room, I faced the couple and their smiling guests and delivered my standard wedding spiel. They exchanged rings, gazed lovingly into each other's eyes, and recited their vows, after which I pronounced them married. Along with their two witnesses, I signed the marriage license, posed for a few photos with them and the dozen or so wedding guests, collected my fee, got back into my car, and headed off to the next wedding on my list. *What a nice couple*, I thought. *That's a forever marriage.*

Monday morning, back at work, Benita told me that she had just received an urgent request from the "forever marriage" bride. Someone had shown her a video of her husband's wedding-eve bachelor party that left her so hurt and enraged that she wanted an immediate do-over. Her husband was going to repeat his vows, or they were through. I told Benita to tell her that I was glad to remarry them but that the repeat wedding wouldn't change anything, legally speaking. The second wedding would, in essence, be pretend. That was fine with her. Later that day, ushered into my chambers by Benita, were the grim-faced bride and her equally grim-faced groom. I asked Benita and Olga Olivas, my courtroom clerk, to stand in as (pretend) witnesses for this (pretend) wedding. After the bride said her vows, she held her husband's hands, looked into his eyes, and directed him to say the vows "this time, like you really mean them." He did just as he was told. The (pretend) witnesses and I looked at one another and did our best to remain poker-faced. Then I pronounced them (pretend) married.

One Saturday afternoon, I drove to a recreation center in a San Jose apartment complex to perform a wedding. When I walked into the large room, a twentyish man and woman, both of who were White, walked up to me. Having introduced myself as Judge Cordell who was here to perform the wedding, they did a quick double take, then smiled and introduced themselves as the bride and groom. It was clear that they were surprised to see that their judge was a Black woman. The double take, the look of surprise, the frown were nothing new to me. I frequently got those reactions, and not just at weddings.

Once, in September 1989, I had driven to a reception honoring the county's female judges. The event, held at a beautiful mansion in the nearby city of Los Gatos, included valet service. I drove along the curved driveway, stopped at the front of the home, and waited as the valet, a young White male, approached. When I opened my car door and started to get out, he pointed to the rear and said, "Ma'am, the catering service is in the back." Seven years a judge, and still . . .

Back at the recreation center, the wedding guests had gathered and were seated in several rows of chairs facing the front of the room where the ceremony was to take place. I pulled the couple aside and said, "You need to know that I don't do 'obey,' and I don't do 'God.'" (In my world, the only people who must obey are military personnel and our children. As for God, she doesn't belong in secular wedding ceremonies.) Both nodded and said that they were fine with this. When I asked if there was anything special that they wanted me to say at their ceremony, a question that I routinely put to couples, their response was anything but routine. "We don't want you to use the word 'love' or 'like' in the ceremony," the groom told me. *Hm,* I thought. Everyone knows that wedding ceremonies have to include the word "love." Love, after all, is the foundation of marriage—well, at least theoretically. So, I asked if they were sure that they wanted me to omit the *L* word, and both nodded in agreement. They weren't joking. I had no idea what this was about, and frankly I didn't want to know.

The wedding guests were now settled in and ready for the ceremony to begin. Robe on, I stepped forward and greeted everyone. "Good afternoon. I'm Judge Cordell and am pleased to be here to preside over this wedding." I had no idea of what I was going to say, but I figured that if I dragged out the wedding spiel long enough, the words would come.

I spoke for a while about commitment and how marriage shouldn't discourage the individuality of spouses. Then I asked them to face each other to exchange rings, telling them that each was to repeat after me: "With this ring, I marry you." The solemnization of a marriage has but one legal requirement: the couple must state their intention to marry in the presence of an officiant. Their "I marry you" fulfilled that requirement. Next, I took a deep breath and wrapped up with: "Do you promise to *tolerate* one another," to which each responded, "I do." I pronounced them married, they kissed, the guests cheered, and I got the hell out of there.

What do you do when you are asked to solemnize the union of a ninety-year-old groom and a twenty-five-year-young bride? The two presented themselves at my courtroom, handed me their marriage license, and were ready to make it official. I wondered, *What's love got to do with this one?* It seemed pretty clear to me that the bride was up to no good. What motivation could she possibly have to marry a man old enough to be her great-grandfather other than the love of his money? I didn't want to be a party to his being taken advantage of. But did I have the right to tell a man more than twice my age whom he should or shouldn't marry? If she made him happy, who was I to stand in his way? I spoke with him for a few minutes and concluded that he understood what he was doing; he was cogent and clear that this marriage was what he wanted. So, I proceeded to pronounce them husband and wife and wished them well.

When the ban on same-sex marriage was still in full force and effect in California, I deliberately violated that ban and presided over the wedding of two women. It was June 2000 when I stood in a spacious backyard before fifty wedding guests, family members and friends of the brides, two women in their twenties—one Black, one White. Even though their marriage would not be recognized by the state, I accepted their invitation to officiate as my way to protest California's ridiculous same-sex marriage ban. It was a perfect afternoon, a perfect ceremony, with the perfect balance of love, humor, and solemnity. I concluded with words that generated nods and a collective chuckle from the gathering: "And now, by the power that *will one day* be vested in me, I pronounce you married." Fifteen years later, that "one day" would come to pass.

In May 2008, we had a brief glimpse of that day when the California Supreme Court overturned the state's ban on same-sex marriages. Six months later, after 52 percent of the electorate approved a ballot initiative reinstating the ban, the decision was overturned. But then, on June 26, 2015, the United States Supreme Court, in the case of *Obergefell v. Hodges,* not only struck down all same-sex marriage bans, but also legalized these unions in all fifty states.

For the most part, I found solemnizing marriages to be entertaining and fulfilling—not so much, though, when it came to undoing them.

II. For Worse

I used to be married . . . but I'm much better now.
—UNKNOWN

After I won a seat on the superior court in a contested election, I was assigned to sit in the family court to preside over divorces. That was when I began to appreciate how emotionally draining judicial decision-making could be. During my previous six years as a municipal court judge, I advised thousands of defendants of their rights at arraignment hearings, presided over dozens of drunk driving jury trials, and ruled in hundreds of cases in criminal court, traffic court, and small-claims court. There was nothing in my experience on the municipal court to prepare me for the drama of family court, not even the time that I went to court for my own divorce, two years earlier. Since my ex-husband and I had worked out an agreement, it took all of five minutes for the judge to sign the order and pronounce us divorced.

Almost 50 percent of all marriages in the United States end in divorce or separation. Most divorce cases are, legally speaking, routine affairs, resolved outside of courtrooms in lawyers' offices where agreements are brokered, final "dissolution of marriage" papers signed and submitted to judges for their final approvals, bringing doomed relationships to their official ends. But when acrimony runs so deep that warring spouses are unable or unwilling to work things out, they wind up in court before black-robed functionaries tasked with sorting out the remains of what was—sometimes in headline-grabbing detail.

In 1934, New York tabloids had a field day with the custody battle over ten-year-old heiress Gloria Vanderbilt (the late mother of CNN's Anderson Cooper), waged between her mother, Gloria Morgan, and her paternal aunt, Gertrude Vanderbilt Whitney. After Ms. Morgan's maid testified that she witnessed her boss in bed with a woman who had been "kissing her just like a lover," the commotion in the courtroom was so loud that the judge was forced to close the rest of the trial to the public. Aunt Gertrude prevailed in that one.

Most family court cases involve people with limited resources and seemingly unlimited problems, financial and otherwise. So, it is left to family court judges to determine the amount of money parents pay for child support, figure out how much spousal support the divorced couple must pay to one another, set visitation schedules for noncustodial parents, and decide whether visits should be supervised. Judges divvy up personal property such as silverware, furniture, cars, and stamp collections. And, on occasion, they respond to allegations that restraining orders have been violated.

In one instance, I presided over a hearing in which the ex-husband, a retired physician, wanted me to hold his ex-wife in contempt of court for violating a mutual restraining order that directed them to stay away from one another. Their lawyers were polar opposites. His was an outspoken feminist who had a take-no-prisoners reputation. Hers was a good ole boy family law practitioner. Both lawyers were smart and well prepared. I settled in to watch them square off. Since these were two very high-priced attorneys, I assumed whatever they were fighting over was of great importance.

Answering questions from his attorney, the ex-husband told his story from the witness stand: A few weeks earlier, he had attended his weekly aerobics class, taught by his current and much younger girlfriend, who, of course, had accompanied him to court. As he told his story, she sat in the front row of the spectator seats, beaming. Asked what clothing he had worn in the class, the doctor described a sleeveless workout shirt and tight-fitting black spandex shorts. Shortly after the class began, he looked around and saw, to his dismay, that his ex-wife was there. They ignored each other and exercised along with the rest of the class. When everyone stopped to check their heart rates, he felt a hand grab his right buttock. Asked by his lawyer to identify whose hand it was, he pointed to his ex-wife. *Well,* I mused, *this was a first.* I'd had defendants appear before me for crimes such as indecent exposure and mooning (indecent exposure is limited to genitalia, which buttocks are not) but never for a butt grab.

His attorney wasn't finished. She asked the doctor to step down from the witness stand so that he could demonstrate for me exactly how he was grabbed. There being no objection from the ex-wife's attorney, I gave him the go-ahead. Wearing a handsomely tailored suit, he turned his back to me, and with his right hand, lifted his jacket and squeezed his right cheek. *Wow, yet another first,* I thought.

Now it was the ex-wife's turn. Questioned by her attorney, she testified that while she knew that her ex attended the aerobics class, she didn't believe that she was violating the mutual restraining order by simply being there. After all, it's a free country. During the session, everything was fine, she said, until her ex walked by her. That was when she "tweaked" his buttock. Holding up the index finger and thumb of her right hand, she squeezed the two digits together in a pinching motion. "Why in the world did you touch his buttock?" I asked. She sighed, looked at me, and said, "Judge, I just couldn't help myself."

In his closing argument, the ex-wife's lawyer stated that it was absolutely absurd and a waste of my time and a waste of his client's money to be dragged into court over such a silly matter. "All of this fuss over a little tweak?" he asked. "Ridiculous!" I was inclined to agree with him.

The ex-husband's attorney stood and responded. "Your Honor, if this had been a woman's buttock, we wouldn't be calling this a waste of time and money, would we?" She continued, "We all know that if *he* had grabbed *her* buttock, no one would trivialize that. Judge, don't use a double standard here. The consequence for tweaking a male buttock should be no different from tweaking a female one. She violated your restraining order, plain and simple."

She was right, of course. Had the roles been reversed, I would have taken the matter somewhat more seriously. I held the tweaker in contempt and issued a new restraining order directed just to her: no more aerobics classes with her ex.

In forty-one of the fifty states, all that an unhappily married person has to do to secure a divorce is assert that irreconcilable differences have arisen in the marriage. In these "no-fault" states, of which California was the first in 1969, it's ask and ye shall receive. Divorce granted, no questions asked. In nine states, people who want out of their misalliances must first establish grounds for their divorces. In these "fault" states, judges *or juries* make those determinations. For example, in Georgia, there are thirteen possible grounds for divorce, including impotency or mental incapacity at the time of marriage, adultery during the marriage, desertion, cruel treatment, and habitual drug addiction. In Tennessee, one ground for divorce is the attempted murder of one spouse by the other. That sounds about right.

The forty non-community-property states follow "equitable distribution" rules, meaning any property earned by a spouse remains that spouse's individual separate property. In other words, If I earned it, it's mine, 'til death do us part. California is a community property state, which means that all assets acquired during the marriage (income, real property, stocks, personal property—everything) are deemed to belong to the marital community and, therefore, must be equally divided between the divorcing couple. There are nine community property states. Make it ten if you count Alaska, where divorcing couples may mutually agree to have their assets classified as community property.

In one case, after a half hour of testimony and arguments from the lawyers, I gave a divorcing couple joint custody of their Mercedes; each got the car on alternate weeks. Not long into my stint on the family court, I presided over a hearing in which a man calmly explained that he wanted his ex-wife to return his dentures, putting my ability to maintain a poker face to the test. The courtroom was filled with litigants who, waiting to have their cases heard, were intrigued by the case of the missing dentures, as was I. To confirm that his uppers were, in fact, AWOL, I asked him to approach the bench so that I could inspect his mouth. His uppers were definitely not there. I then turned to the ex-wife who stood before me, arms folded, scowl on her face, and asked if she did, indeed, have the man's dentures. (I questioned them directly because they were representing themselves.) She looked at me and said, "Yes, Judge, I have his teeth."

At this point, the chuckling of the spectators was so loud that Benita stood up and politely yet firmly directed them to quiet down. It was all that I could do not to chuckle along with them. When I ordered the ex-wife to return his teeth, she said, "I can't, Judge, because I put them in storage with all the rest of his things," which was met with more chuckling from the spectators and, now, Benita. I told the woman to go get the dentures and then ordered both of them back to court that afternoon.

I heard more than twenty cases that morning, took the noon recess, and at 1:30 P.M. was back to business. When I entered the courtroom, every seat was filled, with some people even standing in the rear. I found this strange, since fewer cases were set for that afternoon than I had heard in the morning. I sat down and looked out at the crowd, many of whom looked familiar. That's when I realized that they were spectators from the morning session who came back to see the resolution of the missing dentures case. Right off the bat, I called that case, and as the couple stepped forward, she dragged behind her a large and bulging black trash bag. When I directed her to return the teeth, she opened the bag and slowly removed and dropped onto the floor several pieces of her ex's clothing—his underwear, socks, shirts, and pants. At the bottom of the bag, of course, were the dentures; she reluctantly handed them over to their rightful owner. Case closed. Sure, this hearing gave everyone a chuckle, but at the same time it was sad. The dispute wasn't about teeth. It was about yet another couple who needed the assistance of a stranger in a black robe to bring to a close their fractured marital relationship.

In 2018, California's governor, Jerry Brown, a professed dog lover, signed Assembly Bill 2274, which elevated family pets to the status of family members. The law directs judges to handle custody battles over pets in the same manner that they resolve child custody disputes. Under this new law, pet custody decisions must include consideration of such factors as to whom the pets are most closely bonded, who feeds Fido, who spends the most time with Duke, who takes Princess to the vet, and, well, you get the picture. In one case, I was forced to split up the pups in a canine custody battle. I gave one dog to each ex-spouse—a Solomonic call, since the couple testified that the two dogs were closely bonded and didn't want to be separated. In yet another pet custody dispute, the divorcing couple fought over their cats, all four of whom resided with the ex-husband. Because the terms of the ex-wife's rental agreement forbade pets, she petitioned the court to allow her to visit with two of the cats, her favorites, at the home of her ex-husband. Surprisingly, he agreed, but on the condition that I appoint someone to supervise the visits; he didn't trust his ex to be left alone in his residence. And since he would be providing room and board for her two kitties, he felt it only fair that I order her to reimburse him the costs of their care and feeding. It all sounded fair to me, so I happily gave them what they wanted—cat support for him, supervised cat visitation for her.

No matter how thorny the distribution of assets—be they money, dentures, cars, or cats—those determinations pale when compared to the complexity, difficulty, and pain in deciding issues of child custody. In all states except Texas, where parents can choose to have juries decide who gets the kids, child custody decisions are the exclusive province of judges.

When it comes to these frequently traumatic disputes, reality is subjective: everyone is to be believed and no one is to be believed. While the financial declarations that parents are required to file about their income and expenses are frequently suspect, it was my experience that parents rarely lied about matters of child custody. The problem was that by the time these cases wended their way to the courtroom, parents perceived very differently from one another what it was their children needed or what constituted their children's best interests.

Only eleven days into my family court assignment, I had presided over five child custody hearings where I listened to testimony, considered evidence, ruled, and prayed that I hadn't done too much damage. Day ten ended with a seven-year-old girl who, after I ordered that she was to live with her mother, screamed in protest. It was a wild scene as she ran around the courtroom, crying out for her Bible-toting dad, with her mother, stepsister, and their lawyer in hot pursuit. All the while, across the hall stood her father, yelling and wildly waving the New Testament.

After several bailiffs removed him from the courthouse, Benita escorted the screaming child and her mom outside. I was exhausted. When I reflected on the trauma that our family court process inflicted on this little girl, my heart ached. There had to be a better way.

California Family Laws and Rules requires that judges make custody decisions based solely upon what is in the best interests of children:

> *In making a determination of the best interest of the child . . . the court shall, among any other factors it finds relevant, consider all of the following: (a) the health, safety, and welfare of the child; (b) any history of abuse by one parent or any other person seeking custody against . . . (1) Any child to whom he or she is related by blood or affinity or with whom he or she has had a caretaking relationship, no matter how temporary. (2) The other parent. (3) A parent, current spouse, or cohabitant of the parent or person seeking custody, or a person with whom the parent or person seeking custody has a dating or engagement relationship . . . (c) The nature and amount of contact with both parents . . . (d) The habitual or continual illegal use of controlled substances or habitual or continual abuse of alcohol by either parent.*

No matter how diligently judges consider and apply the relevant best interest factors, and no matter how much evidence is thrown at them in embattled courtrooms, judges have only secondhand information to work with. And even when that information is relatively complete and reasonably objective (which is as good as it gets), it can't adequately address the dynamics unique to each family. In the words of Tolstoy in *Anna Karenina,* "All happy families are alike; each unhappy family is unhappy in its own way."

To compound the problem, whereas in most civil litigation judges can take their time ruling on motions or in criminal cases—where judges frequently grant long continuances—delay in child custody matters can be disastrous. For families in crisis, time is of the essence. In the end, judges must take it on faith that they've made the right decision.

A "best interest" case left me in a quandary. The mother resided in Southern California with her five-year-old son, along with her twelve-year-old daughter from another relationship. The boy's father, who lived in Santa Clara County, had only recently reappeared in his son's life. For several months, he requested that the mother let the boy visit with him; she refused, insisting that visits with him would be detrimental to the child. She came up with all manner of excuses to stop the visits: the boy had a cold and couldn't travel, her car broke down en route to the airport, the weather was too inclement to travel, and on and on. As a result, they had been to court eight times.

On their ninth court appearance, albeit their first time in my court, I referred them to an evaluator with Family Court Services, an arm of the family court staffed by licensed social workers and family therapists, whose role is to assess the family dynamics of the parents and to make custody recommendations to judges. Even though the evaluator found that the boy was thriving with his mother and had very real attachments to his half sister, his recommendation was to change custody to the father. His thinking was that Dad would be more willing than Mom to comply with visitation orders. While that was likely true, would it really be in the boy's best interest to change custody to the father if he was clearly thriving in his mother's custody? It didn't seem right. And yet, time with the father was important for the boy's development. Depriving him of visitations with his dad—that didn't seem right, either. And if I were to follow the recommendation of the evaluator and place the child primarily with his father, would I be punishing the child for his mother's noncompliance? That didn't seem right, either. So, what was in the best interests of this little boy? Damned if I knew.

According to the family code, all I had to do was simply assess how well the child was doing and consider "any other factors I found relevant." Any other relevant factors? What did that mean? I was no closer to figuring out what to do. But what I did figure out was that lawyers-turned-judges with no training in child psychology or child development are in no position to decide what is best for children. And there I was, a lawyer-turned-judge with no such training, whose only experience with children was raising my two daughters. I had to wing it and try something outside of the box.

Since it was the mother's noncompliance that needed to be addressed, I ordered her to deposit into a trust account sufficient money to cover a round-trip plane ticket to Southern California (economy class), from which only the father could make withdrawals. If she were to refuse to allow the father his scheduled visitation, he could withdraw money from the account to pay for a round-trip flight to pick up his son. Then the mother was required to replenish the account before the child's next scheduled visitation with his father. It turned out that the mother's aversion to paying for her ex's plane fare outweighed her aversion to his visits with their son. Her initial deposit into the trust account remained untouched.

Divorcing parents tend to fall into three categories: (1) two wonderful parents, (2) two rotten parents, and (3) one good parent and one lousy parent. The last scenario is the easiest to address; the good parent gets primary custody, end of story. Unfortunately, judges are rarely presented with this constellation. That would make their work way too easy.

Two wonderful parents? That's a hard one. You might ask, Why not joint physical custody? (There is also joint *legal* custody, where both parents participate in decisions about their children's health, safety, education, and welfare, such as choosing a pediatrician or where the children go to school.) With joint *physical* custody, each parent has equal time with the children—one week with one parent, then one week with the other. A win-win for the parents, yes, but not so much for the kids. Imagine a child having to move back and forth between two residences every week. (In the typical primary custody arrangement, the child lives in one home and on alternate weekends, some holidays, and summers resides with the other parent.) The disruption caused by the weekly shuffle of children between residences in joint physical custody arrangements is not, I think, in the kids' best interests.

It is said that Sigmund Freud opted to sit behind his patients and out of their view to spare himself the fatigue of continuous eye contact with them. I get it. To look into the eyes of two good parents, well-meaning and committed to their children, and to tell them that only one of them would have primary custody was one of the most painful aspects of my job. But the knowledge that the children would be nurtured by good parents—no matter to which parent I gave primary physical custody—offered me some solace.

Finally, when it is bad parent vs. bad parent, think mission impossible. Choosing between two lousy parents is a no-win for the children, the parents, and the judge. What is in the child's best interest in this situation? Do you pick the least bad parent? If so, how does that work? Time to bring in the experts.

Since judges are strictly limited to considering the evidence that is presented in the courtroom, they are left to rely on court-appointed clinicians and therapists to give them accurate and objective evaluations. Once having completed an evaluation of a parent who is requesting custody of a child, an evaluator will come to court and offer the judge an assessment.

I recall one case where the therapist/evaluator gave the mother a diagnosis of avoidant personality disorder and urged that I not give her custody of her daughter. Given that the average judge's knowledge of psychology ranges from slim to none at all, the concepts and vocabulary peculiar to mental health professionals are of very limited value. Fortunately for me, my partner, Florence, is a clinical psychologist, so I knew to look to the *DSM* (*Diagnostic and Statistical Manual of Mental Disorders*), the bible of mental health professionals, for explanations.

According to the *DSM*, avoidant personality disorder is "a pervasive pattern of social inhibition, feelings of inadequacy, and hypersensitivity to negative evaluation, beginning by early adulthood and present in a variety of contexts" such as being "unwilling to get involved with people unless certain of being liked" or "avoids social or occupational activities that involve significant interpersonal contact."

I understood that the evaluator was telling me that the mother was someone with serious social constriction. But did that render her an inadequate parent? A clinical diagnosis is a *conclusion*. The law, however, requires specificity for the judge, the trier of fact, to arrive at a conclusion. For example, when a court-appointed therapist describes a parent as obnoxious or hostile, what does that really mean? Does it mean aggressive? Does it mean assertive? Does it mean demanding? Does it mean that the parent is reacting to a highly stressful situation? Or does it mean that the parent simply rubbed the therapist the wrong way? And how did this obnoxious behavior relate to the quality of parenting? What judges need to hear is evidence— what clinicians observe, what they see, and what they hear from the parents and children. What judges need to know is the thinking behind therapists' conclusions and the specific behaviors that cause therapists concern.

It is the responsibility of court-appointed evaluators to limit their evaluations and their testimony to matters about which they have substantial knowledge. Unfortunately, not every evaluator recognizes her limits. I heard about the testimony of a psychologist who served as an expert witness in a custody dispute in the courtroom of one of my colleagues. The child involved in this particular custody battle, a little girl, was African American, as were her parents. The mother was light skinned with curly hair. The father was darker skinned with kinkier hair. The psychologist, a White female, when interviewing the mother for the evaluation, asked her to draw a picture of a woman; the psychologist subsequently concluded that the mother had drawn a self-portrait.

According to the court transcript of the hearing, this was the testimony of the psychologist/evaluator, a sixtyish White woman, when questioned by the mother's attorney:

Attorney: You indicated earlier this morning that the mother didn't identify with her African American heritage. Is that your contention?

Doctor: My contention was mainly that she didn't have a strong identification as an African American woman, that's correct, and I had some concerns with regard to her daughter's sense of identity as she entered adolescence.

Attorney: And what leads you to that conclusion?

Doctor: Mainly the drawings which she did for me in part of the testing process.

When questioned about the drawing, the evaluator testified that she believed it showed that the mother did not have a strong identification with African Americans. When asked what the picture would look like if the mother had had a stronger Black self-identification, she testified: "The hair would be more coarse and curly."

Doctor: My concern about the racial identification was only that the child has a strong resemblance to her father, her father's coloring, father's hair. There are a lot of things about her which are different than her mom. That's my concern.

Attorney: Did the mother give you any background in her history at Stanford University in regard to what extent she was involved in the Black movement at the time?

Doctor: I could look through my notes to see . . . I will look through here and see if she said anything.

Attorney: Do you recall a conversation you had with the mother in regard to her living at the Black dormitory at Stanford?

Doctor: I guess I didn't write it down in my notes.

Attorney: Do you recall that the mother told you that while she was at Stanford, she organized the very first Malcolm X Day at Stanford?

Doctor: No, she did not tell me that.

Attorney: Do you recall her telling you that she was a member of the National Black MBA Association at Stanford?

Doctor: Yes, she told me that . . . There's a real serious conflict introduced in a child under such circumstances particularly when she herself looks more like her dad than her mom.

As a consequence of that testimony, the family court judge, a White male who was apparently no better informed than was the psychologist about things African American, adopted the psychologist's recommendation and changed primary custody of the little girl from her light-skinned, curly-haired mother to her darker-skinned, kinky-headed father. Of course, omitted from this absurd construal of racial identification was the issue of gender identification. Apparently, for this psychologist, in determining custody of a child, shades of Blackness trumped being female.

Some attorneys have perfected the art of turning custody matters into adversarial circuses. In their seemingly endless armamentarium is the therapist as hired gun. Consider the case that came before me after a lengthy custody trial before another judge who had given primary custody of a seven-year-old girl and her nine-year-old brother to their mother. The issue I had to decide was the father's request that the children, who had been with him for the summer, should remain with him.

The one witness, a clinical psychologist retained by the father, had sound credentials. However, I noted that he had not interviewed the mother. His only observations of her were those garnered in the waiting room of the courthouse *after* he had completed his written evaluation report. Not surprisingly, it was the psychologist's assessment that his client, the father, was the parent of choice for the children. In his testimony, he described the mother in this fashion:

> *There was a small altercation between myself and the mother. The children were running very, very quickly around the [waiting] room, which I thought was getting too rambunctious and dangerous. They could fall and be in danger. She told them they could run for one more minute. I asked them to come and see a movie at the moment. She became very upset with me. Her words to me were: "Why are you always contradicting me?" We have had no time to be contradictory to each other. So, she became— obviously very upset.*

As I listened to his testimony, I thought: Imagine a woman locked in a custody battle with her ex-spouse, a battle that has persisted for three years. She finds herself confined in a courthouse waiting room in consort with a psychologist hired by her ex who is shortly going to testify that her ex is a fine, upstanding human being and that she is not. There are at least three possible responses that the mother might have to that psychologist: (1) she might be interested in his profession and engage him in a scintillating conversation, (2) she might be pleased to find another adult in the waiting room with whom she could strike up a friendly conversation, or (3) she might fantasize screaming at him at the top of her lungs. But rather than act on that fantasy, she redirects her anger and allows her children to engage in rambunctious play in the courthouse waiting room. I found the psychologist's adversarial stance in rooting for the father, while never bothering to evaluate the mother, to be of little value. The opinions of hired-gun clinicians—advocates for one side or the other—who square off in custody disputes are rarely, if ever, useful to judges making custody decisions.

The question that should concern all of us is whether child custody matters have a place in an adversarial setting. Combat may be fit for the criminal justice arena where the goals are to weed out the truth, punish the guilty, and free the innocent. Similarly, combat is useful for civil litigation where lawyers battle mightily over money. But when the goal is to determine the best interests of children, a system in which (privileged) parents resort to hired-gun advocates who duke it out before judges with limited or no formal training in child development is, at best, of questionable value. To level the playing field and to reduce the combative nature of custody disputes, why not adopt a collaborative team approach where judges refer difficult custody decisions to mental health professionals, approved and funded by the court, who, together, conduct thoughtful and well-reasoned evaluations for judges' consideration?

Shortly after beginning my assignment on the family court, I audited a course at Stanford Law School taught by renowned child psychologist Eleanor Maccoby and Michael Wald, a nationally recognized juvenile law professor. While I continued to struggle with child custody decisions, at least the class gave me a rudimentary framework and vocabulary with which to think about the best interests of children. Having attended this class, I believe that judges who preside over child custody cases should be required to take courses on child development and child psychology.

A no less compelling question is why the newest and greenest of judges, as was I, are handed this assignment in the first place. Why are family courts so often the province of the least experienced? Why are life-altering child custody decisions thrust upon judicial neophytes?

For starters, there's the excitement factor. Judges delight in presiding over interesting and intellectually challenging cases; a lawsuit that presents novel legal issues or involves high-profile personalities is a judge's dream. There is, alas, nothing particularly exciting about distributing community property or calculating child support payments or issuing restraining orders. When you have twenty, thirty, or forty of these hearings a day, as I had, the process of decision-making begins to resemble an assembly line.

And there's the exhaustion factor. Family court is a pressure cooker. When I concluded my three-year tour of duty in the family court, having spent seven to eight hours a day, four to five days a week, dealing with combative lawyers, dueling experts, fretful children, and warring parents, I was physically and emotionally drained. Rancor, heartbreak, confusion, bitterness, despair, outrage—all are visited on family court judges who daily render decisions that immediately and forever impact the lives of families. It is no wonder that civil and criminal trials, where juries, not judges, are the deciders, are the preferred assignments. Newer judges must take a backseat to the more senior judges; family court is at the back of the bus.

In 1989, my second year on the family court, I was the supervising judge, which meant I had oversight over my three colleagues who also served on the family court, as well as some latitude to do what I felt was needed to ensure that our court would run smoothly and fairly.

Many of the custody cases in our court involved angry noncustodial parents, most frequently fathers frustrated by the strenuous opposition of the mothers to their attempts to visit their children. Some of the fathers had abused alcohol or were drug dependent; others had histories of child abuse; still others were virtual strangers, having only recently reappeared in their children's lives. In many instances, I allowed the dads their visits but only on the condition that their visitations would be supervised, at least initially. Exactly who would provide the supervision, where the visits would take place, and how the supervision would be arranged, I didn't know. I didn't think much about it.

Judges order people to do things; that's what they do. They demand that litigants pay fines, attend counseling sessions, vacate apartments, make restitution, and much more. But rarely, if ever, do they contemplate *how* their orders will be carried out. Does the defendant have the wherewithal to pay that fine? Can the woman with an alcohol addiction afford the fee for the court-ordered counseling? Where will the evicted family end up? There's no time to ponder these questions; judges are, after all, very busy people. But when some of these dads returned to court, they educated me: they had not visited with their children because they didn't know who would supervise the visits and when or where the visits were to take place. They hadn't the faintest idea how to comply with my orders. While I had determined that it was in the best interests of the children to spend time with their dads, I realized that there was no one to ensure that my orders would actually be carried out. This got me thinking.

Trial judges are in a unique position to improve our legal system. They can introduce innovative programs to make the system more responsive to all of its participants. Take juvenile dependency court, where judges must decide how to address the needs of children who have been abandoned, neglected, and abused. In 2017, San Francisco County Superior Court judge Nancy Davis introduced a "comfort" dog in the San Francisco juvenile dependency courtroom to provide support and company to traumatized children while they waited to hear their fate. Would they be placed in foster homes, in group homes, or with relatives? In a similar vein, after noticing an increasing number of veterans on his docket, New York judge Robert Russell created the first Veterans Treatment Court to meet the specialized mental health, drug, and alcohol needs of veterans.

Charles Hamilton Houston—a pioneering African American civil rights attorney, architect of the legal strategy that led to the decision in *Brown v. Board of Education,* and the first dean of Howard University School of Law—famously said, "Lawyers are either social engineers or parasites on society." This was my philosophy when, as a lawyer, I chose to devote my law practice to representing the underserved. And in the judicial arena, I believe that judges are either activists for justice or black-robed do-nothings. My notion of judicial activism differs from the widely promulgated caricature of activist judges as outliers who ignore long-standing court decisions or who make rulings entirely suited to their own political beliefs. In my world, judicial activists implement and support changes to improve our legal system, while maintaining a deep and abiding respect for judicial precedent.

Returning to the family court, with funding from the Judicial Council of California and private foundations and with the invaluable assistance of the late Professor David Rosenhan, a Stanford psychology professor, in 1990, I created the Supervised Visitation Program, the first in the nation that trained volunteer seniors to monitor visits between noncustodial parents and their children at seven senior community centers. The training consisted of sessions where the seniors role-played a variety of possible visitation scenarios. For example, Dr. Rosenhan or I portrayed a contentious dad who resented that his visit was supervised, an argumentative mom who arrived late to pick up her child from the visitation, and a dad who ignored the supervising senior's directions. Fortunately, rarely, if ever, did these kinds of problems actually arise. Our Supervised Visitation Program was a win-win. Noncustodial parents and their kids got to know one another, and seniors felt useful.

Thereafter, when our family court judges issued orders for noncustodial parents to have supervised visits, they actually could. In no time, more than fifty families, many of them highly conflicted, had been referred by judges for noncustodial parental visitations. The cost to the visiting parent was just $10 per hour for a one-hour visitation. The following year, the neighboring county of San Mateo created a Family Visitation Center. By 1992, supervised visitation services had become a cottage industry. Hundreds of independent service providers sprang up across the country. Ultimately, the Supervised Visitation Network was formed, a nonprofit organization that established minimum practice standards for professional supervised visitations and serves as a resource for the courts and educators.

The road to reform was not nearly as smooth when I turned my attention to legislating change within the family court. Actually, it was a disaster. In early 1990, as I began year three of my family court assignment, after speaking at a statewide conference about problems in the family court system, I was contacted by Rebecca Morgan, a highly respected, moderate Republican state senator from Silicon Valley. She told me that if I could think of a way to improve the family court, she would propose legislation to make it happen. I had an idea.

When couples split up, the payment of child support becomes an urgent matter. Since most noncustodial parents don't simply volunteer to pay child support, it is important that parents secure a court order as quickly as possible. Typically, a parent seeking support must retain an attorney who files the necessary paperwork and gets a court date for the hearing. Those parents with limited incomes, who cannot afford lawyers' retainer fees, are left to muddle through the child support thicket on their own.

So, why not help indigent and low-income parents navigate the child support system by providing them with child support advisers, free of charge? No need to hire lawyers; instead, the court could provide law clerks or specially trained court assistants to help parents complete the appropriate forms, calculate the initial child support payments that were likely to be ordered, and then assist the parents in securing their court dates. I pitched the idea to the senator, and she liked it.

Senate Bill 680 (SB 680), introduced by Senator Morgan, called for a pilot project to be implemented in Santa Clara and San Mateo Counties that would provide child support advisers to assist low-income custodial parents in need of initial child support orders. Several months later, in October, Governor Pete Wilson signed SB 680 into law, the first legislation of its kind in the nation.

But there was a problem. Unbeknownst to me and to Senator Morgan, SB 680 had been amended *seven times* as it worked its way through the legislature. The final version, approved by the Assembly Judiciary Committee, had been expanded to allow judges to make initial orders for child custody and the division of property, along with child support, all without the involvement of lawyers. This version of SB 680 was not the bill that the senator and I had envisioned or wanted.

Lawyers were outraged that they had been excluded from family court hearings. I got that. The judges who joined in the fray were never really comfortable with my presence on the court, no matter what I did. So, when the presiding judge advised me that I could stay on the family court but no longer as the supervising judge, I reluctantly decided that it was best that I move on to another assignment.

After word of my departure from the family court appeared in a local newspaper column, lawyers immediately took sides. Some were infuriated; others were pleased. I was a beacon for change or a menace to the well-being of the court. I was a staunch fighter for greater legal access for the poor and increased efficiency of the judicial system or the poster child for out-of-control judicial activism. JUDGE REASSIGNMENT STIRS TROUBLE and CORDELL BIDS FAMILY COURT A FOND, AND FIERY, FAREWELL were the local headlines.

On Friday, December 14, 1991, at a noontime gathering of more than one hundred members of the Santa Clara County Bar Association's Family Law Section at San Jose's Fairmont Hotel, I bade farewell in a ten-minute speech. "It was the best of assignments; it was the worst of assignments," I began. After praising the family law bench and bar, I turned to the attacks from the handful of attorneys that had plagued my tenure as the supervising judge. "I hope that before these lawyers would bring complaints against judges to the likes of the Commission on Judicial Performance [California's judicial disciplinary body], they would either convey their concerns to the judge or follow appellate procedures if our decisions do not please them." Many of the lawyers in the audience were clearly shocked on learning that some of their colleagues had subjected me to frivolous albeit time-consuming investigations. I continued, "The energy that I have had to expend in fending off these personal attacks would have been far better spent on attending to the needs of this court."

Next, I addressed the harassment to which I had been subjected by special interest groups. "I wish that the parents of my successors will be spared the copies of hate mail, of which my own parents have been recipients." While on the family court, I had been a longtime target of a hate mail campaign by the National Congress of Men, a group that claimed family court judges were biased against men. They frequently picketed the family courthouse, handed out flyers attacking me, and mailed hit pieces about me to the media and even to my parents on the East Coast. Once again, there was an audible gasp from the audience. I concluded, "It would be so easy for the bench leadership to occasionally acknowledge the family court judges, who are isolated from their colleagues, and to commend them for their good work. I challenge anyone to find a family court system anywhere in this state—make that in this country—which is more efficient, more innovative, and more user-friendly than is ours." Fighting back tears, I received two standing ovations.

SB 680's pilot project never saw the light of day.

Where There's a Will

Court Battles Over the Dearly Departed

Death is not the end. There remains the litigation over the estate.
—AMBROSE BIERCE, AMERICAN AUTHOR

By the time that I was assigned to the probate court in January 1994, I had already presided in criminal court, juvenile court, family court, small-claims court, and traffic court. But none of those assignments prepared me for the highly specialized world of probate. The probate court oversees the transfer of property from the estate of a person who has died. Simply put, it is the legal process for determining who gets the decedent's spoils, but simple it isn't. The *California Probate Code,* a tome that exceeds six hundred pages, contains the laws that govern probate. When I began my two-year probate assignment, I had only a generalized idea of what probate was about. After perusing the probate code, I was no closer to finding out. Take, for example, Section 80:

Section 80. Totten trust account
"Totten trust account" means an account in the name of one or more parties as trustee for one or more beneficiaries where the relationship is established by the form of the account and the deposit agreement with the financial institution and there is no subject of the trust other than the sums on deposit in the account. In a Totten trust account, it is not

essential that payment to the beneficiary be mentioned in the deposit agreement. A Totten trust account does not include (1) a regular trust account under a testamentary trust or a trust agreement which has significance apart from the account, or (2) a fiduciary account arising from a fiduciary relation such as attorney-client.

I had no idea what that meant then; I have no idea now. When I asked one of my more seasoned colleagues to explain a Totten trust to me, he told me: "Don't worry about it. The lawyers will educate you about all of this stuff." He didn't have a clue, either. So, I'd just have to wing it until I got the hang of things. If that didn't work, the probate lawyers would quickly learn that their judge was a fraud.

What little I knew about wills was that everyone should have one. Many of us don't. Celebrities are no exceptions—Aretha Franklin, Prince, Amy Winehouse, Bob Marley, Jimi Hendrix, and Sonny Bono all died without leaving wills. Forty years after Bob Marley's death in 1981, the heirs are still battling over his estate. Death is not a subject about which most of us care to think, let alone prepare. Truth be told, it wasn't until I presided in the probate court that I finally got around to preparing my own will.

The purpose of a will is to ensure that your postdeath directives are followed and that your beneficiaries get all that you have chosen to leave them. When you are dead, you obviously have no say in such matters, so you have to trust that the person whom you have selected, your executor, will abide by your wishes. So, what happens when your directives are not followed? It's time to head to probate court.

In one of my cases, the beneficiaries had a problem: they couldn't stand each other. The deceased left an estate of about $400,000 in cash to wife number two and the adult daughter of wife number one. In his will, he directed that the two women were to share equally in the estate, on one condition—they were to expend $2,000 for two parties ($1,000 per party) that they were to throw in his memory, at each of his two favorite bars. The beneficiaries wanted no part of it; neither wanted to spend the cash on the bash, which was the only thing on which they agreed. The executor, tasked with implementing the will's directives, brought the two to court with a request that I put the kibosh on the postmortem parties. At the hearing, the executor told me that after the decedent's second marriage, wife number two had succeeded in alienating not only the man's daughter but also each and every one of the decedent's buddies; there was simply no one left to invite to the festivities. "So, Your Honor," he asked, "how can you have a party if nobody comes?" Made sense to me. With a stroke of my pen, I buried the whole affair.

In California, as is the case in most states, a valid will has two basic requirements: (1) the testator (the author of the will) must be of sound mind when executing the will; and (2) two adults, unrelated to the testator and who are not beneficiaries, must witness the testator's signature and then sign their own names. (Witnesses shouldn't read the wills because the contents are none of their business.) Once a person dies, the executor or executrix (the female of the species) takes charge by hiring a probate attorney who presents the will and the death certificate to a probate judge, who then orders the executor to distribute the assets as specified in the will. It's a simple and straightforward process—usually.

In what I assumed was a routine probate matter, the sole beneficiary of a will was a woman who stood ready to inherit a substantial sum of money and several businesses from her deceased husband. But there was a hurdle. She was accused of murdering him. If convicted, the only thing that she would inherit would be a very long prison sentence; murderers cannot inherit from their victims. Since no other beneficiaries were named in the will, were a jury to find her guilty, her spouse's estate would be distributed as if there were no will at all. It would be handled according to the laws of intestacy that determine how an estate is distributed when a person dies without a will or when a will is deemed to be invalid. The rules of intestate succession vary from state to state, but generally, the first in line to inherit is the decedent's spouse, then her children, followed by her parents, then her siblings, grandparents, cousins, and so on. I ended up postponing the alleged murderer's probate hearing until the conclusion of her jury trial.

Two years later, when my probate assignment had ended, her trial had yet to begin.

Probate court is also a forum in which the disgruntled can challenge or contest wills. At one hearing, a young woman objected to the provision in her father's will that left everything to her stepmother, his wife of twenty-eight years, and nothing to her, his only child. Arguing that his wife had pressured her dearly departed dad into excluding her from the will, she accused the wife of exerting undue influence over him. "Undue influence," a legal term, happens when someone uses her relationship with another person to pressure that person to do her bidding. In the world of wills, undue influence is a big no-no.

His daughter had left out one important piece of information, however. Her father had filed a complaint with the police accusing her of stealing his jewelry. Little wonder, then, that she wasn't listed as his beneficiary. Still, she continued to insist that there was more to the story and was ready and willing to fight on in court. Since a protracted legal battle could generate substantial legal fees that might easily deplete the estate, I convinced both sides to sit down with me to discuss a settlement. What his daughter wanted was her daddy's money; in the end, she got some.

In California, when will contests go to trial, there are no juries; judges alone have the honor of making final decisions. (Nonjury trials are called court trials.) One weeklong probate trial turned out to be a real-life soap opera. The protagonists, two brothers—forty-three-year-old Bruce L. and forty-five-year-old Steve L.—were in a high-stakes battle over their mother's estate. Having died from Alzheimer's at the age of sixty-five, their mother, Elaine, had written a will leaving everything to Bruce, who for twenty years had lived with her and taken care of her—sort of. Elaine's estate consisted of two run-down houses that, because they were situated in Silicon Valley, were worth several million dollars (location, location, location). She also had $2,000 in a savings account. Steve, on the other hand, had left home in his early twenties and resided in Idaho with his wife and three children. Contending that she was not of sound mind when their mother executed her will, Steve returned to California to contest his mother's will in court.

Three lawyers—one for Bruce and two retained by Steve—called fourteen witnesses to testify, three of whom were physicians who were in agreement that Elaine's dementia had been so advanced that she could not possibly have understood the will that she had signed. Bruce, of course, disagreed.

When it was time for the brothers to testify, Steve went first. Since he was the one contesting the will, the burden was on him to prove to that his mother had been incompetent when she signed the document. Steve answered his lawyer's questions in a straightforward manner and weathered the rigorous cross-examination by Bruce's attorney. I was left with the impression that Steve was a credible witness. Since this was a court trial, and I could ask my own questions, I queried Steve about the brothers' relationship. My inquiry had clearly touched a nerve. Sobbing, he told me, "I love him. But we lost our mother, and then our dad died just two months ago. We shouldn't be going through this." It was time to take a break. I adjourned for fifteen minutes.

Back in court, it was Bruce's turn in the witness stand. Answering questions from his attorney, he angrily accused Steve's wife, Brenda, as the person responsible for the litigation. "She's greedy and wants Mom's houses and her money. This is all her fault." Determined to convince me that his mother had been of sound mind when she executed her will in 1995, Bruce testified that at the time, his mom had been sufficiently competent to pass the written test required to renew her driver's license. Indeed, he produced the renewed license. *But,* I wondered, *hadn't the doctors testified that Elaine suffered from an advanced stage of dementia? But she passed the written driver's test? How could that be?* I got the answer when one of Steve's attorneys produced a surprise rebuttal witness—an employee of the DMV who brought records showing that while Elaine had, indeed, renewed her driver's license, she hadn't been required to take a written test. *Now, that's good lawyering,* I thought.

One of Bruce's several witnesses was Ziggy, a notary public who testified that he recalled placing his official notary stamp on the will immediately after Elaine signed it. According to Ziggy, Elaine was cogent and aware of what she had signed. Bruce then attempted to bolster Ziggy's testimony with the testimony of four witnesses, all of whom were, no surprise here, Bruce's close buddies. Each testified that Elaine was sharp as a tack and able to take care of her affairs. However, on cross-examination by one of Steve's lawyers, each was forced to admit to being unaware that on at least one occasion, Elaine had been discovered by the police wandering in a field in her underwear. They also professed ignorance about an episode when Elaine was found lying in the street with a fractured forehead. I quickly concluded that his buddies' testimonies had been a bunch of "testi-lies" and a waste of my time.

What a contrast when Steve's lawyers produced the testimony of a county health department inspector. He stated that over the years, he and some of his coworkers had made several unannounced visits to Elaine's home where they found hoarded bottles, cans, clothing, towels, and cardboard retrieved from an array of Dumpsters. He testified that mother and son were habitual Dumpster-diving buddies, who for the last six years had spent four to five hours every night of the week digging through neighborhood Dumpster bins. So alarmed was the county health department about the amount of debris and junk on the property, they had issued citations for a variety of code violations. *Well,* I quietly concluded, *so much for Bruce's good care of his dear mother.*

Following five days of testimony, I determined that Elaine's will was invalid; Steve had proven, by a preponderance of the evidence, that their mother had not been of sound mind when she signed her will. With no will, I declared that Elaine had died intestate. Since both of the brothers' parents were deceased, next in the line of intestate succession were her surviving children, Steve and Bruce. I ordered Elaine's estate divided equally between the two brothers. Perhaps their mother really did want Bruce to inherit everything, but the law is the law. An unsound mind does not a valid will make. It came as no surprise to me that Bruce's attorney was subsequently disbarred for providing wills to obviously incompetent people.

When wills are filed with the probate court, they are public records; anyone can read them and even copy them simply by perusing files in the clerk's office. In probate proceedings, private affairs become glaringly public ones—not so when the information is in a living trust. Known in legal parlance as "revocable inter vivos" trusts, living trusts created by a not-yet-deceased person called a settlor are private because they are not subject to probate proceedings. Inter vivos, literally "between the living," allows a settlor to revoke or change the terms of the trust at any time until the settlor's death. Additionally, during the settlor's lifetime, he can manage all of the property in the trust. There are also tax advantages for those who place their assets into living trusts, which is likely why so many wealthy people have them.

The McDonnell trust became a public affair because of a dispute among the beneficiaries. Funded with $500,000, the McDonnell parents established a trust to benefit their four sons and one daughter. When their father died, Ms. McDonnell, the wife of the deceased, appointed her son Michael to replace him as the trustee. She also amended the trust to add the following provision: "If, at the date of my death, Dennis has not entered an alcohol treatment program and pursued that program consistently so that there is a substantial probability that he will be a recovered alcoholic, he should receive no portion of the trust estate." By 2000, when Ms. McDonnell died, the five siblings, including their alcoholic brother, Dennis, were adults.

It was left to Michael to determine if Dennis was, in fact, a "recovered alcoholic." *What crazy lawyer came up with this language?* I wondered. What does "a substantial probability that he will be a recovered alcoholic" mean? And who in her right mind would advise the mother to leave this decision to a beneficiary of the trust? If Michael decided that his brother wasn't a recovered alcoholic, Dennis's share of the trust would go to his four siblings. So, it would be to their benefit if Michael were to conclude that Dennis was still in the throes of alcoholism and not a recovered alcoholic, a clear conflict of interest. To no one's surprise, Michael declared that his brother was not in recovery; he had even gone so far as to hire a private investigator to search for discarded beer cans in Dennis's trash cans. There didn't appear to be much brotherly or sisterly love in the McDonnell family. The battle lines had been drawn. So, it was all that I could do not to throw them big kisses when the lawyers walked into court and announced that they had settled the case. Under the terms of the settlement, Dennis would annually receive payments from his share of the trust for five years. Thereafter, any remaining money would be given to him outright, to do with as he pleased.

The living trust of the estate of Laverne Shinkle was yet another public affair that taught me everything I ever wanted to know about the world of ombudspersons. When Ms. Shinkle died at the age of eighty, she left an estate that consisted of $200,000 in cash and two parcels of real estate. C. J. Thompson, a retired schoolteacher, was an ombudsperson who worked at the nursing home at which Ms. Shinkle had been recuperating from a broken hip. Not long after befriending her and before you could say, "Laverne, give me your money!" Ms. Shinkle executed a living trust, leaving everything she owned to Mr. Thompson.

Claiming that C.J. had taken advantage of her by using his role as an ombudsman, three of Ms. Shinkle's relatives contested the trust; and they asserted that Ms. Shinkle had not been of sound mind because, at the time, she had been taking Haldol, an antipsychotic medication that left her experiencing hallucinations. More strikingly, they alleged that C.J. had forged Ms. Shinkle's signature on the trust. C.J.'s lawyer countered that his client was Ms. Shinkle's dear friend and that she had signed the trust of her own free will. Sixteen witnesses would testify before I could sort things out.

I had a general idea about ombudspersons, but at this trial I learned a whole lot more. In California, all long-term care facilities must have ombudspersons. Ombudspersons are volunteers who must be at least eighteen years of age; they are required to complete a forty-hour certification program and attend twelve hours of training annually to maintain their state certifications. Once certified, ombudspersons advocate for the residents of the long-term facilities, field patient complaints, and protect the welfare of the residents. Importantly, they are cautioned never to befriend the residents, never to accept gifts from them, and never to become personally involved with them.

After the nursing home staff concluded that C.J. was paying too much attention to Ms. Shinkle, he was assigned to another long-term care facility. But that didn't stop him. When Ms. Shinkle returned home, C.J. visited her regularly and handled her finances, writing her checks and making her bank deposits. Then, after C.J. enlisted an estate planner to meet with Ms. Shinkle, she signed the living trust that designated C.J. as the sole beneficiary.

In response to the claim that his client had violated his duties as an ombudsperson, C.J.'s lawyer argued that once Ms. Shinkle was again living at her home and no longer a resident of the nursing facility, C.J. was no longer acting as an ombudsperson. Rather, he maintained that his client had simply become her friend, which made it entirely proper for him to inherit her estate.

The attorney for Ms. Shinkle's relatives pointed out that but for his status as an ombudsperson, C.J. would never have met Laverne. He also noted that just sixty days after Ms. Shinkle's death, C.J. had withdrawn all her money, deposited it into his own bank account, and promptly paid off the $70,000 mortgage on his home. It wasn't looking good for C. J. Thompson.

One of the more interesting witnesses at the trial was a handwriting expert who testified that C.J. had forged Ms. Shinkle's signatures on both the will and the living trust. (Wills are included in living trusts.) The problem with handwriting experts is that there are no statewide standards, no required training, and no state-mandated certifications. Before deciding to become a handwriting expert, the witness, Ms. Fisher, had been a forensic photographer; before that, she was a graphologist. A graphologist, she explained, examined handwriting samples to evaluate the writer's personality, sort of like reading palms.

When cross-examined by C.J.'s attorney, Ms. Fisher admitted that in 1982 she had been hired by Hewlett Packard to investigate whether an employee had been sending lewd notes to female employees. After Ms. Fisher erroneously determined that the male employee had been the culprit, the wrongfully maligned employee sued the company, along with Ms. Fisher. Still, even though her judgment had been found wanting in 1982, Ms. Fisher's testimony at this trial made sense to me. She had enlarged the exemplars of Ms. Shinkle's signatures and demonstrated quite clearly that the signatures on the will and the living trust were markedly different. I wasn't yet convinced, though, that these signatures were forgeries.

But even if the signatures hadn't been forged, there remained the issue of whether C.J. had been acting as an ombudsperson. If, when Ms. Shinkle returned to her home, C.J. had continued in that role, he would be disqualified from inheriting from her. If, on the other hand, their relationship was nothing more than a simple friendship, he was in the clear.

Over the weekend, I researched cases about undue influence and the role of ombudspersons. I concluded that C.J. had been more than a friend to Ms. Shinkle and penned a seventeen-page decision in declaring the living trust to be invalid. C.J.'s relationship with Ms. Shinkle had not changed after she left the nursing home; he had improperly continued in his ombudsperson role.

When I subsequently mentioned to one of my colleagues, a nice man who had been on the court for more than twenty years, that I had spent several hours writing the decision in this case, he was aghast, telling me: "I never write decisions. I rule from the bench right then. So, I never take work home. You just have to rule and be done with it." When I asked him about cases involving complex legal issues or ones with convoluted facts, he said, "Just rule from your gut. They'll never appeal, and if they do, who cares?" I don't know about that. I figured that if the attorneys put so much time into presenting their cases, I should, at the very least, give them more than a simple "denied" or "granted." When I was a lawyer, those one-word decisions drove me crazy. No one should have to guess the reasons for judges' rulings.

The most entertaining case that I had the pleasure to hear in my time on the probate court concerned a living trust created by Marvin Walton, a Yale graduate (class of 1949) who subsequently attended Stanford Graduate School of Business. While his vocation was the management of his family's extensive investments and real estate holdings, he also tinkered with tools and even held a few patents. Before his death in 1989, Mr. Walton placed all of his property—$600,000 in cash and $3 million in real estate holdings—into a living trust. Since he had neither married nor sired children and had no known relatives, there were no familial heirs. So, to whom, I wondered, had he bequeathed all of his wealth? What lucky person had just become a multimillionaire? And when I asked the attorney representing the Walton estate to please stand and identify himself, why did *four* lawyers rise?

This quartet of lawyers stood because there were four primary beneficiaries of Mr. Walton's trust—Tom, Dick, Mary, and their mother, Kim. They had no last names because the beneficiaries were cats. I kid you not. Incredibly, four feral felines had inherited $600,000, the maximum amount that Mr. Walton could bequeath them, at the time, without the cats having to pay federal estate taxes. A battle royal among the cats and a few other beneficiaries was about to unfold. I couldn't wait.

Pet living trusts are not all that uncommon. Perhaps the most famous was one created by Leona Helmsley, a wealthy hotel heiress, who died in 2004. Into her living trust she placed $12 million for the care of her dog, Trouble, a Maltese. She also provided that Trouble's remains were to be buried next to hers in the Helmsley mausoleum at Woodlawn Cemetery in the Bronx. With that bequest, Trouble became the third-wealthiest dog in the world. (The wealthiest canine was Gunther III, a German shepherd who inherited $106 million in 1992 from Countess Karlotta Libenstein.)

When Ms. Helmsley's brother and grandson, upon whom she bestowed the responsibility of caring for Trouble, declined to take custody of the dog, Carl Lekic, the general manager of a Helmsley hotel in Florida, stepped up. Upon negotiating an agreement with the estate to be Trouble's keeper, Mr. Lekic landed in fat city with a payout of $5,000 per month, an annual payment of $100,000 for Trouble's security, $8,000 for her grooming, $1,200 for her food, and $18,000 for the dog's veterinary needs. It took a New York probate judge to eventually bring a modicum of sanity to the situation by reducing Trouble's inheritance to a meager $2 million. In 2011, Trouble passed away at the age of twelve; the remainder of his fortune was donated to charity.

The Walton trust provided that the $600,000 was to be used to maintain the cats "in a most pleasant manner and pleasing atmosphere that as I have been accustomed to give them during my lifetime." *What lawyer came up with that wording?* I wondered. The trust also bequeathed $3 million in real estate to seven animal charities. Now, five years after Mr. Walton's death, the attorneys for the charities were unhappy with the trustee, one Dewey Turner. Mr. Turner, an avuncular seventy-six-year-old attorney, had been designated by Mr. Walton to be the trustee—the person to oversee the trust. (A trust has a trustee; a will has an executor/executrix.) The three lawyers who represented the seven animal charities contended that Mr. Turner had improperly used the trust assets to pad his pockets and those of his friends. In order to resolve this issue, I needed to understand the terms of Mr. Walton's trust and what he had intended.

I had lots of questions. Why had it taken the trustee almost a year to inform the charities about the bequests to them? Was it proper for Mr. Turner to pay himself *$300,000* in trustee fees and legal fees in the four and a half years since Mr. Walton's death? Was the $300,000 that the charities had been belatedly paid from the trust too little, too much, or just right? Was it necessary for the trustee to subscribe to two cat magazines? And what about Gloria? I had a whopper of a soap opera on my hands.

Gloria Friedman, Marvin Walton's longtime friend, was named in the trust to feed and entertain the cats. For said services, trustee Turner had already paid Gloria $30,000 from the trust—in addition to the *$50,000* that Mr. Walton had separately bequeathed to her.

The attorneys for the charities asked me to remove Mr. Turner as the trustee and direct him to repay the trust a substantial portion of the money that he had paid to himself. Unsurprisingly, Mr. Turner contended that he had done nothing wrong and blamed the charities' lawyers. "Your Honor, their ridiculous legal wrangling is using up the trust's assets." He continued, "It's their fault that I've had to devote every minute of my time fending off these meritless attacks. I bill the trust for my time because that's what the trust says the trustee should do. They need to back off, Judge."

Preferring mediation to litigation, as is always my wont, I spent several hours in discussions with the attorneys trying to work out a settlement. Eventually, we reached a resolution that provided a sensible division of Mr. Walton's wealth among all of the beneficiaries. Most important, I ordered that Tom, Dick, Mary, and Kim should continue to live in the comfort and care to which they had grown accustomed.

Sic transit gloria mundi.

Would You Be Mine?

Adoptions

I have four children. Two are adopted. I forget which two.
—BOB CONSTANTINE

Wednesday mornings I presided over adoptions, of which there are a variety of types—stranger or nonrelative adoptions, stepparent adoptions, adult adoptions, same-sex adoptions, and international adoptions. According to Adoption.org, of the 140,000 children who are adopted annually by American families, 59 percent are from the foster care system, 26 percent are from other countries, and 15 percent are from mothers who voluntarily relinquish their babies at birth. Girls are adopted at a faster rate than boys and infants more quickly than older children.

Approximately seven million Americans are adopted, the more famous of whom are celebrities such as actor Jamie Foxx, reality star Nicole Richie, country music singer Faith Hill, actor Ray Liotta, singer Anita Baker, football great Colin Kaepernick, singer/actress Keyshia Cole, and actor/comedian Keegan-Michael Key.

Parents—infants and toddlers in tow—filed into my courtroom to await the moment I would sign orders that officially enlarged their families. Adoption Wednesdays were a welcome break from the daily tedium of probate court, with lawyers arguing over fees and litigants fighting over their deceased relatives' estates. The day before the adoption hearings, I reviewed the court files containing confidential home studies. Unavailable to the public, these studies revealed detailed information about the backgrounds of the children and the adoptive parents, as well as descriptions of the birth parents' situations. The information in these reports was intended to assure me that I was acting in the best interests of the children when I signed orders approving their adoptions.

Because I wanted to make each adoption a warm and inviting event, I handled each case in my chambers, one at a time. Sitting at my desk with the child on my lap—if he or she were willing (or in the case of the adoption of triplets, with all three on my lap)—and surrounded by adoptive parents, relatives, and friends, I smiled and said the magic words: "Having reviewed your petition for the adoption and having read the home study recommending that the adoption go forward, it is with pleasure that I now sign the order granting your petition. Congratulations, you are now a family, forever!" With that, cameras clicked, family members applauded, and tears flowed.

Adoptions bring together three distinct groups—birth parents, children, and adoptive parents. In most instances, the adoption process goes smoothly: birth parents agree to give up their children, adoptive parents agree to raise the children as their own, and the children, well, they do what they're told. However, when one of the groups isn't in agreement, things can get ugly.

In October 1994, a birth father petitioned to stop the adoption of his one-year-old daughter. At the two-day court trial, I listened to the testimony of the birth parents, each of whom had lawyered up. (There are no juries in adoption trials.) Their relationship had been a rocky one; she was the breadwinner and he was unemployed. Additionally, he was the father of two children from another relationship. He visited them regularly and occasionally paid child support to their mother. In this case, when the birth mother became pregnant, she told the birth father that she wasn't sure that the baby was his. Then, two months before her due date, she kicked him out and cut off all communication with him. Unbeknownst to the birth father, the birth mom had secretly made arrangements for the baby to be adopted; her newborn was quietly placed with the prospective adoptive parents. When she returned home from the hospital, the birth mom lied to her mother and her friends, telling them that the baby had died at birth. Then she enlisted a friend to give the birth father the (fake) bad news.

A few months later, the birth father got wind of a rumor that the baby was alive and began investigating. By surreptitiously (and illegally) copying the confidential information from the adoption file at the courthouse, he had been able to locate the adoptive parents and the date of the adoption hearing. Now, he was in court demanding that I give him custody of his daughter. The birth mother angrily testified that he didn't really want custody of the baby; what he wanted was the return of his "property," which he claimed had been stolen from him. Besides, she asserted, "He has no intention of raising the child. I know this because his mother told me that his girlfriend, who has three teenagers, wants the baby because she can't have any more children!" "Objection! Judge, this is hearsay," was the angry response from the birth father's attorney. I agreed. "Sustained."

What to do? On the one hand, here was the birth father who had been lied to and, as a result, deprived of a child on whom he had yet to lay eyes. On the other hand, there were the adoptive parents with whom the infant had lived her life from day one. And, from all accounts, the child was thriving in their care. After two days of testimony, I advised everyone that I would issue a written decision in a few days; I needed to buy some time to figure out what to do.

I researched adoption decisions issued by the appellate courts to see if there were any that fit the facts of the case I was considering. Trial court judges must follow the decisions issued by courts of appeal. In California, there are six appellate districts, each with a court of appeal that hears appeals from the decisions of trial judges in the counties within their districts. The highest of the appellate courts is the California Supreme Court, whose seven justices have the final say. It is the court of last resort.

Once the supremes rule, the appeal is over, at least within the state courts. (Some cases can thereafter be appealed in the federal courts.) When appellate courts choose to publish their opinions, their rulings become "case law," to which all trial court judges must adhere. (Not all appellate decisions are published.)

My research led me to a recent California Supreme Court decision in an adoption case with facts similar to the case before me. The court ruled that if a biological father fails to take steps to immediately gain custody of his child, starting at the time of pregnancy, he forfeits his right to custody. I believed that the court's reasoning applied to the birth father in my court and issued a written decision concluding that the birth father's efforts had failed to meet the standard set by the California Supreme Court. The facts, I wrote, demonstrated that the birth father urged the mother to abort the pregnancy, did not contribute to the expenses of the pregnancy, and had disappeared from the birth mother's life throughout her pregnancy. I terminated the birth father's parental rights, denied his petition to halt the adoption, and ruled that the best interest of the child—that she be adopted—outweighed his claim to be her parent. Understandably, the birth father's attorney objected and filed a request that I reconsider my decision. After reconsidering his arguments, I declined to change my ruling, whereupon his lawyer filed an appeal. During the nearly two years that the case was before the appellate court, the birth father waged a vicious campaign against me in the newspapers and on local television news programs. In May 1997, the appellate court finally ruled. In a lengthy opinion, the justices held that my decision to allow the adoption to go forward was the right one. My ruling had been upheld.

Adoptions in the United States weren't always decided by judges; at first, they weren't considered to be legal proceedings at all. When parents ran into financial or other difficulties, they'd simply send one or more of their children to live with relatives or, in some instances, to temporarily reside in orphanages. It was not until the mid-1800s that state legislatures began to take an interest in adoptions. England, for example, didn't pass adoption laws until 1926. Massachusetts, in 1851, was the first state to regulate adoptions when it enacted the Adoption of Children Act giving probate judges the sole authority to adjudicate them. In 1917, Minnesota became the first to require home studies and the first to mandate the confidentiality of adoption records.

Today, while all states and the District of Columbia have laws that regulate adoptions, there is little consistency among them. For example, when prospective adoptees reach a certain age, they must consent to their adoptions. Most states and the District of Columbia set the age of consent at twelve or fourteen years. However, in Alaska, Arkansas, Hawaii, Maryland, New Jersey, and North Dakota, adoptees' consent is required starting at age ten. In Vermont, only adoptees who are eighteen years and older need consent. And adoptees in Louisiana and Wisconsin are never asked for their consent, no matter what their ages.

There have been attempts by Congress to bring uniformity to the adoption process by replacing the states' wide-ranging criteria with one set of federal standards. In 1994, the National Conference of Commissioners on Uniform State Laws proposed the Uniform Adoption Act that would establish one standard set of rules for all domestic adoptions. (This was the third attempt to bring uniformity to state adoption laws; efforts in 1953 and 1971 went nowhere.)

The Uniform Adoption Act has been endorsed by the American Bar Association and the American Academy of Adoption Attorneys; it is opposed by more than a dozen national adoption organizations, including the Child Welfare League of America, the National Association of Social Workers, and Catholic Charities USA. To date, Vermont is the only state that adheres to the Uniform Adoption Act.

In 1965, Congress enacted the Immigration and Nationality Act to regulate international adoptions that grew out of orphan rescue missions, "baby lifts," stemming from four military conflicts—the Second World War, the Korean War, the Bay of Pigs debacle, and the Vietnam War. Prior to that, federal law had limited these adoptions to two foreign-born children per couple. But it was a request from an evangelical couple from rural Oregon—Bertha and Harry Holt—that set the wheels in motion for Congress to pass the Bill for Relief of Certain War Orphans in 1955. This legislation allowed the Holts to adopt eight mixed-race Korean orphans—four boys and four girls, ranging in age from infancy to three and a half years. (The Holts, both fifty years old, already had six children of their own.) The following year, in 1956, Holt International Children's Services opened its doors to promote international adoptions. Utilizing proxy agents to represent American adoptive parents, they petitioned foreign courts to approve adoptions. Once the adoptions were ordered, the adoptees, upon entering the United States with the proxy agents, were handed over to the adoptive parents sight unseen. The Holts were to arrange hundreds of proxy adoptions for American couples. In the belief that a childhood in America was superior to a childhood in any other country, their agency even recruited adoptive parents who had been rejected by conventional adoptive agencies. Additionally, the Holts disapproved of race matching children with adoptive parents (except for children whose parents were African American).

While praised by the press and Christian communities as humanitarians, the Holts were considered by child welfare policy makers and social workers to be religious zealots who lacked the requisite skills to properly supervise adoptions. With no home studies, no background checks of the adoptive parents, no inquiries into the circumstances of the birth parents, and no attempts to develop cultural awareness of the adoptees' situations with the adoptive parents, travesties were inevitable. According to an official of the International Social Service, in one instance, a woman from Texas "appeared to be drunk and she appeared to be over 50 years of age" when, in 1957, she first greeted the Greek baby adopted for her by proxy.

With the enactment of the Immigration and Nationality Act of 1965, the Holts were forced to accept standard professional adoption practices. Today, their Oregon agency, which no longer promotes evangelicalism, is one of this country's leading international adoption agencies.

I believe that the Holts' commitment to the adoption of biracial children, stigmatized and abandoned in their home countries, was well-intentioned. However, their utter lack of understanding and appreciation of the native cultures of these children, their failure to investigate the backgrounds of the families into whose homes the children were placed, and their refusal to place children of African American parentage with White adoptive parents leave me wondering whether they did more harm than good.

In raw numbers, the United States is the largest of the receiving countries (although Spain and Norway adopt more children per capita). In 2004, the peak year of international adoptions, 22,884 adopted children from more than ninety nations came to the United States. By 2011, due to restrictions imposed by several countries, including China and Russia, international adoptions declined to 9,319. And by 2018, the number of these adoptions had dropped even more, to just 4,059.

In 1994, I presided over an international adoption that involved refugees from the war-torn country of Iraq. During the Gulf War (August 1990–February 1991), the United States had joined with a coalition of countries to drive out Iraqi forces who had invaded Kuwait. Among the one hundred thousand to two hundred thousand civilians killed in the conflict were the wife and parents of Ibrahim B., a well-educated Kurd who, with his two children, ages two and three, had fled Iraq. Nearing starvation, Ibrahim brought his son and daughter to the home of friends who introduced him to two American Christian missionaries, both White and in their forties. The couple persuaded Ibrahim to leave his children with them until such time as he would be able to provide for them. Placing his trust in them, that's what he did. Not long thereafter, he was captured and imprisoned in a Turkish camp.

At the end of the war, he was released and fled to the Netherlands, where he was given sanctuary by the Dutch government. At that point, he began a three-year search to regain custody of his children, which eventually led him to Germany, where his son and daughter had been living with the missionary couple. He was devastated to learn that the couple was now living in the United States and that their petition to adopt his children had been granted by a Santa Clara County judge (not me). Now five and six years of age, Ibrahim's children were American citizens with American names; they had no memory of their father. The Dutch government, at Ibrahim's request, provided him a legal aid lawyer who filed a petition in the Santa Clara County Superior Court requesting that the adoptions be set aside.

At the set-aside hearing in April 1994, Ibrahim and his attorney were in attendance, both having flown in from the Netherlands. A local attorney retained by the adoptive parents was there but without his clients. He assured me that the couple and the children would be in attendance at the next court hearing. However, he said that he had evidence that would make another court appearance unnecessary. He definitely had my attention; I told him to explain. The couple's attorney then said that because Ibrahim had consented to the adoptions, there was no basis to set them aside. As proof of the consent, he handed me a consent form with what appeared to be Ibrahim's signature. I looked up at Ibrahim, who had a stunned look on his face. I then looked to his attorney, who stood and told me that since Ibrahim would never have given up his children, the signature on the document had to be a forgery. Outraged, the couple's attorney stood and demanded an apology. I told both to calm down and sit down. To get to the bottom of this, I appointed a handwriting expert to analyze the signature on the consent form and directed Ibrahim to provide handwriting samples for the analysis. I also ordered the expert to expedite her report; I needed to resolve this as quickly as possible. Within a few days the expert sent me her written findings: Ibrahim's signature had, indeed, been forged. After sending copies of her report to the attorneys, I ordered everyone—the lawyers, Ibrahim, the adoptive parents, *and the children*—to be present at the next hearing, set for the following week. I had lots of questions, starting with the phony consent form.

When we reconvened, Ibrahim and his attorney were all smiles, hopeful that I would set aside the adoptions and return the children to their father. But it was not to be. The adoptive parents and the children were no-shows. Their lawyer shrugged and told me that he had no idea of their whereabouts. I was outraged and ordered him to call the couple's home telephone number in Germany right then. To no one's surprise, the number was disconnected; the adoptive parents and the children were on the run. Ibrahim cried, his attorney fumed, and the couple's lawyer looked down and smirked.

I issued an order giving Ibrahim temporary custody of his children and scheduled another hearing the following month. While I could have set aside the adoptions right then, if I had, the children would no longer be American citizens. (A set-aside voids everything; it means that the children were never adopted.) Without their being citizens of this country, our courts would not have had jurisdiction over this case, which would mean that should they return to this country, there would be no authority to punish the adoptive parents for their wrongdoing. The next hearing, thirty days later, was a repeat of the one before it—no children, no adoptive parents. A year later, when I completed my assignment in the adoption court, Ibrahim's children and the adoptive parents were still nowhere to be found.

While Ibrahim's separation from his children was the result of fraud, the separation of American children from their families is most frequently occasioned by parental neglect and abuse, resulting in foster care placements. Annually, of the more than 400,000 children in our foster care system, approximately 114,000 who cannot be returned to their families await adoption; annually, nearly 20,000 are never adopted. Sadly, they simply age out of the foster care system and are on their own. According to Joe Carter, writing for the Ethics and Religious Liberty Commission, "On average, a child will spend 32.3 months in foster care awaiting adoption. About 55 percent of these children have had three or more placements with foster care families, and 33 percent had changed elementary schools five or more times, losing relationships and falling behind educationally." In contrast, 62 percent of children (usually newborns) placed by private adoption agencies have their adoptive families within one month of their births.

When a child is actually adopted out of foster care, it is cause for celebration. That's what happened when I presided over the adoption of three Mexican American children—two sisters and their brother, ages five, seven, and nine, who had been in foster care for nearly a year. Their foster parents, a White couple in their sixties, wanted to keep the siblings together, so they petitioned to adopt all three. It is highly unusual for foster parents to take in multiple siblings from one family and even more unusual for foster parents to adopt all of them. The fact that this was a transracial adoption did not bother me in the least.

Transracial adoptions have long been controversial in the United States. Because they are seen as promoting the intermingling of the races, until the 1960s and 1970s Texas and Louisiana flat out prohibited them. The Texas law specifically targeted African Americans: "No white child can be adopted by a negro person, nor can a negro child be adopted by a white person." The Louisiana statute was broader: "A single person over the age of twenty-one years, or a married couple jointly, may petition to adopt any child of his or their race." (Both laws were subsequently found unconstitutional—Texas in 1967, Louisiana in 1972.)

In the states where the law did not ban transracial adoptions, judges filled the void. A Washington, D.C., judge, in 1955, denied the stepparent adoption petition of a Black man who, with the child's White mother, had reared her six-year-old White child. In finding the transracial stepparent adoption to be inappropriate, the judge reasoned:

Another problem arises out of the fact that the stepfather is a colored man, while the mother and boy are white people. This situation gives rise to a difficult social problem. The boy when he grows up might lose the social status of a white man by reason of the fact that by record his father will be a negro if this adoption is approved. I feel the court should not fashion the child's future in this manner.

In a 1950 divorce proceeding between a White wife and her Black husband, a Washington State family court judge granted the divorce to the husband and, finding the mother unfit to parent them, gave custody of the couples' two small children to him. The Washington Supreme Court upheld the custody decision as being in the best interests of the children while lamenting: "These unfortunate girls, through no fault of their own, are the victims of a mixed marriage and a broken home. They will have a much better opportunity to take their rightful place in society if they are brought up among their own people."

"Race matching," a policy that prefers matching children as closely as possible to the race of their adoptive parents, is at the core of the transracial adoption debate. In 1972, with the publication of a position paper by the National Association of Black Social Workers (NABSW) that was highly critical of transracial adoptions, the debate heated up considerably. Founded in 1968, the NABSW addressed social issues of importance to the Black community. According to the Adoption History Project, the organization "took 'a vehement stand against the placements of black children in white homes for any reason,' calling transracial adoption 'unnatural,' 'artificial,' 'unnecessary,' and proof that African-Americans continued to be assigned to 'chattel status.'" Incredibly, the organization's president took the position that it was better for Black children to remain in foster care or in group homes than for them to live in permanent homes with White adoptive parents.

In a 1984 case involving a divorcing White couple in Florida, the United States Supreme Court weighed in on the role of race in transracial placements. A year after a family court judge had given custody of a three-year-old daughter to her mother, the father petitioned for custody because the child's mother had remarried to a Black man with whom she and her daughter lived. The trial judge, even though finding the mother and her spouse to be fit parents, ordered the child's removal and placement with her biological White father, stating: "This Court feels that despite the strides that have been made in bettering relations between the races in this country, it is inevitable that [the child] will, if allowed to remain in her present situation and attains school age and thus more vulnerable to peer pressures, suffer from the social stigmatization that is sure to come." A unanimous United States Supreme Court disagreed, ruling that the change in custody was unconstitutional because the judge "made no effort to place its holding on any ground other than race," adding that "whatever problems racially mixed households may pose for children in 1984 can no more support a denial of constitutional rights than could the stresses that residential integration was thought to entail in 1917. The effects of racial prejudice, however real, cannot justify a racial classification removing an infant child from the custody of its natural mother found to be an appropriate person to have such custody." Bottom line—race can never be the sole factor in determining what is in the best interest of a child.

A decade later, Congress enacted the Multiethnic Placement Act (MEPA) of 1994 prohibiting states that receive federal assistance for their child welfare programs from delaying or denying foster and adoption placements on the basis of the child's or the prospective parents' race. Still, MEPA requires the states to diligently recruit foster and adoptive parents who reflect the race or ethnicity of those children needing foster care and adoptive homes.

I believe that when children have the opportunity to be adopted by adults who look like them and share a common culture, it is, generally, a good thing. I also believe that it is criminal to leave children languishing in foster care when there are suitable adults of any race who can provide them permanent loving and caring homes. So, returning to that morning in my courtroom, with a full house that included the social worker and lots of family and friends, I was delighted to put my stamp of approval on the adoption of the three Latinx siblings by their loving White parents.

The following month, I presided over an adoption that was a judge's nightmare in the making. *Six* lawyers—one for the birth mother, one for the proposed adoptive mother, one for the birth father, one for the paternal grandmother, one for the fifteen-month-old, and one for the county's department of social services—had gathered in my courtroom. The demographics of the birth parents and adoptive parents were unusual. The proposed adoptive mother was Asian American, and the birth mother, a drug addict, was White. Both were in their thirties and had been lovers. The paternal grandmother, also a lesbian, wanted the toddler placed with her and her female partner. Her son, the birth father, a White man in his forties, had a long drug and theft criminal history. The father and paternal grandmother had squared off against the biological mother and the adoptive mom, with the lawyers for the child and the social services department somewhere in between. The tension in the courtroom was palpable. I realized that a full-blown hearing would have dragged on for three, four, or five days. There had to be a better way.

I asked everyone to come into my chambers. As they filed in, the lawyers (five of whom were women) took seats at my conference table; their clients stood or sat on the nearby sofa. I needed to get everyone talking and focused on what was best for this child. After nearly two hours, we worked out a settlement where the biological parents agreed to terminate their parental rights, leaving the little boy to be adopted by the birth mother's former lover and the grandmother guaranteed visitation rights. With a little bit of judicial persuasion, the adoptive mom and grandmother agreed to attend counseling—together. To close the deal, I reluctantly volunteered to serve as a mediator for the next three months, should any disputes arise between the adoptive mom and the grandmother. Lucky for me, I heard nothing more from any of them.

Most children in foster care have it rough. Even when they are placed with loving foster parents, they know that their "real" parents have abandoned them, either voluntarily or by court order. Irene, a biracial girl, was born to a fourteen-year-old White mother who refused to identify the African American father. Upon her birth, Irene *and* her mother were placed in foster care, and for three years the two were moved from foster home to foster home. The one saving grace was that they had been able to stay together. However, when her then seventeen-year-old mother was sexually abused at one of the foster placements and not surprisingly fell into the throes of depression and drug abuse, the Department of Social Services (DSS) quickly removed Irene from her mother. Thereafter, DSS filed a petition with the court to terminate her mother's parental rights. A judge (not me) granted the petition and issued an order prohibiting any contact between three-year-old Irene and her mother. Parentless, Irene was placed into a succession of foster homes where, like her mother before her, she was the victim of sexual abuse.

When all seemed lost for this girl, an angel appeared in the form of one Sylvia R., a single African American woman in her forties, who had been persuaded by a social worker to become the now six-year-old Irene's foster mother. Sylvia took the little girl into her home and, four years later, she made the big decision to adopt her. The adoption petition was granted, and for the first time in her life, ten-year-old Irene had a loving mother and a stable home. However, the good times were short-lived.

When Irene entered the fifth grade, her behavior changed dramatically. She became assaultive, became sexually active, repeatedly skipped school, and physically attacked Sylvia. To her credit, Sylvia didn't give up. She took Irene to therapist after therapist and enrolled her in a succession of special schools, ever hopeful of finding a way to turn things around for her daughter. Things got markedly worse after Sylvia learned that Irene was engaged in prostitution for a pimp who had made it clear that if Irene didn't work for him, he would kill both of them.

The horror of this situation was compounded when Sylvia discovered that the Department of Social Services had known of the depth of Irene's emotional problems but had never revealed that information to her. Now, fearing for her own safety, Sylvia decided that she could no longer be Irene's mother; she reluctantly petitioned the court to end the adoption.

Irene, unaware of Sylvia's request to terminate the adoption, had been removed from Sylvia's care by DSS and placed in a group home that predictably hadn't gone well. After brutally assaulting a girl at her group home placement, Irene ran away, only to become the victim of a brutal gang rape.

Now, sitting in my courtroom was a teary and traumatized fifteen-year-old Irene, upon whom I was about to inflict perhaps the worst trauma of all. Sylvia, who had been sitting quietly in the courtroom, got up, walked to Irene, and hugged her; both were in tears. How was I to tell this girl that she was no longer adopted? How could I tell her that she was, once again, abandoned? I took a deep breath and asked to meet with Irene and her attorney in my chambers. With that, Sylvia nodded at me, stood, and slowly walked out of the courtroom.

Once in my chambers, I did the dirty deed. Irene was devastated and sobbed uncontrollably. Her female attorney, a public defender, was in tears. I sat on the couch next to Irene and told her that none of this was her fault, that she needed help, and that I was determined to do what I could to make things better for her. She grew silent, stared at me, looked away, and said nothing more. How could she trust me or anyone else in a system that had failed her so miserably? My heart broke for her, but I did what I had to do. Parentless once again, Irene left my court and was taken to the county's children's shelter. Not surprisingly, she ran away the next day, eventually ending up in a group home in nearby Oakland. What she didn't know was that her attorney had located her birth mother—the two hadn't seen each other for twelve years—and had arranged for them to reconnect. Twenty years later, I'm left to wonder where and how they are.

Adolescents and teens in foster care are far more difficult to place for adoption than are cute and cuddly infants and toddlers. As a result, social services caseworkers, under a great deal of pressure to locate permanent homes for these hard-to-place foster children, sometimes cut corners. In Sylvia R.'s case, DSS, in their eagerness to place Irene, withheld negative information about the girl's history. Had Sylvia known of the depths of Irene's mental and emotional problems, it is highly unlikely she would have adopted her. Cutting corners to move children out of the foster care system is unacceptable; anyone who engages in this kind of behavior should face serious consequences. But, all of this notwithstanding, I think that the system's gravest failure was in terminating the parental rights of Irene's young mother before finding a permanent home for her. With that termination, Irene literally had no one in her life; she was alone and adrift in a system filled with abandoned children. How anyone—the judge who approved DSS's petition and the social worker who recommended it—could have viewed the termination of parental rights as being in the best interest of Irene without first finding her a home, even a temporary one, baffles me. Then, DSS made matters worse by obtaining a restraining order that prohibited Irene and her mother from having any contact with one another. In the end, our legal system had victimized Irene, her birth mother, and Sylvia. I hope that they can forgive us.

Another instance of institutional failure is the well-documented and shameful history of the treatment of Native American families by the federal government. Adoption laws are no exception. In the 1800s, the forced removals and mass assimilation of Native children resulted in the creation of boarding schools whose goal was to indoctrinate Native youngsters in the ways of the White man. From 1958 to 1967, the federal government's Indian Adoption Project (IAP) was mandated to promote the adoption of as many Native children as possible by White parents. An April 14, 1966, press release proclaiming the IAP's success touted:

> One little, two little, three little Indians—and 206 more—are brightening the homes and lives of 172 families, mostly non-Indians, who have taken the Indian waifs as their own . . . At the time of adoption, the Indian children have ranged in age from birth to 11 years, with more than half under the age of 1 year. Five sets of twins, and a number of other groups from the same families have been adopted. . . . The 209 Indian adoptees have come from 11 States, with the majority from South Dakota (64) and Arizona (52). Almost all the placements have been in the east and Midwest, with 49 in New York alone. . . . Indian children adapt happily to a non-Indian environment in almost all cases—even the older ones. While the adoptive parents have sometimes been overly protective at first, they have soon found out that the Indian youngsters slip easily into family and neighborhood patterns.

Enter New York attorney Bert Hirsch, who by 1978 had led an unprecedented effort to collect data in all fifty states about the adoptive placements of Native children. Hirsch was especially appalled at the manner in which judges approached cases involving tribal children, saying: "[Judges] had no trouble just taking tribal kids away from their families and putting them in foster care, because they didn't like Indians and they didn't like their way of life. Ostensibly, they were removed for neglect, but really it was all about poverty. If you're poor and you're Indian, you lose your kid." Heroically spearheading an eleven-year grassroots effort involving thousands of people, Hirsch ensured the passage of the Indian Child Welfare Act (ICWA). As reported in *The Chronicle of Social Change,* the legislation dramatically passed "at the 11th hour, just before the 95th Congress would come to a close, on October 24, 1978."

My ruling in the adoption of a biracial Native American infant (African American/Native American) took on a life of its own in August 1994. The newborn boy had been given to a White couple by the birth mother, a Native American who resided in New Mexico. However, six months later, she changed her mind and demanded that they return her child. When they refused, she, along with her Pueblo (a sovereign Native American group also known as a Tribe), filed a petition claiming that the ICWA applied. They argued that the law required that the child be returned to his mother or, in the alternative, placed with another Native American family. The attorneys for both parties, the adoptive couple and the child's Pueblo, had squared off, ready to fight to the end. This was war. The ICWA requires the Native child's Tribe to be notified as soon as any proceedings concerning the child's welfare are filed in court. Once notified, the Tribe has the right to be present and represented in the courtroom at all of the proceedings, the idea being that only Tribes have the right to decide what happens to their children. The ICWA gives a custody preference to the child's family, then to the child's Pueblo/Tribe, and finally to other Native American Tribes.

My first task was to determine if the infant was an "Indian" child as defined by the ICWA. If he were, then I would be required to give the custody preference to his birth mother, who now wanted him back. The adoptive parents' lawyer passionately argued that the ICWA did not apply here because the Pueblo he had contacted informed him, in writing, that the child wasn't a member. Indeed, the letter he presented to me said just that. However, the letter also advised him to check the child's possible membership with two neighboring Pueblos. When I asked him if he had done so, he said no. The Pueblo's lawyer then said that their records proved that the infant was a member of their adoptive tribe, which is why they had intervened and joined with the birth mother in seeking the child's return.

The ICWA provides a child must be returned to the birth mother if she changes her mind *any time before the adoption is final.* Since I was now convinced that the ICWA applied to this case, I reluctantly ruled that custody of the baby was with his birth mother. I knew that my decision would upend the lives of the adoptive parents who had parented the nine-month-old infant since his birth and, of course, the infant. But, under the ICWA, I didn't have a choice.

After I issued my order, the adoptive parents and their attorney dug in their heels and refused to relinquish the child. The attorney for the birth mother and the Pueblo asked me to immediately order the parents back to court with the child; and should they fail to appear, he demanded that I issue a warrant for their arrest. Because their lawyer had filed an emergency appeal asking for an immediate reversal of my decision, it was my guess that the adoptive parents were withholding the child on the advice of their attorney. A few days later, the appellate court ruled, affirming my decision. The child was to be returned to his birth mother. But things were far from over.

Later that month, the attorney for the parents appealed to the California Supreme Court. While that appeal was pending, he did everything in his power to remove me from presiding over the case, filing declarations alleging that I had engaged in all manner of misconduct—issuing orders without giving him an opportunity to be heard, lying, demonstrating bias against his clients, and on and on. His vendetta against me took an even uglier turn when he began bad-mouthing me to the small and tightly knit community of adoption lawyers. Word spread quickly in the courthouse that he had been urging his colleagues to disqualify me from presiding over their adoption cases. At the time, judges were prohibited by judicial canons from defending themselves when their decisions were criticized, no matter how misguided and erroneous the criticism. Judges had no right of self-defense. (That changed in 2020 when the canons were revised to allow judges to defend themselves.) All that I had to rely on was my reputation. As luck would have it, his disparagement of me went nowhere.

At the end of October, the California Supreme Court rejected the adoptive parents' appeal. Still, they pressed on by requesting an emergency hearing before the United States Supreme Court. When that didn't pan out, they had no choice but to comply with my order; they returned the child to his birth mother in early November. By then, the boy had been with the adoptive parents for one year.

The case took a sudden and surprising twist when the birth mother inexplicably replaced her attorney with one who was a friend of the adoptive parents' lawyer. Shortly thereafter, she took up residence in the home of the adoptive parents and claimed that she had been coerced by the Pueblo and her former attorney into taking her son back. This didn't smell right; actually, it stunk. My guess is that she had been bought off by the parents, and, a few months later, when everything would have died down, she'd move out, leaving the child with the adoptive parents who would quietly proceed with the adoption. I had to hand it to them. They did what they had to do to get what they wanted, the ICWA be damned. Perhaps this was the best outcome for the boy who, today, would be nearly thirty years old. I sure hope so.

Today, the controversy over adoptions of Native children continues. In June 2016, a ten-month-old Navajo Cherokee boy was placed in the home of Jennifer and Chad Brackeen, a White, evangelical couple, who resided in Fort Worth, Texas. (The child's Navajo birth mother, who relocated to Texas, had lost custody of the child because of her drug use.) The Navajo tribe invoked the Indian Child Welfare Act and demanded that the infant be placed with a nonrelative Native family. Somehow, the Brackeens succeeded in adopting him. Three years later, in 2019, when the Brackeens applied to adopt the boy's sister, her Navajo extended family declared that they wanted her. In response, the Brackeens lawyered up, filing a federal lawsuit that has yet to be decided, attacking the constitutionality of the Indian Child Welfare Act. Joined by the state of Texas and backed by the Goldwater Institute, a conservative think tank, the lawsuit contends that the ICWA unconstitutionally promotes a racial preference in adoptions. If they succeed, the Brackeens may upend a law that has been in place for more than forty years. The United States Supreme Court will almost certainly have the final say.

What happens when *three* people want to be the legal parents of a child? That was the question before me in the case of sixteen-year-old Adam, who wanted to be adopted by his birth mother's lesbian partner. The parental rights of biological parents can only be terminated with their consent or, if they refuse to consent, by court orders. Adam's father had no interest in giving up his parental rights; at the same time, though, he had no objection to the adoption of his son by his ex-wife's partner. Oddly, everyone was on the same page; all wanted Adam to have two moms and a dad.

In May 1997, when this adoption petition was filed, I had rotated out of my adoption assignment and was presiding over criminal cases. But after the judge then assigned to hear adoption cases made it clear to the family's attorney that he wasn't going to approve the adoption, the lawyer reached out to me. When I told him that I was willing to hear the case, the adoption judge was equally willing to hand it over. After reading the file, I wondered why Adam didn't simply wait another two years when, having attained the age of eighteen, he could petition for an adult adoption.

With the exceptions of Michigan, Nebraska, Arizona, Alabama, and Ohio, in all states, an adult can be adopted by another adult. Once adopted, the adult adoptee has the same rights as the adopter's biological children, including the right to inherit from the adoptive parents. But as with all things legal, even straightforward adult adoptions can get a little messy. In 2006, Virginian Justine Critzer died without leaving a will; what she did leave was a sizable estate. With no spouse, no children, and no living parents, her closest surviving heirs were a niece and a nephew. But even though they were next in line to inherit, there was a wrinkle: Ms. Critzer, at the age of fifty-three, had been legally adopted by her aunt-in-law (Ms. Critzer's deceased uncle's widow). So, the question before the court was whether the adult adoption severed all of Ms. Critzer's legal ties to her biological family. The Supreme Court of Virginia ruled that by becoming the child of her adopting parent, the adoption had severed the ties to her biological parents; she was no longer related to her biological sister. This meant that the niece and nephew, her biological sister's children, could not inherit from Ms. Critzer's estate. Bottom line, their aunt was no longer their aunt, even though she really was.

Back in my courtroom, I asked to speak with Adam and his attorney in my chambers. They walked in and sat at my conference table. Seated at my desk, I asked Adam: "So, what's the rush here? You could wait until your eighteenth birthday and then have your mother's partner adopt you as an adult. That way, you wouldn't have to deal with a three-parent arrangement that may or may not be legal. Why not wait?" Adam was so nervous; he was also very sweet. He told me: "I really want her to be my mom. She's always been my parent, since I was born. If the law says that she is my parent, that will make us a real family." He hadn't answered my question, but I was persuaded that he knew what was going on. I was confident that this was what he really wanted and that no one had put him up to it. So, we went back into the courtroom. I asked the two moms, the dad, and Adam if they consented to the adoption. One at a time, each answered, "Yes, Your Honor." With that, I approved Adam's adoption and quietly hoped that everyone would get along. Imagine the mess if the dad were to decide that he wanted sole custody of Adam or if the two moms broke up and each wanted custody. As they walked from the courtroom into the hallway, Adam shouted, "Hey, everybody! This is my family!"

The Name Game

Name Changes

What's in a name? That which we call a rose by any
other name would smell as sweet.

—WILLIAM SHAKESPEARE, *ROMEO AND JULIET*

Lots of people change their names. Celebrities do it all the time: Elton John was once Reginald Kenneth Dwight; actress Whoopi Goldberg was born Caryn Johnson; John Legend was John Roger Stephens. It is estimated that as many as fifty thousand Americans change their names each year. Women frequently take the last names of their husbands or wives; newly arrived immigrants often take on easier-to-pronounce American names; and others take on new names just because. When I married my husband, I changed my last name, Hazzard, to his, Cordell. It was the 1970s and, hey, that's what some women did—and still do.

In the mid-1990s, for two years, I was the name-change judge. Once a week, I heard requests from all manner of individuals with all manner of reasons to change their names. Because they rarely presented complex legal issues, were noncombative, and were just plain fun, I looked forward to these hearings. The litigants were happy because the judge was surely going to give them what they wanted; and I was happy because most of the time, I gave them what they wanted. For me, the name-change calendar was one big lovefest.

In California, as in most states, anyone eighteen years or older and of sound mind can change her name. There are two ways to do this—usage or petition. "Usage" means that you simply *use* your chosen name. When you have used this name for several years, once it is sufficiently identified with you, then that's your name. Exactly how long this usage takes before the name is officially yours is an open question.

The way to change your name with certainty is by heading to the courthouse to file a name-change petition with the court clerk. Then, you must publish a notice in a local newspaper's legal notices section (the section that no one reads because the print is so small), and it must run for four consecutive weeks. Once that's done, you go to court, where a judge reviews your petition, asks you a few questions, and if no one objects, hands you a court order officially establishing your new name. The process is straightforward and inexpensive, so most people can handle these cases on their own. She who represents herself does *not* have a fool for a client when in court for a name change.

I enjoyed listening to the myriad reasons that people gave for changing their names so much so that even though the reasons were explained in their petitions, I still wanted to hear directly from the petitioners. Besides, giving litigants the opportunity to speak in a forum that is nonadversarial makes them feel good and, I think, leaves them feeling more positive about the courts and our judges. As importantly, their explanations provided terrific entertainment not only for me but for the spectators as well.

For example, there was the fortysomething-year-old woman who had lived her life as Joan McCarthy, a nice enough name, I thought, but not nice enough for her. She wanted to be Summer Johnson. When I asked her why, she said, "It fits my identity better." *Okay.* And a young Vietnamese man, a recent immigrant, wanted the name Lawrence because he had a commanding view of the Lawrence Expressway from his apartment window. *Whatever works.* When I asked Lloyd Eugene Dringenberg why he wanted to change his name to Lancelot Einstein Hunter, he explained that these interesting names were sure to attract attention to his sales business. *You gotta do what you gotta do.*

Occasionally, people want multiple names, like the man who petitioned to change his name to those of six Roman statesmen—Octavius Caesar Augustus Cicero . . . you get the picture. When I gently cautioned him about the difficulty of fitting six names on a credit card, he shrugged his shoulders and said, "It's a free country, Judge." *True*. I granted his petition and off the would-be emperor went, clothes and all.

And then there are those who, rather than change their names, want more of them. I didn't even bother to raise the no-space-on-your-credit-card issue when a middle-aged man's petition requested *eight additional names*. In responding to my question about why in the world he wanted eight more names, he told me: "I have always liked those names, Your Honor. Now, I want them, all of them." Petition granted.

Michael Smith, a man in his forties, told me that he wanted a new name because his birth name was boring. *Agreed*. When he left my court, he was Joshua Peduoa Whiskey. He explained, "Joshua means 'strength'; Peduoa is Greek for 'quick'; and since I grew up in Whiskey Flats, California, Whiskey obviously has to be my last name." *Obviously*, I thought. I loved these cases!

Only once did I deny a name-change petition. The petitioner, a White male in his early twenties, asked to change his name from Charles Franklin to Matthew Blackstone. When I inquired why, he said, "Judge, I owe money to a few creditors. I've got bill collectors coming after me. If I change my name, they won't be able to find me and then I can put this behind me and start over." It is not often that a judge hears such candor in the courtroom. But when I informed him that it was illegal for a person to change his name to commit fraud and that duping his creditors was fraudulent, he was incredulous. "You mean that I can't change my name?!" *That's right, sir.* "You mean that I spent all that money on a filing fee and running that notice in the paper, for nothing?" *Right again, sir.* The spectators in the courtroom chuckled quietly. I told him that I was sorry but that his petition was denied. No name change today. As he exited the doors at the back of the courtroom, I heard him mutter sotto voce but loud enough: "Damn!" As well as fraud, words that are patently offensive, such as racial slurs, are a nonstarter. And while the names of celebrities and public figures are fair game for name changes, the newly named are not permitted to profit from using them.

And then there are some very serious reasons for name changes. One case involved two children whose father murdered their mother. After custody was given to their maternal grandparents, the children, understandably, no longer wanted to bear their father's last name. I granted their request.

Occasionally sticky moral questions arise in the name-change arena. In one instance, I read the petition of an Ethiopian immigrant requesting to change his last name and that of his two small children. (Unlike an adult's name, which can be changed via usage or a petition, a child's name can only be changed by a petition to the court, filed by the parents or legal guardians.) When I called the case, he came forward and sat at one of the two counsel tables. I greeted him. "Good morning. I see that you want to change your last name and the last names of your two children. Is that right?" He smiled and answered yes. "Does the mother of the children approve?" I asked. He frowned and stared at me. That's when I looked up and noticed a woman who appeared to me to be Ethiopian sitting alone in the back of the courtroom. Pointing at her, I asked him: "Is she the mother of the children? Is she your spouse?" He answered yes to both questions, whereupon I asked her to please join her husband at the counsel table. A frown on his face, her husband was clearly unhappy with the direction that this hearing was going. His wife, her eyes cast down at the floor, sat in the chair beside him.

When I asked her name, he immediately answered for her. I leaned forward and said, "Sir, I asked your wife, not you. I'd appreciate you not speaking for her." His frown had now become an angry glare. I again asked for her name. When she told me, I asked why her name wasn't on the name-change petition, since she was the children's mother. Just as her husband was about to answer, I gave him my you-don't-want-to-go-there look. He sat back and remained silent. She quietly told me that she didn't know why her name wasn't on the petition. Looking at her, I asked if she was okay with changing the last name of her children, to which she responded that she was.

In theory, at that point I could have simply granted the petition, but I couldn't. Directing my comments to the father, I said, "If the issue affects your children, *both* of you must have a say in the matter. You are the parents and are equals in my court. Sir, her name should have been included on the petition." Given the outrage on the man's face, I'm willing to bet that this was the first and only time that a woman, no less a woman of color, had ever spoken to him in this fashion. I doubted that female equality was much of a topic of discussion in their household. With that, I approved their petition.

Was it inappropriate for me to lecture them about women's rights? In doing so, had I disrespected their culture? On the one hand, in their culture, the husband was in charge. He was the decider. On the other hand, this was my courtroom where women were not second-class litigants and where *I* was the decider. Did I overstep my bounds? I got my answer when, as they neared the door to exit the courtroom, the woman turned, smiled, and then nodded in my direction.

What about individuals who have transitioned and desire names that reflect their gender identities? Interestingly, even though this was the 1990s, when transgender persons in courtrooms were a rarity, I presided over a few of these requests. I always made it a point to place these cases at the end of the court calendar when the courtroom would likely have no spectators, to avoid any embarrassment or awkwardness these petitioners might otherwise experience. In one case, two transwomen, represented by an attorney, also a transwoman, sought female first names—John to Rebecca and Bruce to Tiffany. As I listened to the lawyer present their name-change requests, I looked at all three and thought how hard it must have been for them to have lived their lives in the wrong bodies and how brave of them to become who they were meant to be. In a matter of minutes, they exited my courtroom with court orders in their hands and smiles on their faces.

One case that touched me deeply was that of a transwoman who, representing herself, stood before me in April 1994 to change her name.

I had, early on, flagged her petition and placed it at the bottom of my stack of the name-change files for that morning. The courtroom was empty of spectators when I called her case. She came forward, stood at one of the counsel tables, and smiled nervously. In no time, the hearing was over. I approved her petition and signed the order, and after my clerk handed it to her, off she went. A few days later, I received this letter:

Lisa. ███ ███ ███
███ ██ ███ ██████

Judge LaDoris H. Cordell
Superior Court
191 North First Street
San Jose, CA 95113

April 13, 1994

Ms. Cordell,

I'm not sure if you recall me, but I appeared in your courtroom only yesterday for a name change. I was so impressed by your concern and sympathy that I felt a need to write to you and thank you.

In the process I have been going through, I have met and had to deal with many intollerant people. People who seem unable to deal with things they can't understand. These people include, for me, an ex-employer and, unfortunately, my parents. Therefore, coming across someone as understanding as you appeared to be is an INCREDIBLY refreshing change for me.

I watched you handle all the other name changes before mine and, at first, thought that you granted them no matter what, until a pair of parents appeared who wanted to change the name of their little girl. You seemed concerned at the effect that this might have on the child's identity and I was touched by the apparent concern that you had for their child as to the effect that this may have on her. This made quite an impression on me.

To be honest, I was terrified that you would call me up and start the procedure as you had with all the others before me: "State your name, please." To my delight, you did not! You simply asked me "You wish to change your name to Lisa ████████. Correct?" I can't express to you the RELIEF I felt when you said that!

To top it all off, you then had your assistant (clerk?) call me aside and ask me if I wished the records to be sealed. I had never even thought or heard of this for these cases. Again, I was pleased.

I know that the standard response to comments like mine is "I'm just doing my job." And, while you ARE, you are doing much more than is required by your job. You are showing a great amount of concern for the well-being of those involved in the proceedings in your courtroom, whether they are present or not. It is people like you who maintain my faith in the human race. Thank you!

Sincerely,

Lisa

Lisa ██ ███████ ← *Officially!* ☺

It doesn't get any better than this.

JURIES AND JUDGES

Thank You for Your Service

Jury Duty

When you go into court you are putting your fate into the hands of
twelve people who weren't smart enough to get out of jury duty.

—NORM CROSBY, COMEDIAN

I. Jury Duty

'm not guilty. There's no way that I can be convicted." Thus spoke twenty-six-year-old Monte Otis, who insisted on representing himself at his jury trial where he was charged with two counts of vandalism, misdemeanors. If convicted, he faced a maximum punishment of one year in the county jail and a fine of as much as $1,000. I had tried to talk him out of representing himself, explaining that he faced a seasoned prosecutor who had tried more than forty cases. I also had warned him that I wouldn't be able to assist him if he proceeded on his own. Still, he was adamant about going it alone. So, that April afternoon in 1987, we began to select a jury.

That morning had been awful. I was assigned fifteen misdemeanor jury trials; I settled a few and continued the rest. It didn't help that the prosecutor, a middle-aged White man, was in a bad mood. "Why are you settling cases by giving lower jail sentences? This isn't the time to make offers on cases," he whined. "Look," I said. "When you have fifteen trials, you are forced to make offers. If I were assigned just one case, I wouldn't have to do this." My so-called lower sentences consisted of:

(1) nine months in jail instead of ten months in a drunk driving case, (2) eight days instead of ten days in jail for a first-time convicted drunk driver, and (3) formal probation and six months in a locked psychiatric facility instead of five days in jail for a prowler.

At one point, the prosecutor got into it with a female defense attorney when she told him that she needed to continue her client's case for a month. So, when we took a break for lunch, I pulled him aside and asked, "Are you okay? You seem like you're on edge." He sighed and said, "No, I'm all right. I'm just unreasonable. You thought I was reasonable, but I'm not." I shook my head; this didn't bode well for the afternoon when he would return to prosecute Mr. Otis.

At 2:10 P.M., about eighty people were ushered into my courtroom by one of the sheriff's deputies, filling the spectator seats on the side closest to the jury box, directly behind Benita's desk. They had been sitting in the jury assembly room on the first floor of the courthouse for God knows how long, waiting to be assigned to a courtroom. My staff and I stood as they entered and when all were seated, I sat, smiled, then welcomed them to Department 8 by introducing myself, my court staff, the prosecutor, and the defendant. I briefly described the case that fourteen of them would hear (twelve jurors and two alternates). "Mr. Monte Otis is charged with two counts of vandalism, misdemeanors. It is alleged by the prosecutor that Mr. Otis slashed the tires of two cars owned by Ms. Long and Ms. Dremer. Because Mr. Otis is presumed to be innocent, it is the burden of the prosecution to prove, beyond a reasonable doubt, that he committed these offenses. Your job, if you are selected as jurors, will be to determine if the prosecution has met that burden. Mr. Otis has chosen to represent himself."

I saw that this jury pool consisted of two Latinx (both men), one Asian American woman, lots of Caucasians, and not one African American. (In the late 1980s, Santa Clara County's Black, Brown, and Asian populations were small. Today, the county's demographics are dramatically different: 23 percent Latinx, 37 percent Asian, 31 percent Caucasian, and 3 percent African American.) Since Mr. Otis was Caucasian, he was surely relieved to know that his jury would look very much like him, a feeling that defendants of color in our county rarely, if ever, experience.

Even though the word "jury" appears nowhere in the document, the guarantee of a jury trial was enshrined in England's Magna Carta of 1215: "No free man is to be arrested, or imprisoned, or disseised [removed from one's property], or outlawed, or exiled, or in any other way ruined, nor will we go against him or send against him, except by the lawful judgment of his peers or by the law of the land."

Before 1215, disputes in England were resolved in one of three ways:

(1) Trial by battle, where litigants engaged in physical combat; whoever won the fight prevailed in the dispute.

(2) Trial by ordeal, where the accused carried a hot iron in his bare hand or removed a stone from boiling water. If, after three days, the wound healed, he was declared innocent; if not, then he was guilty as charged.

(3) Trial by compurgation, where eleven or twelve men, known as compurgators or oath helpers, swore to the credibility of the accused and by doing so, secured his acquittal.

The seeds of the independent jury in America's legal system were planted in the 1670 landmark decision in *Bushell's Case,* in which William Penn and William Mead, two Quaker activists, were tried before an English jury for the crime of unlawful assembly. The jurors, led by Edward Bushell, refused to convict them, whereupon the trial judge ordered the jury to continue deliberating—this time without food or water. When the jury again refused to bring back guilty verdicts, the judge fined them and ordered them to prison. The jailed jurors successfully appealed to the Court of Common Pleas, which freed them, declaring that jurors cannot be punished for their verdicts.

Inspired by the *Bushell* ruling, the authors of the Declaration of

Independence included the principle of an independent jury in their twenty-seven grievances against King George III, who insisted on "depriving us in many cases, of the benefits of Trial by Jury."

Today, the right to a jury trial is enshrined in three places in the United States Constitution: Article III, the Sixth Amendment, and the Seventh Amendment.

Article III of the U.S. Constitution provides: "The trial of all crimes except Cases of Impeachment, shall be by jury."

The Sixth Amendment in the Constitution's Bill of Rights more explicitly addresses juries in criminal cases: "In all criminal prosecutions, the accused shall enjoy the right to a speedy and public trial, by an impartial jury of the State and District wherein the crime shall have been committed."

Jury trials in civil cases are the focus of the Seventh Amendment: "In Suits at common law, where the value in controversy shall exceed twenty dollars, the right of trial by jury shall be preserved and no fact tried by a jury, shall be otherwise re-examined in any Court of the United States, than according to the rules of the common law."

(The Sixth Amendment applies to the states, but the Seventh Amendment doesn't. This means that the states are required to provide the right to jury trials in criminal cases. However, the Seventh Amendment's right to civil jury trials is optional, leaving it to individual states to require them or not. Today, all of the states have laws that guarantee the right to jury trials in civil cases.)

Because I'm a people person, I loved presiding over jury trials. My favorite part of the trial was voir dire, the time when I got to engage directly with potential jurors by asking them about their backgrounds and explaining to them the various moving parts of the legal system.

I began by asking general questions of the entire jury panel and advised them that if their answers were yes to any of my questions, they should raise their hands so that I could follow up with them. These were standard inquiries that trial judges utilize to set the stage for the jurors, to give them the lay of the land. The judges on our court used a trial handbook with guidelines for handling jury trials and suggested questions for voir dire.

Before the start of the trial, I had gone over my questions with the prosecutor and Mr. Otis in my chambers, and neither of them had any objections.

I began: "Does anyone have a problem understanding English?" No hands raised. "Does anyone have a problem sitting for long periods of time?" Nothing yet. "This trial will take approximately two days. Is there anyone who believes he or she cannot be a juror in this case?" A bunch of hands shot up into the air. I wasn't surprised. Jury duty is like the plague: no one wants it. I can't tell you how many times I've fielded frantic phone calls from friends and neighbors desperate for advice about how to get out of jury duty. What did surprise me were the people who *didn't* raise their hands.

Websites abound with advice about how to avoid jury service, including: "Want to Get Out of Jury Duty? Here's How." Two "tricks" addressed juror attitudes—the good and the bad. First, the bad: "Sometimes, just having a bad attitude can be enough to get you dismissed. If you are going to be negative and difficult the whole time, the judge and/ or attorneys might decide to send you on your way."

Juror questionnaires, commonly used in lengthy civil and criminal trials, speed up voir dire by providing the lawyers with juror background information. For example, in the 1994 O. J. Simpson double-murder trial, potential jurors filled out a mammoth seventy-five-page questionnaire that had 302 questions. In 2000, I encountered the jerk of all jurors in a civil trial involving an Asian American man who sued his former employer for racial discrimination. The jerk, a middle-aged White male, had written several offensive answers on his juror questionnaire:

(1) Occupation: *pimp.* [In fact, he was a sales manager.]

(2) Duties at work: *pimpin, slackin, taking customers to strip bars, abusing co-workers.*

(3) Have you ever disciplined employees? *I yell at a lot of people; yelling is fun; I once kicked an employee's ass.*

When asked how he felt about the use of profanity in the workplace, he wrote: "Often I admire it and add to my own lexicon. I really like the way it makes my mouth feel when I say, 'fuck you.'"

Other of his responses included:

I worked with a lot of women at the GAP. They sucked. . . . affirmative action kept me from getting into UCLA. . . . I have been investigated for sexual harassment twice. Beat the rap both times. I would be kinda pissed if you picked me. I want to go to Vegas and get laid. If O.J. can get acquitted, isn't that enough to tell you that this whole system is bullshit?

I was livid but adhered to my thick-of-skin and long-of-fuse mantra; my thought bubble was going crazy. I calmly called him and the two lawyers to the bench, leaned forward, and looked him in the eyes. Lowering my voice, I said, "Sir, your answers to these questions are offensive and insulting. You are excused; get out of my courtroom. Now." He blushed, started to say something, apparently thought better of it, turned, and stormed out.

And there's the good-attitude trick: "Believe it or not, if you are especially enthusiastic about serving on a jury, there is a good chance that you will be dismissed. If you seem overly interested in being on the jury, there might be some question about whether or not you are biased or have an agenda." According to Philip K. Anthony, chief executive officer of DecisionQuest, a trial consulting firm: "We are wary of people who are trying to get on a jury." After surveying more than one hundred thousand jurors, his company estimated that 17 percent are "stealth jurors," people who want to further their hidden agendas by serving on juries. So, his firm cautions lawyers to avoid the especially enthusiastic. In my view, there are reasons having nothing to do with hidden agendas for which individuals might be excited about serving on juries. I, for one, would love to be a juror because I am fascinated by the entire process. (I was summoned for jury duty once, but at the time I was presiding over a jury trial, so, predictably, I was dismissed.) Although I'd have a hard time hiding my eagerness to serve, I think that I'd make a good juror. I remain ever hopeful that one day my summons will come.

Senior citizens have a get-out-of-jury-duty card. Even though there are no upper age restrictions for jury service, in most states, seniors can opt out simply by informing the court that they have medical or physical conditions that render them unable to serve. And for the most part, no documentation of any kind is required—no doctors' notes, no questions asked.

Why do so many people dread serving on juries? It is my guess that the answer lies in the inordinate amount of time wasted sitting around, waiting to find out which of those summoned will be chosen. As a consequence, most people come to view jury duty as a nuisance and an inconvenience. It frequently is. Case in point was the assignment to me that morning of the fifteen jury trials that I had to handle before I could summon the prospective jurors for the *Otis* trial, all of whom waited, utterly in the dark about why. The notion of jury duty as a noble civic responsibility frequently gets lost in the waiting.

Also, it doesn't help that compensation for each day of jury duty (the time waiting in the jury room, during jury selection, and actual jury service) is a pittance. Juror fees range from a high of $50 per day (Arkansas, North and South Dakota, and federal trials) to $5 a day (New Jersey, Kentucky) to nothing (Delaware and South Carolina), and everything in between. New Mexico, which ties its juror compensation to the state's minimum wage, pays jurors $7.50 per hour of service. California is near the bottom, coming in at just $15 per diem. When full-time employees are called for jury duty, only eight states and the District of Columbia require employers to pay their regular wages during jury service.

Most judges see the jury trial as an opportunity to lecture prospective jurors about the importance of jury service as a civic responsibility; it is. But when jurors are paid as little as $5, $15, or $50 a day for their service, what does that say about the perceived value they bring to our legal system? How can judges realistically expect jurors to willingly serve when service frequently means lost wages for days, weeks, and sometimes months? The courts need to put their money where their mouths are and provide meaningful compensation to jurors. Until then, our legal system does little more than pay lip service to the importance of juries and to the Sixth Amendment in which they are enshrined.

Approximately thirty million Americans receive jury summonses each year. Their names are drawn primarily from lists of registered voters and from licensed drivers and identification cardholders registered with departments of motor vehicles. California also permits names to be utilized from state tax returns, customer mailing lists, telephone directories, and utility company lists.

It is the view of Andrew Guthrie Ferguson, author of *Why Jury Duty Matters,* that "a jury summons is an invitation to participation. Jurors are asked to involve themselves in some of the personal, sensational, and terrifying events in a community . . . Participation in jury service teaches the skills required for democratic self-government." I'm hard-pressed to regard any kind of summons as an "invitation." But based on the overwhelmingly positive reactions of jurors who served in my more than seventy-five jury trials, I believe that participation on a jury can be an eye-opening experience that teaches people about the legal process and instills respect for it. Indeed, in a survey commissioned by the American Bar Association in 2004, 87 percent of those who had been called for jury duty agreed with the statement: "Jury duty is an important civic duty I should meet even if it is inconvenient." The hard part is getting them into the jury box.

While I relished jury trials, there are judges who find them to be unpleasant experiences and jurors to be irritating nuisances. Voir dire, in particular, tries their patience, occasionally landing them in hot water. In one instance, a judge was disciplined for causing prospective jurors to wait in the hallway for several hours and, in another, for accusing two prospective jurors, in front of the other jurors, of lying to get out of jury duty.

Returning to the *Otis* trial, when hands went up in response to my questions about who felt that jury service wasn't for them, I settled back to listen to their litany of excuses with a poker face and my thought bubble on full alert: "My work can't do without me." *But you run the copy machine.* "I may get married soon." *I do weddings.* "I have asthma." *And?* "I am uncomfortable with crime." *Who isn't, unless you're a criminal?* "I have to urinate a lot." *Ah, a juror with no inhibitions.* "I'm nervous." *Take a Xanax.* "I gave in on a jury because the other jurors harassed me, so I'm not going through that again." *This is an entirely different case with an entirely different jury.* "I can't understand you [meaning, me] because of your accent." *My accent?!* "My wife told me that if the trial ran into our vacation, I would have hell to pay." *I do divorces.* "Since the Simpson trial, I believe that the system is a joke, so I don't want to be a part of it. The guilty always go free." *Do I look like Judge Ito?*

I released a handful of people "for cause"; their excuses were legitimate reasons for their inability to serve. There was a single mom who couldn't afford to miss work, a man whose business had just one employee—him, an older Vietnamese woman with an extremely poor grasp of the English language, a young woman who recognized one of the alleged vandalism victims, and a sixtyish White male whose faith as a Jehovah's Witness prohibited him from sitting in judgment of others.

Next, I asked my clerk to randomly draw from a small, black metal container twelve slips of paper, on each of which was printed the name of a member of the jury pool. As she plucked each piece of paper from the box and called out the name, I directed the lucky person to take a seat in the jury box. When the twelve seats were filled, it was time for voir dire by the lawyers.

II. Voir Dire

In theory, voir dire (translated from French, "to see them say") is a process to ascertain information to enable the selection of fair and impartial jurors. In practice, it's much more than that because lawyers use voir dire to give jurors a preview of their sides of the cases (almost like opening statements), to generate juror sympathy for their clients, and to romance the jurors. The thinking is, if you like me, then you'll like what I have to say or at least you'll be willing to listen.

Law professor James J. Gobert, author of a treatise on jury selection, has analogized voir dire to a job interview: "The job is that of juror in the case; the applicants are members of the panel. Voir dire provides jurors with a general understanding of the nature of the job for which they are being interviewed, allows them and their employers the opportunity to learn something about each other, and provides sufficient background information to enable the identification of those who are unsuited for the job."

Since 1961, federal court judges have been allowed to conduct voir dire entirely on their own, with the option of permitting attorneys to participate. In state courts, individual practices vary; some courts follow the federal model, while others simply give voir dire over to the lawyers. In California, it's a mix of both: judges are required to question potential jurors orally and/or by written questionnaires, after which they must allow lawyers to conduct their own voir dire.

One criticism of voir dire is that when the lawyers get involved, it takes on a life of its own—sometimes a long, long life. Voir dire dragged on for *six weeks* in the trial of Albert Greenwood Brown, Jr., accused of the rape and murder of a California teenager. When, to protect the privacy of the jurors, the trial judge ordered all but three days of the six-week voir dire closed to the public, the Press-Enterprise Co., a local newspaper covering the trial, asked for the release of the voir dire transcript. When the judge refused, the newspaper appealed. This situation escalated and eventually made its way to the United States Supreme Court. In ordering the release of the voir dire transcript, the court held that the constitutional guarantee of open public proceedings in criminal trials includes the voir dire of potential jurors. As significantly, the justices condemned the six-week-long voir dire, writing: "We cannot fail to observe that a voir dire process of such length, in and of itself, undermines public confidence in the courts and the legal profession. . . . Properly conducted, it is inconceivable that the process could extend over such a period. We note, however, that, in response to questions, counsel stated that *it is not unknown in California courts for jury selection to extend six months.*" (Emphasis added.) A year before the *Press-Enterprise* decision, the New York Governor's Commission on the Administration of Justice analyzed 462 felony jury trials and found that in 20 percent of those cases, voir dire took longer than the trials and, on average, consumed 40 percent of total trial time.

The most vocal proponents of excluding lawyers from participating in voir dire are judges, prosecutors, and jurors. In opposition are criminal defense attorneys who contend that judicially controlled voir dire is ineffective in rooting out bias when race, ethnicity, sexual orientation, age, and religion are inevitably involved. Their view is that lawyers know the issues in their cases better than anyone and are, therefore, far better equipped than are judges to select jurors who will listen objectively and return just verdicts.

It is my belief that lawyers should have great latitude in their questioning of jurors in trials where guilty verdicts could result in extremely serious punishments such as lengthy years of imprisonment, lifetime confinement, and imposition of the death penalty. But I think that in trials with less serious consequences, for example where the punishment is not more than a year in jail, while judges should allow lawyers to meaningfully participate in jury selection, they should set tighter time limits on voir dire.

It is also my belief—after teaching judicial bias and ethics for more than a decade at California's B. E. Witkin Judicial College in Berkeley with retired judge David Rothman, author of *the* book on the subjects— that judges alone cannot competently ferret out juror bias. Judges, as do all of us, harbor conscious and unconscious biases and, like all of us, can become defensive when their own biases are called into question. The most enlightened jurists may lack the capacity to recognize biases in themselves, rendering them ill-equipped to undertake the delicate and extremely difficult task of eliciting those biases from prospective jurors. I think it best to leave the bulk of voir dire to trial attorneys (and their trial consultants), who are surely as competent as are judges in rooting out bias.

Returning to the case of the misbegotten Mr. Otis, the prosecutor was first up, beginning his voir dire with a question that he appeared to pose to the entire jury panel. "Now, let's say you're downstairs in your house and a friend comes in the front door. He is carrying an umbrella, it's open, and it's wet. The person upstairs yells down to you and asks if it is raining. Do you think it's raining?" He called on Juror #4, a middle-aged White woman, who answered, "Yes, I think it's raining." The prosecutor followed up with: "You don't need to look out the window to make sure it's raining?" At this point, Juror #4 looked unsure, as if she may have given a wrong answer, and said, "Well, I could check, too." The prosecutor raised his voice and told her: "You don't have to check anything. You saw the wet umbrella, so you can rely on circumstantial evidence, right?" *Not good,* I thought. He just lectured a juror and embarrassed her when he could have simply explained to all of the jurors that circumstantial evidence is admissible in a trial, just as direct evidence is admissible, and then asked, "Does anyone have a question about that?" Next, he turned to Juror #10, a thirtysomething male. "What if I curse? Will that be a problem for you?" Benita did all that she could not to chuckle; I did all I could not to roll my eyes. His questioning went on like this for thirty grueling minutes.

Mr. Otis's voir dire was all over the place. "Do you believe in the Constitution of the United States?" and "Do you rent or own your home?" While belief in the Constitution and one's status as a homeowner had no apparent relationship to his vandalism case, I gave him some latitude and let him go on for a bit until, after a juror said that she could be fair to both sides, he pointed a finger at her and shouted, "I don't like your answer!" That was it. I ordered him to sit down and told him that his voir dire was over.

Now that voir dire was completed and the "for cause" folks excused, it was time for the peremptory challenges that allow each side in a criminal (or civil) case to excuse potential jurors for any reason or for no reason at all, as long as they have not been removed because of their race, gender, sexual orientation, or religion. (In the legal world, "peremptory" means final, conclusive, not open to challenge or appeal.) Just how one can detect if a lawyer has a discriminatory motive when she uses a peremptory challenge has long been grist for discussion and hand-wringing in the legal community and among the justices on the U.S. Supreme Court. More on that in a bit.

III. Peremptory Challenges

Peremptory challenges were instituted in England in 1305, although rarely used. Defendants were given thirty-five challenges; the Crown (the prosecution) had none. Over the years, the number of defense "peremptories" in England steadily decreased, going from thirty-five to twenty in 1530, to seven in 1948, to three in 1977, until they were entirely abolished in 1989. American colonies followed England's seventeenth-century practice of allowing peremptory challenges but differed among themselves about whether or not to allow the prosecution to utilize them. Some did; some didn't.

There is no constitutional right to peremptory challenges in the United States. Because our Constitution is silent on them, it was left to Congress and state legislatures to enact rules for the use of peremptory challenges in jury trials—and enact they did. Today, "peremptories" are utilized by all state and federal courts in civil and criminal cases (allotted to both the defense and prosecution). In federal courts, defendants charged with felonies have ten peremptory challenges; prosecutors get six. The number of peremptories in the states varies. For example, in California, in felony trials, each side gets ten challenges; Idaho allows six peremptory challenges for each side; in Michigan, the defense and prosecution in felony cases are permitted five challenges each; and Hawaii allows just three apiece. Since 2015, misdemeanor trials in California limit each side to six peremptory challenges; but when the *Otis* trial was before me, each side had ten opportunities to excuse the jurors.

Mr. Otis used none of his ten peremptory challenges. I wasn't sure if he understood that he even had the challenges or if he simply didn't want to exercise them. The prosecutor, on the other hand, used all ten of his challenges.

In 1986, a year before the *Otis* jury trial, the U.S. Supreme Court issued a ruling in the case of *Batson v. Kentucky* that dramatically changed the peremptory challenge landscape. Before *Batson*, peremptories were completely discretionary and subject to no second-guessing about what motivated the dismissal of a juror. In the *Batson* case, the prosecutor had used his peremptory challenges to remove all four of the Black jurors in a trial so that Mr. Batson, a Black man charged with burglary and possession of stolen goods, was left with an all-White jury. Batson's attorney objected and asked that the jury be disbanded because the prosecutor's removal of all of the Black jurors violated his client's right to a fair trial. The trial judge denied Mr. Batson's request because the parties could use peremptory challenges "to strike anybody they want to." After the jury convicted Mr. Batson of both counts, he filed an appeal that eventually reached the Supreme Court. The high court ruled that peremptory challenges could be second-guessed only when a prima facie case (a case of first impression) had been made that racial discrimination was the motivation. "We have confidence that trial judges, experienced in supervising voir dire, will be able to decide if the circumstances concerning the prosecutor's use of peremptory challenges creates a prima facie case of discrimination against black jurors."

Under *Batson*, when a defendant contends that the prosecutor's peremptory challenge was racially motivated or motivated by other types of discrimination—ethnicity, religion, sexual orientation, or gender—the prosecutor must offer to the judge a neutral explanation for removing the prospective juror. Then it is up to the judge to determine if the prosecutor's race-neutral explanation is plausible.

So, how has the Supreme Court's confidence in trial judges' ability to uncover racial bias panned out? Not well. More than thirty years after the *Batson* decision, trial judges continue to accept superficial and outright ridiculous excuses from prosecutors for their peremptory challenges. For example, in 1995, a prosecutor struck two prospective Black jurors because of their mustaches and goatee-type beards, explaining: "Those are the only two people on the jury with the facial hair. . . . I don't like the way they looked." The trial judge found the explanation to be race neutral. Consider this jaw-dropping exchange in a Pennsylvania federal court between the judge and the prosecutor in 1989:

> **Prosecutor:** For the record, I believe that this juror No. 2 . . . my impression is that he is . . . East Indian. He is not a black man, so—at least, not by heritage, I believe. My impression is blacks come from Africa, whereas Mr. Das, Juror No. 2, is clearly, to me, an Indian. And my reasoning in striking him was that I feel that he is probably Hindu in religion, and Hindus tend, in my experience and in talking it over with my counsel, to have feelings a good bit different than ours about all sorts of things . . . and I can be more certain with an American juror, and that was my primary reason for striking him. He may have religious beliefs that may affect his thinking.

> **Judge:** Well, let the record show that, according to the Court's own observation, Mr. Das is not of the black race. However, we will not question him about his race. We will not question him about his religion. I think that he probably is Indian or some other race. There is one man of the black race, according to my observation, on the jury panel, and only one, and, of course, he is not in controversy here, so I think [the prosecutor's] explanation is sufficient, so we need not make any other inquiry.

In another case, a California judge saw nothing wrong with the following explanations offered by the prosecutor, who used her peremptory challenges to strike all four of the prospective Black jurors:

> **Prosecutor:** Your Honor, the jurors [sic] Mr. Conte [the defendant's lawyer] is referring to, Cynthia King and Annie McMullen, Marvin Young and Carlos Davis . . .
>
> My reason [sic] for excluding Cynthia King is she is a social worker. I just wouldn't put a social worker on the jury.
>
> Annie McMullen looked—she glared at me. She looked really sullen, and she just, I mean it was like a glare. I felt very uncomfortable with her, and I wouldn't put her on.
>
> Marvin Young lives in the defendant's neighborhood. He came to court in jeans, and I just thought—I felt uncomfortable. I don't like to pick people who come in in jeans, in the first place, because I think it shows that they don't have that much respect for the system. . . . I thought he lived in the neighborhood— he's black, too, and he was dressed casually, and I thought he might identify with him too much so I excused him.
>
> Carlos Davis I kicked because he acquitted in a case just a couple of weeks ago.

And then, there was the judge in Louisiana who accepted the prosecutor's peremptory challenges against all five prospective Black jurors. About one of the five, the prosecutor told the judge:

> I thought about it last night. Number 1, the main reason is that he looked very nervous to me throughout the questioning. Number 2, he's one of the fellows that came up at the beginning [of voir dire] and said he was going to miss class. He's a student teacher. My main concern is for that reason, that being that he might, to go home quickly, come back with guilty of a lesser verdict so there wouldn't be a penalty phase. Those are my two reasons.

Even though the defense attorney disputed both reasons, and even though the prospective juror's professor had confirmed to the court, by telephone, that the trial would not pose a problem for the juror, the trial judge was unbothered by the prosecutor's he-looked-nervous explanation: "All right. I'm going to allow the challenge. I'm going to allow the challenge." This was during voir dire in a death penalty case. You tell me, who among us wouldn't be nervous?

The most recent U.S. Supreme Court pronouncement about the peremptory challenge was in the high-profile case of *Flowers v. Mississippi.* On July 16, 1996, four people were murdered at the Tardy Furniture store in Winona, Mississippi. Curtis Flowers, a Black man, was arrested, convicted of the murders, and sentenced to death, after *six jury trials*, some of which ended with deadlocked juries and some reversed for prosecutorial misconduct, unrelated to jury selection. The first four times Doug Evans, the White prosecutor, tried Flowers, he struck every Black panelist he could, thirty-six in all. After a deadlocked jury in the fifth trial, Evans used his peremptory challenges to excuse five of the six Black jurors; Flowers was convicted in trial number six. In each of those trials, the judges accepted the prosecutor's explanations for removing Black jurors.

In June 2019, the U.S. Supreme Court reversed Curtis Flowers's conviction in his sixth trial (7–2) and, in a superbly reasoned opinion by Associate Justice Brett Kavanaugh, strongly criticized the prosecutor's abuse of peremptory challenges. In 2020, the state of Mississippi dropped further prosecutions of Mr. Flowers.

Do trial judges who defer to prosecutors' sometimes implausible "race-neutral" explanations harbor racist attitudes? Maybe, but I prefer to believe that most do not. Rather, I think that it is unreasonable and just plain silly to expect judges to figure out the hidden agendas of those who exercise peremptory challenges. Associate Justice Thurgood Marshall said as much in his concurring opinion (an opinion in agreement with the majority opinion) in *Batson*, writing: "Merely allowing defendants the opportunity to challenge the racially discriminatory use of peremptory challenges in individual cases will not end the illegitimate

use of the peremptory challenge. . . . Any prosecutor can easily assert fa-
cially neutral reasons for striking a juror, *and trial courts are ill-equipped to
second-guess those reasons.*" (Emphasis added.) Similarly, Associate Justice
Kavanaugh cautioned in the *Flowers* decision that trial judges "must not
allow the spirit of *Batson* to be diminished by misguided allegiance to
the peremptory challenge."

How many lawyers will admit that their motivations are to rid the
jury of individuals because of their race or ethnicity? And how many
judges are willing to find discriminatory intent, when by doing so they
are in essence calling these lawyers liars? Imagine reversing a prosecutor's peremptory challenge because her explanation was implausible and
then having to deal with that same prosecutor throughout the trial—not
a pretty picture.

There are those (mostly lawyers) who think that the peremptory
challenge is a good idea because it allows lawyers to maintain control
over the jury selection process. They contend that since lawyers know
their cases better than anyone, it is they who have a better sense of which
prospective jurors can fairly evaluate the evidence.

Those who condemn the peremptory challenge (mostly legal scholars)
label it "a charade whose protections are illusory," "a cloak for discrimination," a "weapon of prejudice," and "probably the single most significant
means by which . . . prejudice and bias [are] injected into the jury selection system." Some academics and judges, including Thurgood Marshall
(in his concurring opinion in *Batson*), have called for its abolition. In
2001, the Supreme Court of Florida's *Report of Jury Innovations Committee* went so far as to recommend that a comprehensive study of the
peremptory challenge include whether it should be eliminated.

I'm of two minds on the subject. On the one hand, the peremptory
challenge invites lawyers to invent explanations to cover their discriminatory motives. On the other hand, the peremptory challenge gives lawyers
an opportunity to dismiss prospective jurors for reasons not in any way
related to discrimination but instead based on a gut feeling that some-

thing about that person just doesn't feel right. Having been a litigator, I know the feeling. When, as a trial attorney, I had a bad feeling about a prospective juror but couldn't put my finger on exactly why, I knew that I had a peremptory challenge to fall back on. It could have been a dismissive frown or a scowl in response to my questioning or a hostile glance at my client—insufficient to remove the person "for cause" but enough to satisfy me that the person might not be a good juror for our side.

Back to the *Otis* jury trial: "The People thank and excuse Juror #3 [a White male construction worker]." Each time the prosecutor excused someone, the clerk chose another slip of paper from the black box and the person whose name she called sat in the excused juror's empty seat to be questioned by both sides. The next person up was a White male computer programmer. "The People thank and excuse Juror #11 [a middle-aged white female librarian]." She was replaced by a thirtyish White female clothing store sales manager. By the time the prosecutor had used his ninth peremptory challenge, there were twelve people seated in the jury box. I announced that he had just one peremptory remaining. (Both my clerk and I had been keeping a tally of the challenges.) "The People thank and excuse Juror #7 [a White woman in her fifties who worked at a skilled nursing facility]." With that, the prosecutor had used his tenth challenge. This meant that the person whose name was called next, whoever she or he was, could not be excused by the prosecutor with a peremptory challenge; he had run out of them. So, unless that juror were to be excused "for cause" (a specific reason), we would have our jury. Filling the seat was a White male security officer in his fifties who was employed at a nearby mall. When questioning by the prosecutor and by Mr. Otis gave no reason to excuse him from serving, the security guard became our twelfth juror. Done!

We ended up with a jury of eight men and four women. (Since the trial was going to take no more than a day, it seemed unlikely that any of the twelve jurors would drop out; both sides agreed to proceed without alternate jurors.) I directed the twelve chosen ones to stand and raise

their right hands, and then asked them: "Do you, and each of you, understand and agree that you will well and truly try the cause now pending
before this court and a true verdict render according only to the evidence
presented to you and to the instructions of the court?" They answered in
unison: "I do." Let the trial begin!

IV. The Trial

Because the accused is presumed to be innocent, the burden is always on
the prosecution to prove beyond a reasonable doubt that the defendant
is guilty of the charges against him, which is why the prosecution goes
first. In the *Otis* trial, the prosecutor began by calling as his first witness
one of the alleged victims, Ms. Long. She swore to tell the truth, the
whole truth, and nothing but the truth. Then she sat at the witness stand
directly to my left, the jury box on her left, and began answering the
prosecutor's questions.

Ms. Long testified that she worked in a bar called the Savoy Lounge
and that on the night in question, Mr. Otis entered the bar and almost
immediately began harassing the female patrons. When she told Mr.
Otis to leave, he argued with her, then abruptly and angrily left the bar.
She watched him walk into the parking lot and witnessed him cut the
tires of her car, using a knife that he had removed from his jacket pocket.
Seated in a large and intimidating courtroom, telling her story to a
bunch of strangers, that she was nervous was understandable. The court
reporter took down her every word. I believed her, but my opinion was
irrelevant; the jurors would have to make that call.

The purpose of cross-examination is to test the credibility of the witness's testimony. Mr. Otis's questioning of Ms. Long was as I expected—
not challenging and not very good:

> You say that I demanded food? Did you tell me that you didn't want
> men in the bar? How long have you known me? Isn't that bar a women's
> club? Why aren't there any other witnesses around?

The next witness was Ms. Dremer, the owner of the lounge and Ms. Long's employer. They were also roommates. Ms. Dremer claimed that Mr. Otis slashed one of the tires on her car, an Cadillac Eldorado. On direct examination by the prosecutor, she said that Mr. Otis kept yelling about not being served because he was a man. She testified that she told him that the lounge was a women's club but that men were allowed and that no one refused to serve him. Mr. Otis's cross-examination of Ms. Dremer was brief and, in my view, pretty ineffective.

Next, Officer Scaletta testified that he arrested Mr. Otis in the parking lot of the lounge. On cross-examination, Mr. Otis asked the officer, "What's the width of the slits in the tires?" The officer referred to his police report and answered, "One inch." Next, Mr. Otis asked Officer Scaletta to measure the width of the knife that was confiscated from him. The officer removed the knife from the evidence envelope and using a ruler that my clerk handed to him, measured it. "One-half of an inch," he answered. "So how could the punctures in the tire be a full one inch wide, Officer?" "Well," responded Officer Scaletta, "because you likely moved the knife back and forth when you plunged it into the tires." Mr. Otis then said, "No further questions, Your Honor."

The trial started at 3:00 P.M.; by 3:30 we were already up to the fourth witness. Officer Gunn testified that he found the knife in Mr. Otis's jacket pocket. On cross-examination, Mr. Otis asked, "Do you know anything about the club with a hatred of men?" Officer Gunn answered, "I know it has a substantial number of women, but I don't know about a hatred for men." Mr. Otis had no further questions of the witness.

Throughout the trial, I worked hard to monitor my facial expressions; every time that I glanced at the jury box, there were at least two or three jurors looking at me. Jurors watch judges all of the time, and when they do, they pick up cues, real or imagined, from judges' behaviors. I was particularly aware of this because in 1985, I had coauthored a groundbreaking study with Peter Blanck and Robert Rosenthal entitled *The Appearance of Justice: Judges' Verbal and Nonverbal Behavior in Criminal Jury Trials*. (Today, Peter Blanck is *the* leading authority on judicial nonverbal communication.) We videotaped and studied thirty-four actual misdemeanor trials, each conducted by one of five judges (three men and two women), involving 331 jurors and sixty-one attorneys. The charges against the defendants included vehicular manslaughter, drunk driving, carrying a concealed weapon, assault, and prostitution.

Among the many things we learned was that trial judges may inadvertently "leak" or reveal their underlying feelings or expectations about defendants to juries through nonverbal channels. We pinpointed specific nonverbal "micro-behaviors," such as the pace at which the judge reads the jury instructions, the amount of eye contact with the jurors, head nods and headshakes, hand movements, and fidgeting. Several studies have since confirmed our findings that subtle nonverbal behaviors can be interpreted by jurors as signals for how they should consider the testimony of witnesses. The American Bar Association's Model Code of Judicial Conduct even includes a warning that "facial expressions and body language . . . can give to parties or lawyers in the proceeding, jurors, the media and others an appearance of judicial bias."

In a few instances, judges' nonverbal behaviors in jury trials were so egregious that defendants were granted new trials. That's what happened when a Missouri trial judge placed his hands to the sides of his head, shook his head, and leaned back, swiveling his chair 180 degrees during the testimony of a defendant's alibi witness. In another trial, when a prosecution witness testified, a judge in Iowa smiled approvingly, nodded his head in agreement, and muttered, "Uh-hum." During the testimony of another defense witness, the judge shook his head and uttered negative-sounding words such as "hump" and "no." All judges would do well to heed the prescient words of renowned jurist Learned Hand who, in 1933, wrote: "Justice does not depend upon legal dialectics so much as upon the atmosphere in the courtroom, and that in the end depends primarily upon the judge."

By 3:48 P.M., the final witness in the *Otis* trial took the stand—Mr. Otis himself. He testified, "I went in the club to play pool. The owner said we are closed to men. Other women were at the bar. I was yelled at and ordered out. I bought some liquor and left, and that was it. I didn't slash anyone's tires. I wouldn't do that."

The prosecutor's cross-examination was brutal:

Prosecutor: Isn't it true, sir, that you yelled and cursed at the victims?

Mr. Otis: No way. Look, I walked in and first thing, these women were yelling awful things, so I said fuck you and left.

Prosecutor: Isn't it true that you were so angry that you slashed their tires?

Mr. Otis: No. I wasn't angry. Well, I was a little angry, but not angry enough to cut their tires.

Prosecutor: You had a knife on you, so do you want the jury to believe that it was just a coincidence that you just happened to be standing there by the cars with the slashed tires?

Mr. Otis: Yes. Because that's what happened. I'm innocent. They hate men and that's why I'm here.

Prosecutor: No further questions. The People rest.

We took a ten-minute break before the closing arguments but not before I instructed the jurors, as I always did, that they were not to discuss this case among themselves or with anyone else.

Just as with the opening statement, the prosecutor goes first with closing arguments. Next, the defense gives a closing argument, after which the prosecutor has one last chance to argue to the jury. However, in this case, the prosecutor elected to give just one closing argument and to do so after Mr. Otis gave his. So, Mr. Otis went first and delivered his closing remarks in just three minutes, pointing out to the jurors what he believed were inconsistencies in the testimony of the four witnesses. I didn't see any, but perhaps the jurors would. The prosecutor's closing argument took all of five minutes. He told the jurors that there was an eyewitness to the tire slashings, there was motive—the defendant's anger at being told to leave the lounge—and there was the knife that had been found on the defendant. In my view, this was an open-and-shut case for the prosecution, but you never know what a jury will do once they mix it up in their deliberations. At 4:45 P.M., I read the jury instructions to the jurors, the final step before they retired to deliberate.

Judges utilize jury instructions to provide guidance to jurors about how they should consider the evidence to determine the facts and to outline for them every element of the crime that the prosecution must prove. Judges are the lawgivers; jurors are the fact finders. States and the federal government have their own instructions for criminal and civil trials. In California, criminal jury instructions, approved by the Judicial Council of California, are contained in volumes titled *California Criminal Jury Instructions*.

For example, one of the instructions that I read to the jurors in the *Otis* trial explained how they were to assess the credibility of each of the five witness:

> *You alone must judge the credibility or believability of the witnesses. In deciding whether testimony is true and accurate, use your common sense and experience. You must judge the testimony of each witness by the same standards, setting aside any bias or prejudice you may have. You may believe all, part, or none of any witness's testimony. Consider the testimony of each witness and decide how much of it you believe. In evaluating a witness's testimony, you may consider anything that reasonably tends to prove or disprove the truth or accuracy of that testimony. Among the factors that you may consider are:*

> - *How well could the witness see, hear, or otherwise perceive the things about which the witness testified?*
> - *How well was the witness able to remember and describe what happened?*
> - *What was the witness's behavior while testifying?*
> - *Did the witness understand the questions and answer them directly?*

- *Was the witness's testimony influenced by a factor such as bias or prejudice, a personal relationship with someone involved in the case, or a personal interest in how the case is decided?*
- *What was the witness's attitude about the case or about testifying?*
- *Did the witness make a statement in the past that is consistent or inconsistent with his or her testimony?*
- *How reasonable is the testimony when you consider all the other evidence in the case?*
- *Did other evidence prove or disprove any fact about which the witness testified?*
- *Do not automatically reject testimony just because of inconsistencies or conflicts. Consider whether the differences are important or not. People sometimes honestly forget things or make mistakes about what they remember. Also, two people may witness the same event yet see or hear it differently.*

If you decide that a witness deliberately lied about something significant in this case, you should consider not believing anything that witness says. Or, if you think the witness lied about some things but told the truth about others, you may simply accept the part that you think is true and ignore the rest.

And that was one of the shorter instructions. I always provided hard copies of my instructions to the jurors so that they could refer to them during their deliberations. How else could they possibly remember all of this legalese? Oddly, in some states, jurors are not permitted to have physical copies of their instructions. California leaves it to the judge to decide if written jury instructions ought to be provided to jurors; but should jurors request hard copies, the judge is required to hand them over.

The jury instruction that defines reasonable doubt, an instruction that must be given in every criminal jury trial, has an interesting history. It

was first penned in a decision authored by Chief Justice Shaw of the Massachusetts Supreme Judicial Court in the 1850 murder case of *Commonwealth v. John W. Webster*. Professor John Webster, a chemistry professor at a medical college, was indicted for the murder of Dr. George Parkman, to whom he owed money. After beating the doctor in the head with a hammer and stabbing him, Webster dismembered the victim's body, burning some of it and storing the limbs in a vault. In upholding Webster's murder conviction, Chief Justice Lemuel Shaw addressed the issue of reasonable doubt:

> *What is reasonable doubt? . . . It is not mere possible doubt; because everything relating to human affairs, and depending on moral evidence, is open to some possible or imaginary doubt. It is that state of the case, which, after the entire comparison and consideration of all the evidence, leaves the minds of jurors in that condition that they cannot say they feel an abiding conviction, to a moral certainty, of the truth of the charge. The burden of proof is upon the prosecutor. All the presumptions of law independent of evidence are in favor of innocence; and every person is presumed to be innocent until he is proved guilty . . . the evidence must establish the truth of the fact to a reasonable and moral certainty; a certainty that convinces and directs the understanding, and satisfies the reason and judgment, of those who are bound to act conscientiously upon it. This we take to be proof beyond reasonable doubt.*

Shorter versions of Chief Justice Shaw's reasonable doubt definition have been used ever since by our state and federal courts. California's reasonable doubt jury instruction, the one I read to the *Otis* jurors in 1987, went like this: "Reasonable doubt is defined as follows: It is not a mere possible doubt; because everything relating to human affairs, and depending on moral evidence, is open to some possible or imaginary doubt. It is the state of the case which, after the entire comparison and consideration of all the evidence, leaves the minds of the jurors in that condition that they cannot say they feel an abiding conviction, to a moral

certainty, of the truth of the charge." Wait! What exactly is "moral evidence"? What does "an abiding conviction to a moral certainty" mean?

In 1994, the reasonable doubt instruction was questioned in *Victor v. Nebraska*, a case that went all the way to the United States Supreme Court. Defendants Victor and Sandoval had each been convicted of murder. Mr. Sandoval fatally shot two men in a gang-related incident in Los Angeles, California, in 1984; two weeks later, he murdered an informant and the informant's wife. In 1987, Mr. Victor murdered an eighty-two-year-old woman in Nebraska, beating her with a pipe and slashing her throat with a knife. Each appealed his conviction, contending that the reasonable doubt instruction given to their respective juries violated their constitutional right to due process. (Nebraska and California utilized substantially similar reasonable doubt instructions, which is why the court consolidated the two cases.) The Supreme Court upheld the wording of the reasonable doubt jury instructions in both cases but also strongly criticized them. For example, Associate Justice Ruth Bader Ginsburg wrote: "Jury comprehension is scarcely advanced when a court 'defines' reasonable doubt as 'doubt . . . that is reasonable.'"

As well, Associate Justice Sandra Day O'Connor, in her 1999 remarks at the first national conference on public trust in the legal system, echoed the need to fashion jury instructions in plain words, saying: "And at the end of the case, [jurors] are finally read a virtually incomprehensible set of instructions and sent into the jury room to reach a verdict in a case they may not understand much better than they did before the trial began."

Associate Justices O'Connor and Ginsburg were on to something. Consider this: forty-five million Americans are functionally illiterate and cannot read above the fifth-grade level; 50 percent of adults cannot read a book written at an eighth-grade level; and "nearly 50 percent of the Americans surveyed cannot read well enough to find a single piece of information in a short publication, nor can they make low-level inferences based on what they read."

As it stands, two lawyers and a judge—professionals conversant in the law—are placed in a courtroom where they present evidence and argue sometimes-complex legal concepts to twelve randomly selected individuals. We then expect them to make sense of it all, guided by jury instructions that even some legal professionals find difficult to comprehend. We need to do better; we can.

Over the years, several states, including California, have heeded the call for reform and revamped their jury instructions. Today, the *Otis* jury would get this reasonable doubt instruction: "Proof beyond a reasonable doubt is proof that leaves you with an abiding conviction that the charge is true. The evidence need not eliminate all possible doubt because everything in life is open to some possible or imaginary doubt. In deciding whether the People have proved their case beyond a reasonable doubt, you must impartially compare and consider all the evidence that was received throughout the entire trial. Unless the evidence proves the defendant[s] guilty beyond a reasonable doubt, (he/she/they) (is/are) entitled to an acquittal and you must find (him/her/them) not guilty." Any better?

V. Jury Misconduct

Deliberations in the *Otis* jury trial began at 9:00 A.M. the day after closing arguments. Since, in my mind, this case was a slam dunk, I assumed the jurors would return with a guilty verdict in thirty minutes, max. Was I ever wrong. They deliberated through the morning, took their ninety-minute lunch break, and returned to continue deliberating into the afternoon. Finally, at 3:00 P.M. they sent Benita a note that they had reached a verdict. Six hours of deliberation?!

According to *Guinness World Records,* the shortest jury deliberation ever was *sixty seconds.* In 2004, a New Zealand jury began deliberating at 3:28 P.M. and had their verdict one minute later, acquitting the defendant of cultivating twenty-three cannabis plants.

The prize for the longest-ever deliberation in the United States goes to *McClure v. City of Long Beach,* where, following a six-month federal trial in Los Angeles's U.S. District Court, a jury deliberated for *four and one-half months.* In their 1992 lawsuit, Shirley McClure and her son Jason sued the City of Long Beach for blocking them from opening a chain of residential homes. As deliberations dragged on, one of the jurors became so disgusted that before walking out, he left a message on the whiteboard in the jury deliberation room. "We should change the name of this court to United States *Dairy* Court because you guys are milking this thing to death." He may have been right. By the end of the deliberations, the court had spent $80,000 on jury pay, $33,000 on mileage reimbursements, and $6,400 for juror lunches. Jurors later admitted that, during deliberations, some of them slept, chatted, read, and joked around. They started their deliberations late, ended early, and ordered more food than they could eat so that they could take the leftovers home. One juror described orchestrating a phony sick call to the court so that he and a few of the jurors could take a "mental break"; they went to the horse races for a day. Their verdict? A record $22.5 million awarded to the plaintiffs who, no doubt, felt that it was well worth the wait.

Weren't these shenanigans jury misconduct? Shouldn't the judge have declared a mistrial or done something in response to all of that bad behavior? Probably not, because what the McClure jurors did, while unseemly, likely did not fall within the legal definition of misconduct. Jury misconduct is typically defined as behavior that is so prejudicial that "a fair and due consideration of the case has been prevented."

Misconduct usually takes one of three forms: (1) a juror communicates about the case with a person who isn't on the jury; (2) during voir dire, a juror deliberately conceals information that could influence the deliberations; or (3) a juror conducts her own investigation about the case. And yes, there are real-life examples of these misbehaviors. All jurors receive some form of the "thou shalt not blab about this case to anyone" instruction. The California version, similar to those used in most of the states, is clear and to the point:

> *During the trial, do not talk about the case or about any of the people or any subject involved in the case with anyone, not even your family, friends, spiritual advisors, or therapists. Do not share information*

about the case in writing, by email, by telephone, on the Internet, or
by any other means of communication. You must not talk about these
things with other jurors either, until you begin deliberating.

Yet the irresistible pull of social media has succeeded in tempting jurors
to flagrantly ignore this instruction. In 2015, Kimberly Ellis, a juror in
a New York robbery case, posted on Facebook several details about the
trial and the deliberations, including: "Everything about this process is
inefficient. I'm trying to remain positive and centered but, truthfully,
I'm dying from boredom." Ms. Ellis got a well-deserved earful from the
judge, who found her in contempt of court and imposed a fine of $1,000;
the defendant got a new trial.

Robert Aronovitz, a juror in Florida, scuttled the second murder trial
of Ronnie Betts, accused of killing a mother of two in a home invasion.
During the trial, Aronovitz surfed the internet; he couldn't wait to tell
his fellow jurors that the first Betts trial had ended in a mistrial because
of a deadlocked jury. The judge was forced to declare a second mistrial, setting the state back $70,000 in court costs. Mr. Aronovitz's self-
described "horrible mistake" left him with a contempt conviction and an
order to perform two hundred hours of community service at a home-
less shelter. Betts eventually pled guilty to murder and was sentenced to
twenty years in prison in 2017.

Juror Johnna Lorraine texted her way into trouble. After a New York
jury convicted Robert Neulander, a physician, of murdering his wife, it was
revealed that Ms. Lorraine, a twenty-three-year-old cheerleading coach,
exchanged seven thousand text messages with her family and friends
during the three-week trial, hundreds of which were about the case. Right
after she had been selected as a juror, she texted her father to let him know,
who promptly texted back: "Make sure he's guilty." After deleting some of
the texts and clearing her internet browsing history, Ms. Lorraine insisted
that they hadn't affected her deliberations. The New York State Court of
Appeals didn't buy it, finding that she had committed "misconduct, deceit
and destruction of evidence," thereby depriving the defendant of his right

to a fair trial. In October 2019, the good doctor's conviction was reversed, and after serving three years of a twenty-to-life sentence, he was released from prison to await a new trial. Ms. Lorraine never faced any civil or criminal repercussions. Social media is fast becoming a trial judge's pain in the neck.

There are jurors who commit misconduct by deliberately concealing their biases during voir dire. Los Angeles–based jury consultant Philip K. Anthony claims that between 15 percent and 18 percent of potential jurors conceal their biased mindsets and seek out jury service as a way to comment on or influence trials. In 2007, Miguel Angel Peña-Rodriguez was convicted of sexually assaulting two teenage sisters in Colorado. After the trial concluded, two jurors came forward and signed affidavits that described racially biased statements made by one of their fellow jurors, a Caucasian male, referred to in the court filings as H.C. They reported that H.C. told the other jurors that he believed the defendant was guilty because, in H.C.'s experience as an ex–law enforcement officer, Mexican men had a bravado that caused them to believe they could do whatever they wanted with women. The jurors reported that H.C. said that Mexican men are physically controlling of women because of their sense of entitlement and further stated, "I think he did it because he's Mexican and Mexican men take whatever they want." According to the jurors, H.C. explained that, in his experience, "nine times out of ten Mexican men were guilty of being aggressive toward women and young girls."

In a 7–2 decision, the U.S. Supreme Court reversed Peña-Rodriguez's conviction, ruling that juror H.C. had engaged in misconduct by making clear and unambiguous statements demonstrating that he relied on racist stereotypes of Latinos to convict Peña-Rodriguez.

Keith Tharpe, an African American defendant, was not so lucky. In a 1991 Georgia trial, a jury of ten Whites and two Blacks convicted Tharpe of murder and voted that he receive the death penalty. Seven years after the trial, Barney Gattie, one of the White jurors, signed an extraordinary affidavit in which he stated:

There are two types of black people: 1. Black folks and 2. Niggers. Tharpe, who wasn't in the "good" black folks category in my book, should get the electric chair for what he did. Some of the jurors voted for death because they felt [Tharpe] should be an example to other blacks who kill blacks, but that wasn't my reason. After studying the Bible, I have wondered if black people even have souls.

Even though Gattie's belated and blatant disclosure of racial animus tainted the verdict, in 2019, a unanimous U.S. Supreme Court refused to hear the case for procedural reasons, thereby letting his execution date stand. Tharpe died in January 2020 from natural causes at the age of sixty-one.

Finally, there are those jurors who can't resist going rogue by conducting their own research or investigations, even though they are cautioned by judges not to. Here's the standard instruction: "Do not investigate the facts or the law or do any research regarding this case. Do not conduct any tests or experiments or visit the scene of any event involved in this case. If you happen to pass by the scene, do not stop or investigate." Couldn't be clearer, right? So, what was forty-seven-year-old Terri Wright thinking? After taking copious notes during a trial, she followed up with her own online research at home. "I would get in the car and write things down," she said. "I would go home and do the research." The jury, of which Ms. Wright was the foreperson, convicted reggae star Buju Banton of setting up a deal to buy and sell eleven pounds of cocaine. He was sentenced to ten years in federal prison. The trial judge found Wright to be in contempt of court, placed her on five months' probation, ordered her to perform forty hours of community service, and, fittingly, directed her to research and write a report about the cost of the high-profile jury trial that she had nearly upended.

Thankfully, the jurors in the *Otis* trial behaved; there was no misconduct of which I became aware. After they filed into the jury box and took their seats, I asked Juror #2, a nurse in her fifties chosen by her fellow jurors to be their foreperson, if they had reached a unanimous verdict. She quietly said that they had. (In 2020, the U.S. Supreme Court made it official, ruling that jury verdicts in state court criminal trials must be unanimous.)

I asked the foreperson in the *Otis* jury trial to hand the one-page signed verdict form to Benita, who in turn handed it to my courtroom clerk, who in turn handed it to me. I loved the drama and suspense of this part of the trial. Everyone in the courtroom would be watching as I read the verdict to myself to see if they could detect anything in my facial expression that might reveal the jury's decision. What they didn't know was that I have a terrific poker face; I give away nothing. I read the verdict, then handed the form back to the clerk to read out loud. She asked Mr. Otis to stand as she read: "Count one: We, the jury, in the case of *People of the State of California v. Monte Otis*, do unanimously find that the defendant Monte Otis is guilty of the charge of vandalism, a misdemeanor." She repeated the verdict for count two. The jury had found Mr. Otis guilty on both counts. Mr. Otis sat, shook his head, and scowled; the prosecutor stood, nodded, and smiled. I thanked the jurors for their service and discharged them. Once they exited the courtroom, I ordered Mr. Otis to return to court for his sentencing in four weeks. While it wasn't my plan to impose a jail sentence, he would definitely have to make restitution for the slashed tires and, of course, no more hanging out at the Savoy.

Judges for Sale

Judicial Elements

Let me put it this way, my reaction is: Money can buy anything.
—CALIFORNIA JUDGE DZINTRA JANAVS, WHO LOST
HER SEAT TO A BAGEL-SHOP OWNER

January 1, 1988

Dear Friend:

I will shortly be declaring my candidacy for election to the Santa Clara County Superior Court to fill the vacancy created by the retirement of Judge James Wright. . . . My decision to run for the Superior Court is a result of my desire to expand my judicial horizons and to become actively involved in areas of law uniquely within the Superior Court's jurisdiction, such as juvenile, family law, and mental health matters. I believe that I will be a good Superior Court judge. With your support I can make it happen.

Sincerely, LaDoris H. Cordell
Judge of the Municipal Court

With that letter, mailed to hundreds of lawyers and judges through-out the county, I launched my campaign for election to the superior court. It had been six years since my appointment to the municipal court; I was itching to move up the judicial ladder. (Ten years later, in 1998, California's municipal and superior courts would consolidate into one superior court trial system, rendering municipal courts a thing of the past. But in 1988, the two-tier trial court system was the status quo.)

State and federal courts are hierarchical with variously labeled "lower courts," "inferior courts," "superior courts," and "supreme courts." In the federal system, the court with the greatest authority is, as its name suggests, the United States Supreme Court, whose decisions impact everyone, everywhere. Beneath the high court are thirteen U.S. courts of appeals, whose rulings affect only those states within their geographic jurisdictions; below the appellate courts are ninety-four U.S. district trial courts. In addition, there are specialized courts, created under Article I of the U.S. Constitution: bankruptcy courts, territorial courts, the U.S. Court of Appeals for the Armed Forces, the U.S. Court of Appeals for Veterans Claims, the U.S. Tax Court, the Patent Trial and Appeal Board, the International Trade Commission, the U.S. Court of International Trade, the U.S. Court of Federal Claims, and the U.S. Foreign Intelligence Surveillance Court.

In the state system, with the exceptions of New York, Maryland, and the District of Columbia, whose highest courts are called courts of appeals, the supreme courts sit atop the judicial ladder. Beneath the state supreme courts are courts of appeals and below them are trial courts, variously dubbed superior, district, circuit, and county courts. On the very bottom rung are municipal or justice courts, trial courts whose range of cases is narrower than their superior, circuit, and county court counterparts. The cases over which I presided for six years in the Santa Clara County Municipal Court, while interesting, were narrowly limited to misdemeanor arraignments and trials, felony preliminary hearings, small-dollar civil lawsuits, and a smattering of traffic court and small-claims trials.

The superior court was where all the action was—adult and juvenile criminal trials, big-dollar civil lawsuits, probate, mental health, adoptions, name changes, juvenile dependency, divorces, and child custody disputes. Courtrooms in the superior court were larger and grander, and the judges were paid more than municipal court judges. As importantly, cases in the superior court attracted far more attention than those in the municipal court. Superior court was the big league, and I wanted in on the action.

Until the late 1970s, California's judiciary was composed no differently from that of the other states in that it was predominately White and male. But with the arrival of Jerry Brown in the governor's office, the complexion of the state's judiciary changed, literally. During his first two terms in office (1975–1983), Jerry Brown appointed to the California Supreme Court its first woman, its first Latino, and its first two African Americans. He also named the nation's first openly gay and lesbian judges to the trial courts. When he appointed me to the municipal court in 1982, I became the first African American female judge in all of Northern California. But because the great majority of women and people of color whom he appointed were assigned to the municipal courts, the superior courts remained dominated by White males.

In California, the governor's choice of judicial nominees is first evaluated by the Commission on Judicial Nominees Evaluation. Unsurprisingly, the commission almost always rubber-stamps the governor's picks. Once appointed, the judges serve specific terms that vary depending on the courts on which they sit. Justices on the appellate courts (courts of appeal and supreme court) are required to face retention elections every twelve years, in which the electorate votes yes or no to retain them for additional twelve-year terms.

When the six-year terms of trial court judges expire, there are no retention elections. Instead, any lawyer who has been a member of the State Bar of California for at least five years can challenge a municipal court judge; and any lawyer with a minimum of ten years' state bar membership can challenge a superior court judge in a contested election. In 1988, I had been a member of the State Bar of California for twelve and a half years, well over the ten-year minimum to run for a seat on the superior court.

The timing of Judge Wright's retirement was such that the law did not permit the governor to fill the seat by an appointment; a judicial election was the only option. This was a good thing for me because there was no way that George Deukmejian, Governor Brown's successor, would have ever considered appointing me. I was an outspoken liberal feminist, the antithesis of Governor Deukmejian, an ultraconservative who had won office on a tough law-and-order platform. As this was likely my one and only opportunity to move up during a Deukmejian administration, I decided to throw my robe into the ring.

Judicial elections were first instituted in the late 1770s and early 1800s, when the territory of Vermont and the states of Georgia and Indiana used them to fill seats on their lower courts. In 1832, Mississippi became the first state to adopt judicial elections for all of its judges. In the rest of the states, governors appointed judges to lifetime terms "during good behavior."

Spawned in large part by "the partisan patronage politics of appointments," over the next two decades (1840s–1850s), judicial elections spread throughout the country. Between 1846 and 1851, twelve states elected all of their judges, five states opted to elect some of them, and by 1860, eighteen of the thirty-three states required all of their judges to undergo contested elections. Today, twenty-two states utilize contested judicial elections. In the other twenty-eight states, judicial selection methods range from merit selection (independent nominating commissions), to retention elections (yes or no votes on whether judges should remain in office), to gubernatorial appointments, to legislative appointments.

When I decided to run for a seat on the Santa Clara County Superior Court in 1988, twenty trial judges in the county (ten judges on the municipal court and ten judges on the superior court) were up for reelection because their six-year terms were about to expire. Their names would appear on the June ballot, but because they faced no challengers, their reelections were automatic, a fait accompli. The only vacant seat on the ballot was the one occasioned by Judge Wright's retirement. I could have challenged one of the ten superior court judges but opted not to, believing that by going after a vacant position, the road would be far less contentious. Was I ever wrong.

I announced my candidacy on January 1, 1988, and filed a statement of intention to run for office with the county registrar of voters. With the help of several friends and neighbors, I set out to collect the signatures of registered county voters that could be submitted in lieu of paying the $850 filing fee. I figured that when word went out that I had gathered the more than three thousand requisite signatures, people thinking about running for the seat would think twice about taking me on. If no one else chose to vie for the seat, I would be the sole name on the ballot and with no opposition, the seat would be mine. A month later, on February 1, I submitted forty-four hundred signatures, over a thousand more than were required. I crossed my fingers and prayed that no one would step forward. No such luck.

I soon learned from my local newspaper, *The San Jose Mercury News,* that there might be another contender. As the paper reported:

> *Behind the scenes, a few judges and prosecutors have begun soundings for an opponent. One problem for her adversaries: Several municipal judges who might run are up for re-election—and unwilling to leave the safe eddies of incumbency for what promises to be a fierce race. . . . Who does this leave? One name that has surfaced recently is Deputy District Attorney Mike Popolizio, longtime prosecutor who has specialized in major felonies. But Popolizio has not committed himself yet. "I don't know what I'm finally going to do," he said. "I'm in the mulling stage."*

Mr. Popolizio mulled it over and just before the filing deadline, he submitted a statement of intention to run for the seat. With that, the judicial race was on—a thirty-eight-year-old liberal, female judge of color vs. a forty-two-year-old conservative, White male prosecutor. And what a race it turned out to be.

Santa Clara County covers 1,312 square miles and is composed of fifteen cities, stretching from my hometown of Palo Alto in the north to San Jose in the middle to Gilroy in the south. In order to reach the county's then-671,000 registered voters, I needed a campaign manager to help me develop a strategy, and I needed a treasurer to assist me in navigating the web of campaign finance rules and regulations. My witty across-the-street neighbor Joan Holtzman, an environmental activist and twelve years my senior, agreed to manage the campaign. Phil Pennypacker, a San Jose attorney, volunteered to be my campaign treasurer. Now, all I needed was money, lots of it.

While the general public had a passing interest in this race, the county's legal community was obsessed with it—and for good reason. Lawyers have a vested interest in who presides over their cases. Prosecutors want a tough judge who will side with them. Criminal defense attorneys want a lenient judge who will side with them. Civil litigators want a judge who favors corporate clients. Probate attorneys want a judge who can navigate the complex probate code. I was ethically uneasy about accepting lawyers' contributions to my campaign, but if I wanted to be competitive, I had no choice. I was a single parent of two with a judicial salary of $57,000. Without an influx of cash, I wouldn't be able to introduce myself to voters throughout the county. So, I held my nose and asked. In response, nearly eight hundred lawyers stepped up, donating $70,000 to my campaign ($155,000 in today's dollars).

Compared to fundraising in current judicial races, the money that Mr. Popolizio and I raised was a pittance. Today, outside special interest groups pour money into contested judicial elections, particularly when supreme court seats are at stake. Why those courts? Because the highest of the state courts have the final word on how state laws are interpreted; as well, they have the last say about whether verdicts in civil and criminal trials are upheld or reversed. According to the Brennan Center for Justice, "One-third of all elected justices currently sitting on the bench have run in at least one $1 million race. . . . During the 2015–16 supreme court election cycle, political action committees, social welfare organizations, and other non-party groups engaged in a record $27.8 million outside spending spree, making up an unprecedented 40 percent of overall supreme court election spending." Unsurprisingly, 56 percent of that money was contributed by lawyers, lobbyists, and corporate interests.

By 2004, candidates backed by the biggest spenders—the business community—won seats in twelve of thirteen state supreme court races. And after the 2010 U.S. Supreme Court decision in *Citizens United v. FEC* allowed an unlimited flood of money into political campaigns, the floodgates to state judges' campaigns opened as well.

Consider the dramatic influence of special interest groups in the 2016 race for a seat on the Louisiana Supreme Court. With a vacant seat on the court up for grabs, two lower court judges squared off against each other. A major issue in that election was the controversy over compelling oil and gas companies to pay for the restoration of land that the companies had damaged. Judge Marilyn Castle was supported by oil and gas interests, and she received donations from the Virginia-based Center for Individual Rights, an organization that refused to disclose the names of any of its donors. Judge Jimmy Genovese was supported by the Restore Our Coast PAC that funneled donations to his campaign from plaintiffs' lawyers. In a close race that topped *$5 million*, Judge Genovese won with 51 percent of the vote.

Independence, fairness, and integrity generate public trust in the judiciary. But as the influence of money in judicial races grows—and as its impact on judicial decision-making increases—that trust is fading fast. Kate Berry of the Brennan Center for Justice analyzed fifteen years of television advertising data for state supreme court elections to gauge the ads' impact on judicial decision-making in criminal cases. Generally, the ads attacked judges for being soft on crime or praised them as tough on crime. Three of Berry's key findings were that (1) the more frequently ads aired during an election, the less likely state supreme court justices were to rule in favor of criminal defendants; (2) closer to their reelections, trial judges in Pennsylvania and Washington sentenced defendants convicted of serious felonies to longer sentences than normally imposed for those crimes; and (3) trial judges in Alabama imposed death sentences more often in election years, sometimes overriding life sentence verdicts handed down by juries.

A candidate in a contested *political* election is accountable to her donors, her constituents, and to opinion polls. Judges, however, are not politicians; they are independent and take oaths to adhere to the rule of law, to legal principles, and to constitutional precedent. Judges are held accountable by appellate courts that review the rulings and decisions of trial court judges, by disciplinary commissions that rein in errant judges, and, in some instances, by independent nominating commissions that evaluate the fitness of judges who seek retention.

Utilizing a public and transparent process, these independent, bipartisan nominating commissions vet candidates for judicial vacancies and evaluate judges who want to retain their seats. They then recommend slates of nominees to their states' governors who appoint or reappoint individuals from those slates. Known as "merit selection," this system has been frequently proposed as an alternative to judicial elections; in all but fourteen states it has been ignored. Merit selection isn't perfect, but it has the potential to maximize public trust in our judges and to minimize the political influences on them.

Back to my contested election: As the race picked up steam, I received more than fifteen hundred endorsements from lawyers, retired judges, local and state politicians, community leaders, unions, and environmental organizations. My campaign held eight major fundraising events and enlisted 126 volunteers who operated phone banks and walked neighborhoods distributing VOTE FOR JUDGE CORDELL brochures. My supporters distributed 1,486 CORDELL FOR SUPERIOR COURT lawn signs. I attended one hundred events at churches, schools, and neighborhood coffee klatches throughout the county. Mind you, because I continued to work full-time at the municipal court, I was forced to schedule these campaign activities after work and on the weekends—for five months. I was exhausted, and my daughters were annoyed. Their mother was either on the run or too tired to give them the attention they deserved. They just wanted this campaign to be over; so did I.

Mr. Popolizio, on the other hand, had taken a leave of absence from the DA's office, freeing him to campaign full-time. I was jealous, and I was worried. But by May, just a month before the election, his financial statement showed that his fundraising lagged substantially behind mine.

He had raised just $20,000, nearly half of which he had loaned to his campaign. I had raised almost four times that amount, without any personal loans.

Meanwhile, the media was having a field day: "Campaign Barbs Fly in Santa Clara County Race," "Superior Court Fight: Judge vs. Prosecutor," and "Judge Cordell Leads in Money" were some of the more than twenty newspaper articles published during the campaign. For six months, our campaigns did battle with competing lawn signs, mailers, fundraisers, and debates. Mr. Popolizio repeatedly labeled me a "judicial activist" and a "Rose Bird clone," comparing me to the defrocked liberal chief justice of the California Supreme Court who, in 1986, lost her seat in a contentious retention election. I countered that he was trying to sidetrack voters by linking me to Governor Jerry Brown and Rose Bird. "The difference is I'm a judge and he's not," I said. "I have judicial experience and he doesn't. I have sentenced thousands of people and he hasn't sentenced anyone."

By June, things had really gotten ugly. Mr. Popolizio's supporters focused on *three* of my decisions—out of the tens of thousands I had made over the past six and one-half years—that had been reversed by the appellate courts. To the Popolizio campaign, these reversals meant that I had abused my judicial discretion and failed to follow the law. I contended that having been reversed only three times was a rousing endorsement of my judicial track record. And what were the three instances in which my decisions had been overturned?

When I sentenced convicted drunk drivers to install ignition interlock devices in their cars and suspended a portion of their fines, the district attorney's office challenged those sentences. A judge ruled that I could not lawfully reduce the fines, even if my purpose in doing so was to make the devices affordable for low-income defendants, whereupon a Popolizio supporter in the DA's office proclaimed, "The point is that at the time that this happened, she did not follow the law. That's like a deputy district attorney filing a death penalty case before it's the law." Seriously?!

In the second case, as part of a sting operation, a woman answered a police officer's phone call to an escort service. She subsequently met him but was arrested before actually engaging in an act of prostitution. At a court trial, I found the woman, an attorney, not guilty. Shortly thereafter, she filed a petition for a finding of *factual innocence,* which, if granted, would allow her arrest record to be sealed, forever closed to the public. I granted her request and the prosecutor promptly appealed. The appellate court reversed my finding of factual innocence, writing: "Had there been consummation, no one could have doubted that an act of prostitution occurred." Yes, but an act of prostitution *hadn't,* in fact, occurred; that was my point.

In the third case, I ordered the return of drug paraphernalia seized by the police pursuant to a search warrant because they did not match the description of the items listed in the search warrant. The appellate court disagreed with me and reversed my order. I didn't see it that way, but so be it. Rather than being defensive about these reversals, I let the voters know these three cases simply reflected differences of opinion between the appellate court and me in the interpretation of the law. Moreover, I told them that a judge who has never been reversed is a judge who plays it safe, who lacks the courage of her convictions. That kind of judge, I insisted, wasn't me.

The distortion of judicial decisions is the new normal in contested judicial elections. And when the decisions involve criminal cases, look out! Consider what happened in these three judicial races: In 2007, William Wilson pled guilty to capital murder and felony child abuse and in a Mississippi courtroom was sentenced to death. Five years later, the Supreme Court of Mississippi unanimously granted him a hearing on his claim that his trial attorney had been incompetent. Justice Jim Kitchens, who sat on that supreme court, wanted to go a step further by granting Wilson a new trial. Later, when Justice Kitchens ran for reelection, he was challenged by a justice on the court of appeals whose campaign was funded by the Center for Individual Freedom, a conservative Virginia-based nonprofit organization. He accused Justice Kitchens of "siding with child predators" in the *Wilson* case and found support from the Center for Individual

Freedom, which spent $270,000 on a television ad declaring: "On our Supreme Court, Jim Kitchens is putting criminals ahead of victims." When he prevailed in his reelection bid in 2016, Justice Kitchens said, "I hope this will prove to the people who spent nearly $1 million in the last three weeks on negative ads that the people of Mississippi aren't going to stand for it."

In 2015, three justices on the Wisconsin Court of Appeals ruled unanimously that Daniel Fierro, a convicted sex offender, was entitled to a hearing on his claim that he had not fully understood the crime to which he had pled guilty. One of the justices on that court was JoAnne Kloppenburg, who, the following year, ran for a seat on the Wisconsin Supreme Court against one of the justices on that court whose term was up. A television ad, funded by the conservative Wisconsin Alliance for Reform, targeted her by distorting the *Fierro* decision, saying: "We've heard it before: Liberal judges letting criminals off on *technicalities.* . . . Tell Judge Kloppenburg courts should protect children, not criminals." Ensuring that defendants fully understand the charges against them is a *constitutional* guarantee, not a technicality.

But that distortion paled in comparison to the ad the alliance originally aired but was forced to withdraw when it claimed that Justice Kloppenburg had overturned Fierro's conviction—a blatant lie. She lost that race to the sitting supreme court justice who proudly proclaimed to a gathering of corporate and political insiders: "I am your public servant."

And there was the campaign against Louis Butler, the first African American justice on the Wisconsin Supreme Court, who authored a decision in a lead paint poisoning lawsuit that allowed victims to seek compensation from paint manufacturers. Wisconsin Manufacturers and Commerce, a powerful business organization, unhappy with this ruling, spent $2 million backing a challenger. An attack ad funded by the manufacturers placed Justice Butler's face next to that of a Black man named Reuben Lee Mitchell, a convicted child rapist. The ad claimed that Justice Butler found a loophole that allowed Mitchell to go free and molest another child. It omitted the fact that the justice, several years earlier as a public defender, had represented Mitchell and that the "loophole" had been a violation of his client's constitutional rights. The ad worked; Justice Butler was ousted. His White male opponent, a trial judge with no appellate experience, won the seat with 51 percent of the vote.

Returning to my judicial campaign, things intensified as the June 7 Election Day grew closer. My campaign pointed out that Mr. Popolizio had his own baggage. In one case, an appellate court criticized him for implying to the jury that the defendant had a criminal past. The defendant, the court noted, "had no prior criminal record." In another case, he was reprimanded for denigrating a defendant whom he referred to as an "animal." And in a murder trial that resulted in a partial reversal, the appellate court wrote that Mr. Popolizio had improperly told the jury that the defendant had not been insane when he killed his girlfriend but rather that he had reacted violently to women, a tendency of Italian males. (Mr. Popolizio, himself, was an Italian American!) We focused on my opponent's temperament and integrity, noting that he had been chastised for prosecutorial misconduct by appellate courts more than any prosecutor in the DA's office.

Mr. Popolizio didn't deny that he had been admonished by the appellate courts. Instead, he explained that the misconduct cases occurred more than seven years ago and that he had changed since then and learned from his mistakes. He maintained that those instances of misconduct reflected his zeal in the courtroom not a lack of proper temperament. I wasn't buying it and I hoped that the voters wouldn't, either.

Election Day, Tuesday, June 7, 1988, the date of the presidential primary in California with Democratic candidates Michael Dukakis, Jesse Jackson, Al Gore, and Dick Gephardt battling it out, assured that voter turnout would be high. That morning, when I arrived at my designated polling place, a horde of newspaper and television reporters awaited me. I smiled, cast my vote, then drove to the courthouse and attempted, without much success, to focus on my work. Shortly after five that evening, I drove home. When the polls closed at 8 P.M., I turned on the TV and huddled with my partner, Florence, and my two daughters to watch the returns. About an hour later, I was declared the winner. It wasn't even close; I had won 61 percent of the vote with more than 170,000 votes and 109,500 for Mr. Popolizio. I had become the very first African American on the Santa Clara County Superior Court and the first African American woman to sit on a superior court in all of Northern California.

This race for an open seat on the superior court had been a contest between a judge who contended that her opponent did not have the proper temperament or experience to sit on the bench and a veteran prosecutor who contended that his opponent had a philosophy too closely linked to the liberal era of Rose Bird and Jerry Brown. (In a $10.7 million judicial campaign in 1986, California voters denied retention to its supreme court Chief Justice Rose Bird and two associate justices, Joseph Grodin and Cruz Reynoso. Funded by business interests who were upset with the court's proconsumer decisions, the three justices were attacked as liberal, anti–death penalty proponents, an issue of little concern to the business community but brilliantly exploited to outrage voters. All three justices had been appointed to the state's supreme court by Governor Jerry Brown.)

Since my detractors had been laser focused on the fact that I was a Jerry Brown appointee, their effort to tinge me with a wacko hue and suggest that I was soft on crime led me to spend an inordinate amount of time reassuring voters about who I wasn't. Mr. Popolizio likely believed that associating my name with those of Rose and Jerry would conjure for voters the vision of a cavalier jurist who, in a whimsical and capricious manner, created law in her own image.

This judicial race might have been a vehicle to help voters better understand the workings of the superior court and our roles within it. Instead, I spent unconscionably little time with voters exploring the ways in which our legal system might be more responsive to their needs. And while I am beholden to an electoral process that permitted me to ascend to the superior court, I was and continue to be committed to changing it.

Stories in the newspapers in the days immediately following the election trumpeted my victory: "Easy Victory for Judge Cordell," "Cordell

Wins Superior Court Race," "Cordell Wins Superior Court Post," "Experience on the Bench Tipped Scales for Cordell," and "Popolizio's Bird Call Backfires in Judge Race." I had emerged victorious and was ready to begin my work on the superior court. But the battle for my seat was far from over.

Just two weeks after my election, a story ran on the front page of one of the local newspapers:

> *Municipal Court Judge LaDoris Cordell, buoyed by her impressive show-ing in the June 7 election, has asked Governor George Deukmejian for an early appointment to Santa Clara County's Superior Court. Cordell, 38, was elected to fill the seat that is being vacated by Superior Court Judge James Wright, who is retiring on June 30. Unless an [early] appointment is made, the seat will be left open until January 1, 1989, when Cordell's term technically begins. . . . A spokesman for the governor said no action had been taken on the request as of Monday.*

After two Sacramento County municipal court judges had won election to vacant seats on their superior court the very same day that I had prevailed in mine, the governor swiftly granted their requests for early appointments. So I wondered what was going on. Why was the governor not similarly receptive to my request for an early appointment? His spokesperson didn't make it any clearer when he told a reporter: "The only light I can shed on that is that the two judges in Sacramento were very strongly supported by the law enforcement community and those are the kinds of endorsements the governor is looking for."

The truth was that I had received the unanimous endorsement of the Sunnyvale Public Safety Officers Association with its membership of 225 police and firefighters, the Latino Peace Officers and Black Peace Officer associations of Santa Clara County, along with forty individual endorsements from members of the Deputy Sheriff's Association of Santa Clara County. Anyway, what did law enforcement endorsements have to do with it? I had won the seat, end of story.

By July, the governor still hadn't responded to my request for an early appointment. Superior court judges on our bench were not pleased; they were down one judge, and the workload mounted. As concern among the judges on our superior court and within the county's legal community grew, Presiding Judge Peter Stone reached out to the governor's office by letter and by phone, seeking my appointment. He told a reporter: "Judge Cordell has been elected, and Judge Wright is gone. If he doesn't make the appointment, the only loser will be the public. I would hope to get quick action on this." After a rumor surfaced that the governor might require me to undergo the lengthy process of review by the Commission on Judicial Nominees Evaluation—a process reserved for candidates for judicial appointment to vacancies and not for someone who has won a seat on the bench—the Santa Clara County Bar Association, the county bar's Committee on Women Lawyers, and the California Association of Black Lawyers went public, demanding my appointment.

The governor's stalling continued for six weeks until, on July 18, he made it official:

Personal and Confidential

Dear Judge Cordell:

*   Governor Deukmejian has carefully considered all of the relevant factors bearing on your request for judicial appointment and has decided not to appoint you to the Santa Clara County Superior Court.*

Cordially,
Marvin R. Baxter
Appointments Secretary to the Governor
cc: Presiding Judge Peter Stone

"Relevant factors"? What did that mean? A few days later I learned what it meant. In response to a reporter's question about why he had turned down my request for an early appointment, moments before departing for a Far East trade mission, Governor Deukmejian answered, "Now there are some individuals I would not want to appoint because of my understanding of their philosophy, of their background and the like. I don't want them at some point in the future to say they were appointed by George Deukmejian."

And if there were any question that the governor had placed his political interests above the interests of the voters of Santa Clara County, his spokesperson made it clear when he stated, "The governor didn't want Cordell to be able to tout herself as a 'Deukmejian appointee' in future elections." When asked by the press for a comment, I thought for a moment and then responded, "At last, the governor and I have something in common. It would be a source of great embarrassment for both of us, if I were to be known as a Deukmejian appointee."

Meanwhile, Judge Stone was beside himself. "The situation here is absolutely critical. We have to have a replacement. We were expecting an immediate appointment and had always assumed we would not be down one judge. That means we have lost about twenty percent of our civil trial capabilities," he told a reporter. A raft of newspaper articles and op-eds followed: "Deukmejian Won't Elevate Judge Cordell," "No Early Seat for Judge Cordell," "Superior Court Needs Cordell Now, Judge Says," and my favorite, "Let the Judge Be Seated."

Since the governor refused to expedite my elevation to the superior court, Judge Stone tried a different tact. He asked the Judicial Council of California to temporarily assign me to the seat until January, when I could officially claim it as mine. The judicial council, established by the California Constitution, is the policy-making body of the courts and is headed by the chief justice of the California Supreme Court. At that time, the chief justice was Malcolm Lucas, a former law partner of Governor Deukmejian.

The judicial council's approach was a no-go; they refused to temporarily assign me but not without suggesting another approach—a "blanket assignment." Assuming that the presiding judges of the municipal court (where I still sat) and the superior court (where I should sit) agreed, I could sit via a blanket assignment on the superior court. However, the municipal court's presiding judge was not on board. "We are taking a look at our judicial needs," he said. "We really don't have the spare manpower. It is now a question of whether our court is in a position to do this and still meet our calendar needs." Who knew that I was such a valuable asset to the municipal court?

But then, a few hours later, the judicial council's spokesperson made a surprising announcement. "The Chief Justice has decided to issue an order assigning Judge Cordell to Superior Court, effective September 1, 1988. The assignment is not a blanket assignment. The Chief Justice is issuing it as a regular assignment. His staff said this was to put the issue to rest and for administrative convenience."

God bless Chief Justice Lucas! Common sense had prevailed. My temporary assignment to the superior court seat to which I had been elected began on September 1 and ended January 5, 1989, when, at my investiture, Judge Stone officially swore me in. We high-fived and then, with a big hug, he welcomed me to the superior court, where I would preside *unchallenged* for the next eleven years.

Bad Judges

Judicial Misconduct

*Take all the robes of all the good judges that have ever
lived on the face of the earth, and they would not be
large enough to cover the iniquity of one corrupt judge.*

—HENRY WARD BEECHER, ABOLITIONIST,
"WORKS MEET FOR REPENTANCE"

t was Friday, January 2, 1998, when *The San Jose Mercury News* ran an
article titled "Court Calendar Offers Irreverent View of Law." It read,
in part:

> *When Santa Clara County Superior Court Judge LaDoris H. Cord-
> ell gets bored on the bench, she doodles. But what she scribbles is any-
> thing but boring. It's clever, hilarious, often downright wicked. In her
> courtroom cartoons, Cordell skewers just about anything and anybody,
> including herself, and then titles her art with legal references. . . . Ten
> bucks will buy a copy of 'Court Dayz,' a collectible calendar of Cordell
> wit. . . . Proceeds from the sale of the calendars goes to Legal Advocates
> for Children and Youth (LACY), an organization that provides free
> legal and related social services to the youth of Santa Clara County.*

My "Court Dayz" calendar was a bestseller. Proceeds from the sales
raised more than $11,000, all of which I donated to Legal Advocates
for Children and Youth, a nonprofit organization. So popular was the
calendar that the original cartoons were on display for a year on a wall in

our court's jury assembly room. And, even better, I had been encouraged by jurors, lawyers, judges, and court personnel to produce another set of cartoons for a 1999 calendar.

The calendar had a gimmick: each cartoon depicted a common legal term. The challenge was to figure it out from clues in the drawings. For example, I drew a caricature of former Republican House Speaker Newt Gingrich standing in a courtroom and staring at a cross that he held in his hand to illustrate the legal term "cross-examination." In another cartoon I had drawn caricatures of Johnnie Cochran, Marcia Clark, and Judge Lance Ito, all of O. J. Simpson–trial fame, frolicking at a school playground to depict "take a recess." And in another cartoon, I drew pop singer Sonny Bono tap-dancing on a courtroom witness stand before an applauding and cheering audience. The legal term was "pro bono." All good fun.

I've been cartooning since I was a kid. I read comic books constantly. I loved to draw the cartoon characters and eventually began creating original cartoons—and not just on paper. The sidewalk in front of our family home in Ardmore, Pennsylvania, frequently served as a canvas on which I sketched colorful chalk images of flowers, rainbows, and neighborhood characters. In the early 1970s, when I was a Stanford law student, my cartoons appeared regularly in the school's student newspaper. I poked fun at law professors and lampooned a variety of hot-button topics, among them the law school's affirmative action and admission policies. Years later, before the 2008 national election, when our OBAMA FOR PRESIDENT lawn signs were repeatedly stolen or vandalized, I solved the problem by drawing a large chalk replica of the sign on our concrete driveway.

Two of my favorite cartoonists, Charles Bragg and the renowned Frenchman Honoré Daumier, brilliantly skewered their legal systems. Satirical cartoons provoke, make us laugh, and make us think. I was determined to make next year's calendar the best yet.

In late 1998, I completed a set of cartoons for the 1999 calendar that I again donated to LACY for its fundraising effort. The drawings depicted judges, lawyers, jurors, and me in humorous situations that illustrated more common legal terms. In the first three months of 1999, calendar sales generated more than $9,000 for LACY. I took down the previous year's drawings and hung my newest creations on the jury assembly room wall. But then, a few days later, they were gone. Someone had removed them.

Shortly thereafter, on June 10, 1999, I received a letter from the Commission on Judicial Performance (CJP) informing me that an anonymous complaint had been filed against me alleging that my cartoons "impugned the integrity, impartiality, diligence, sobriety and competency of the judges depicted, potentially eroding public confidence and respect."

State court judges and judges in the District of Columbia are subject to oversight and discipline by state agencies known by a variety of names—Judicial Inquiry Commission, Court on the Judiciary, Judicial Retirement and Removal Commission, and Commission (or Board) on Judicial Conduct.

These agencies investigate complaints against judges. When misconduct is found to have occurred, they have the authority to recommend and, in some instances, impose punishments ranging from the most severe—removal from the bench—to suspension with or without pay, public censure/reprimand, private admonishment (a reprimand that is confidential, communicated only to the judge, and published without using the judge's name), counseling, and advisory/warning letters for minor transgressions also deemed confidential and published without identifying the judges.

Judicial disciplinary agencies are fairly recent creations. Before them, bad judges presided with impunity unless their misconduct was so blatant that the electorate voted them out of office. In 1957, Ohio established a Board of Professional Conduct, the nation's first judicial oversight body. Next California, in 1960, created its Commission on Judicial Performance. By the 1980s, all state courts were regulated by independent judicial oversight agencies.

Members of these oversight agencies are chosen by a combination of state supreme court justices, governors, and state legislators. For example,

Alabama's nine-member Court of the Judiciary has four judges, two attorneys, and three public members. In California, the Commission on Judicial Performance is composed of three judges, two lawyers, and six members of the public.

Federal courts are different; they have no independent oversight body to investigate judicial misconduct. Federal judges police themselves. When there are misconduct complaints, the chief judge of the circuit or division in which the accused judge sits then conducts an investigation. (There are eleven circuits throughout the country.) The chief judge can dismiss the complaint or send it to a "special committee" on which the chief judge sits, along with a number of trial and appellate judges from that circuit. The special committee investigates and refers its written findings to a "judicial council," composed of the chief judge and other trial and appellate judges. If the judge has been found to have engaged in misconduct, the judicial council has the authority to impose discipline.

United States Supreme Court justices, however, are not subject to any oversight at all. Should a Supreme Court justice misbehave, impeachment is the only recourse. In the 230-year history of the U.S. Supreme Court, only one justice has ever been impeached. That happened when the House of Representatives, in 1804, impeached Associate Justice Samuel Chase, who was accused of letting his political bias influence his decision-making when he was a trial judge. (Back then, U.S. Supreme Court justices could simultaneously preside as federal trial court judges.) The following year, Justice Chase was tried by the Senate and acquitted.

One modern-day U.S. Supreme Court justice came close to being impeached. In 1969, Representative H. R. Gross of Iowa introduced a resolution to initiate formal impeachment proceedings against Supreme Court Associate Justice Abe Fortas. In the wake of accusations that Fortas had used his influence to seek a presidential pardon for a former client, he resigned before his impeachment hearing got under way.

The commission's complaint against me focused on four cartoons I had drawn for the 1999 calendar. In the April cartoon, I depicted several items of clothing—a man's business suit with a tag hanging from it

that read "corporate attorney" and papers labeled "billables" in the coat
pocket; a woman's business suit with the tag "family law attorney" and
papers labeled "motion for fees" in the jacket pocket; and a pair of over-
alls tagged "pro per" with papers in a pocket labeled "bankruptcy petition." There were a total of eight different suits of clothing, to illustrate
the legal term "lawsuits."

The May cartoon included three figures—a judge asleep at the bench
with a DO NOT DISTURB sign hanging below him, a small mouse pushing
a golf ball off a tee near a mousehole at the bottom of the bench, and
a jail inmate tiptoeing away with the witness box in his arms. The legal
term for this cartoon was "take the stand."

In the July cartoon I drew a robed judge with bloodshot eyes and a
silly smile on his face, holding up a fifth of scotch. Behind him on the
shelves in his chambers were a golf trophy and several books on judicial
ethics draped in cobwebs. Hanging on his chambers wall was a calendar
showing the month of July with the word "golf" written on each day of
the month, with July 31 marked with the word "retirement." The legal
term for this cartoon was "take the fifth."

And for October, I had drawn a judge sitting at his desk holding a
book with its title obscured by a rain cloud. I added fishing and golf
awards on the wall of his chambers, a golf hat and club on a coatrack,
and a stack of books on his desk, with the titles *Golf for Judges, Duh!
Judging Made Simple,* and *How to Become a Rent-A-Judge.* The legal term
for this cartoon was "cloud on the title," a common phrase in property
law that means there is problem with ownership of a piece of real estate,
such as a lien on the property.

Interestingly, the anonymous complainants had no problem with the
eight other cartoons in the calendar, one of which depicted the bottom
half of a robed judge dangling over the bench and wearing golf shoes to
illustrate the term "hanging judge." Another was a grinning U.S. Supreme
Court Associate Justice Clarence Thomas holding a large sign on which
were written five random sentences, each containing the word "death"
for which the legal term was "death sentences." And there was a cartoon

that had me sitting at the bench, waving my arms along with a bailiff and six random people all doing similarly weird things with their arms and hands. The legal term was, of course, "make a motion." I intended for my cartoons to be witty and funny. And given the enthusiastic response from judges, jurors, lawyers, and court staff to the 1998 calendar, I couldn't understand what the problem was with these cartoons. (I still don't.) In both, I had parodied judges and the legal system. Why the upset now? Then it hit me.

A few months earlier, in October 1998, our local newspaper ran an explosive front-page exposé, with the headline FRIDAY JUSTICE. The two-part series documented how a few of the judges on our court had been ducking out on Fridays to play golf. Color photos of the men riding golf carts and hanging out at the links adorned the multipage series. The story became the talk of Silicon Valley. So, of course, I had to include references to golf-playing judges in the cartoons for the 1999 calendar. Of course! The "anonymous" complainers were the golfers. I hit a nerve; the golfing judges hit back.

On June 29, 1999, I replied to the commission in a four-page letter, explaining that I had not targeted any particular judge on our court but instead had used as my model a generic, balding White male judge. I also stated that these were satirical drawings donated to a charitable organization. I even attached copies of a few of Charles Bragg's cartoons to show how judges and the courts have long been the subjects of parody and satire. I wasn't worried and figured that this would be the end of things. After all, judges are disciplined for serious matters and certainly not for cartooning.

In December, I received a letter from the commission labeled "Personal and Confidential." Inside was a two-page letter that began: "The Commission concluded that further proceedings are not warranted and determined to close the matter with this advisory letter." *Okay,* I thought with relief. *We're done here.* But wait! Advisory letters are a form of judicial discipline. I was being disciplined because I had drawn a few cartoons? Seriously?!

Judges are disciplined for all manner of misconduct. Case summaries, available in annual reports published on the websites of some oversight agencies, make for fascinating and frequently startling reading. Consider what these four judges did:

(1) Judge John Russo began his tenure on the New Jersey Superior Court in 2015. He was disciplined by the state's Advisory Committee on Judicial Conduct for his grossly inappropriate questioning of a sexual assault victim who, representing herself, sought a restraining order and for his equally inappropriate banter with court staff after the hearing:

Judge: Do you know how to stop somebody from having intercourse with you?

Plaintiff: Yes.

Judge: How would you do that?

Plaintiff: I'd probably physically harm them somehow.

Judge: Short of physically harming them?

Plaintiff: Tell them no.

Judge: Tell them no. What else?

Plaintiff: To stop.

Judge: To stop. What else?

Plaintiff: And to run away or try to get away.

Judge: Run away, get away. Anything else?

Plaintiff: I—that's all I know.

Judge: Block your body parts?

Plaintiff: Yeah.

Judge: Close your legs? Call the police? Did you do any of those things?

. . .

Plaintiff: I told him to stop.

Judge: Did you try to leave?

. . .

Plaintiff: He was like holding me like—there was like a chair and he was like holding me like, you know like he was like forceful, like I really couldn't do anything.

Judge: You answered my questions.

Judge Russo denied the woman's request for a restraining order and then had the following conversation with his court staff that was audio recorded by the court's own backup CourtSmart system:

Judge: What did you think of that? Did you hear the sex stuff?

. . .

Judge: What I lack in handwriting skills, I am the master of on the record being able to talk about sex acts with a straight face.

Court Staff: Without laughing?

Judge: Yup.

(2) Judge Marvin Wayne Wiggins, who, in 2015, had served on an Alabama circuit court (a trial court) for sixteen years, told the indigent defendants in his courtroom: "If you do not have any money [to pay your fines] and you don't want to go to jail, as an option to pay it, you can give blood today . . . or the sheriff has enough handcuffs for those who do not have money." Forty-one defendants, most of them African American and poor, lined up outside the courthouse that day to give their blood. Judge Wiggins justified his treatment of the indigent defendants, saying: "We're trying to find creative ways to help people pay their fees and expenses. Because of our area, we know that the people don't have the kind of income, the salaries to pay the fines and we have to collect them. So, as an option sometimes to paying the fine, you may allow them to do community services."

(3) In June 2019, Vegina Hawkins, a newly seated judge on Florida's Broward County circuit court, was caught on a courthouse surveillance camera in the hallway outside her chambers, putting her hands around the neck of a court employee and shaking him because he had failed to provide documents to her in a timely fashion.

(4) Finally, California judge Edmund Clarke Jr. joked about two prospective jurors' limited financial resources and revealed their personal financial information in open court. One juror had written on her hardship form that she had $25 in her checking account. The judge commented it was "an impressive and convincing figure" and remarked, "Well, every one of these lawyers spent more than that on lunch today." After the juror was excused and left the courtroom, the judge stated in open court: "She has twenty-five dollars in her checking account. I know you all eat for less than twenty-five dollars. Sometimes we don't. That's cutting it close." Another juror wrote on his hardship form that he had $33 in his checking account. Judge Clarke said to him: "[You have a] little bit more than the other gal. [Thirty-three] bucks" and "You are putting her in the shade with that big account." He also ordered another female juror who had complained to him that his clerk had been disrespectful to jurors: "Go to the hall and stay and come in, act like an adult, and you can face her and tell me everything she did wrong." The juror went into the hallway, where she was seen crying. After the next juror remarked, "Hate to follow that," Judge Clarke responded: "Trust me, it would be hard not to look good after that."

How were these errant judges disciplined? Judge Russo, who humiliated a female sexual assault victim and joked with his staff about her, received a three-month suspension without pay and was ordered by the Supreme Court of New Jersey to undergo training on proper courtroom demeanor. The Alabama Judicial Inquiry Commission publicly censured Judge Wiggins for requiring jail or blood donations from indigent defendants who were unable to pay their court fines. Judge Vegina

"Gina" Hawkins was suspended without pay in July 2019 for assaulting a court employee following a recommendation by the Florida Judicial Qualifications Commission. More than a year later, in April 2020, still on suspension and with her term set to expire at the end of the year, the judge filed for reelection to keep her seat. An attorney in private practice filed papers to run against her. On November 3, 2020, Judge Hawkins lost her reelection bid to her challenger. And Edmund Clarke, the California judge who demeaned and humiliated jurors in his courtroom, was publicly admonished by the state's Commission on Judicial Performance.

In my advisory letter, the Commission on Judicial Performance explained its reasons for disciplining me, writing:

> *In making this determination, the commission expressed disapproval of your submitting for publication in a 1999 charity calendar, drawings that appeared to denigrate participants in the justice system including judges, attorneys, court employees, and litigants* . . . [It's satire, people!] *The commission also disapproved of your displaying the 1999 illustrations in the court's jury assembly room. You apparently assumed that you were authorized to do so, since you had been permitted to hang those for the previous year's calendar, and, in your opinion, the 1999 and 1998 illustrations were similar.* [Yes. Exactly.] *Given the content of the 1999 drawings, however, it was the commission's view that displaying them in the court's jury assembly room had the potential to undermine juror respect for that court and for the judicial process* [By "content," you mean golf, right?]) . . . *The matter is now closed.*

Oh, no it wasn't closed. Not by a long shot.

With the assistance of a highly respected First Amendment attorney, I submitted a nine-page, single-spaced letter to the commission asking that my advisory letter be rescinded. I began by more fully addressing their criticism of the cartoons, writing:

[T]he April illustration is not an insult to attorneys but is simply a play on words which is evident from a fair-minded examination of the cartoon. . . . The commission's negative interpretation of the May illustration is strained. The cartoon depicts an individual taking the witness stand out of the courtroom while a judge is sleeping on the bench to illustrate the wordplay "take the stand." [T]he sleeping judge is simply a prop to make the thief's act of absconding with the stand more daring and humorous. . . . The illustration is obviously intended to be humorous rather than to bring disrepute upon the bench or other participants in the justice system. . . . The July illustration which depicts a judge in chambers holding a fifth of scotch and smiling broadly . . . is "take the fifth." In context, the illustration is obviously not a suggestion that all judges are drunk and derelict but merely another illustration to form a play on a common legal term . . . [T]here is nothing inherently demeaning or degrading in suggesting that a judge enjoys either golf or fishing.

Importantly, the gravamen of my letter focused upon the commission's attack on my First Amendment right of free expression. I wrote:

A judge does not relinquish his or her First Amendment rights on ascending to the bench. Although limitations may be placed on a judge's free speech rights, those limitations are subject to the same constitutional scrutiny applicable to speech limitations on public employees generally. My interest in supporting charitable work and expressing myself artistically outweighs any interest the state may have in protecting judges from misinterpretation of my drawings. The commission's judgment would necessarily chill my expression of protected speech.

I concluded by asking the commission to retract its decision that infringed on my First Amendment right of expression. In March 2000, I received a letter from the commission informing me: "The Commission respectfully declines to withdraw its Advisory Letter."

The commission's 2000 Annual Report on judicial discipline listed nineteen advisory letters. And sure enough, there I was, on page twenty-one, right after: "7. A judge engaged in a pattern of extensive use of court secretaries and other resources for purposes unrelated to court business, the law, the legal system or the administration of justice." I was number 8: "A judge engaged in off-bench activities that appeared to denigrate the judicial system and had the potential to undermine juror respect for the court and public confidence in the judicial system." I noticed, with amusement, that advisory letter number nineteen had gone to a judge who "appeared to be sleeping during court proceedings," the very conduct that I had lampooned in one of my cartoons.

Judges whose behavior in the courtroom is obviously egregious are easy to spot. Overtly bad judges get lots of attention. In 1997, Joseph Troisi, a forty-seven-year-old trial judge in West Virginia, made the front page of the newspapers after he denied defendant William Witten's request to lower his $40,000 bail bond. As he was being led from the courtroom, Mr. Witten repeatedly and loudly cursed at the judge, whereupon Judge Troisi ripped off his robe, leapt from the bench, and proceeded to bite the twenty-nine-year-old Mr. Witten with sufficient force to remove a chunk of the man's nose. Thereafter, Judge Troisi promptly and wisely resigned from the bench, pled "no contest" to a charge of battery, and served five days in jail. He later explained that he was caught up in "waves of feeling" and not thinking when he bit the nose that jailed him.

And there were the two Pennsylvania judges who traded kids for cash. Over a period of five years (2003–2008), Judges Mark Ciavarella and Michael Conahan, Pennsylvania state court judges, took payoffs to lock up juvenile offenders in private detention centers. After Judge Conahan ordered the shutdown of the state-run juvenile detention facility, the two judges sent more than five thousand youthful offenders to serve time in these private for-profit centers for committing acts like making a joke about a vice principal on the internet and taking change from an unlocked car. The more children they ordered sent away, the more money flowed into the judges' pockets—to the tune of more than $2.6

million. Following a federal investigation, the judges, having pled guilty to fraud, racketeering, and tax evasion, were disbarred; each was sentenced to more than seven years in prison.

But what about judges who subconsciously hold racial, sexual, LGBTQ, or antireligious prejudices? What is to be done about judges of goodwill who make decisions that reflect biases they don't even realize they have? Doesn't that constitute judicial misconduct? Implicit biases are stereotypical attitudes so subtle that we don't even know that we harbor them. A 2009 study, the first to explore implicit racial bias of state trial court judges, determined that judges possess implicit racial biases that influence their decision-making.

For example, when a person is arrested, a judge has the discretion to order her to post bail or to release her outright. The purpose of requiring an arrestee (or her surrogate) to cough up bail money is an attempt to ensure that she will make all of her court appearances. If she posts bail and then fails to show up, she loses it all; if she returns to court as required, she gets the money back (after the bail bond company takes its share, of course). Courts typically publish schedules with guidelines suggesting bail amounts for a variety of crimes. For example, a schedule might recommend setting bail between $1,500 and $5,000 for the crime of burglary. The amount is left to the discretion of the judge. And how has that worked out? Not well.

As far back as 1994, a bail-setting study revealed that when Connecticut judges used their discretion, the bail for Blacks was 25 percent higher than for Whites accused of committing similar crimes. Similarly, a 1995 review of bail-setting decisions of New York trial court judges revealed that in some parts of the state, African Americans were 33 percent more likely to be held in custody awaiting felony trial than were Whites facing felony trials. And lest you think that the racial bias in bail/release decisions is exclusively the province of White judges, think again. One of the conclusions of a 2018 study conducted in courts in Miami and Philadelphia was that both Black and White judges demonstrated bias against Black defendants in their bail decisions.

Implicit bias is at play when it comes to sentencing and with similar consequences. Judges size up defendants whom they hardly know, consider the mitigating and aggravating factors, listen to the arguments of counsel, and then impose sentences that they deem to be fair. Yet, studies examining sentencing decisions consistently reveal that racial bias looms large. In 2014, an American Civil Liberties Union study concluded: "Sentences imposed on Black males in the federal system are nearly 20 percent longer than those imposed on white males convicted of similar crimes. Black and Latino offenders sentenced in state and federal courts face significantly greater odds of incarceration than similarly situated white offenders and receive longer sentences than their white counterparts in some jurisdictions." According to a 2017 report by the U.S. Sentencing Commission, "Judges are less likely to voluntarily revise sentences downward for black offenders than for white ones . . . And even when judges *do* reduce black offenders' sentences, they do so by smaller amounts than for white offenders."

What about the role of gender in judicial decision-making? In 2018, researchers enlisted the participation of more than five hundred judges from an unnamed state court to analyze two hypothetical scenarios—a child custody case and a sex discrimination lawsuit. They concluded:

> *[M]any judges are not able to factor out their personal beliefs while they are considering court cases, even when they have the best possible intentions. In both of these cases, support for traditional gender roles was associated with decisions that encouraged women to engage in more family caregiving at the expense of their careers and discouraged men from participating in family caregiving at all . . . The significant expertise that judges possess doesn't inoculate them against decision-making biases, and we can't expect much change until we see policy reforms that address decision-making procedures in the courtroom.*

It is my experience that most judges are well-meaning people who take their oaths to uphold the law seriously. They do their best to be fair. But the fact is their best isn't good enough; the numbers don't lie. Racial and gender disparities exist, and judges are a big part of the problem. We should be concerned when female litigants, fighting for custody of their children, go before judges who, while polite and respectful, are wedded to the notion that a woman's place is in the home. We should worry that Black defendants seeking pretrial releases are facing judges whose bail/release decisions are influenced by racial stereotypes.

What is to be done with the judge who is clueless or, worse, denies his biases? Take the case of Timothy Stafford, a California superior court judge who presided over a hearing where a woman sought a civil restraining order against a male coworker. At one point, the woman testified that she had sent a text message *to her own husband* in which she offered to provide him sexual favors in exchange for a new car. Judge Stafford responded, saying, "And she knew it, and she liked it, because she got things. And don't—counsel, you're giving me a frown. Look [at] it. If I got a letter from someone, or a phone call saying, 'I'll give you a blow job every day for the rest of your life for a car,' we will be at the Mercedes dealer pretty soon, but not because I'm married, all right." And when the woman's lawyer interjected that the particular text message to which the judge had alluded had been directed to her own husband, Judge Stafford responded, "It came out of your client's mouth, out of her brain onto a piece of paper, didn't it?"

The Commission on Judicial Performance issued a public admonishment to Judge Stafford. For the commission, that was the end of the affair. But should it have been? If Judge Stafford did not appreciate that his comments were sexist and insulting when he uttered them, what about other women who may have come before him? How had he treated them? His conduct in this case should have alerted the commission to review the judge's decision-making history to determine if there existed a pattern of belittling female litigants or of denying restraining orders to women. Even where a judge retires mid-investigation, as was the case with Judge Stafford, past miscarriages of justice mustn't be ignored.

Disciplinary investigations into complaints of bias must be handled differently than investigations into other allegations of judicial misconduct.

Intemperate courtroom conduct, improper communication with only one of the parties in a case, or delay in performing judicial duties requires inquiries into the specific incidents that gave rise to the complaints. Investigations into claims of bias demand far more. Biased behavior isn't a onetime occurrence; it's not biased today, unbiased tomorrow. Quite the contrary, without proper intervention, it's biased today, biased forever.

One conclusion of the 2009 study that looked at implicit racial bias of trial judges was that judges who are "internally driven or otherwise motivated to suppress their own biases" are able to make judgments "free from bias, even implicit ones." In other words, when judges are made aware of their biases, they can work to limit the influence of those biases in their decision-making. There's hope.

The matter of Judge Stafford came to light only because someone filed a complaint against him. What about judges who fly under the radar screen, who are not the subjects of bias complaints? We know from the studies that judges, as do all people, harbor implicit biases. And common sense tells us that there are likely many disgruntled litigants who are too cowed by the legal system to register complaints. So, how do we protect ourselves from an implicitly biased judiciary?

One way is to mandate that all judges—state and federal, trial and appellate—undergo periodic audits of their discretionary rulings. Such an audit could include an examination of a judge's pretrial release/bail-setting orders, his restraining order decisions in domestic violence and harassment/stalking cases, and his sentencing orders involving defendants of color and White defendants. And all judges, no matter their color, ethnicity, or gender, should be required to take implicit bias training. Some state courts have implemented courses on this subject. For the rest, it is time to board the antibias train. Justice demands no less.

J'Accuse!

Judges Under Attack

It is a lie! And it is all the more odious and cynical
that they lie with impunity without one being
able to convince others of it.

—ÉMILE ZOLA, JANUARY 13, 1898,
LETTER TO THE PRESIDENT OF
THE FRENCH REPUBLIC IN DEFENSE
OF ALFRED DREYFUS

There is frequently no warning or signal that a judge's decision is destined to blow up in her face. It could be her umpteenth sentencing decision in her umpteenth criminal case, but for whatever reason, one decision takes on a life of its own—with disastrous consequences. That's what happened to Santa Clara County Superior Court judge Aaron Persky.

In 2016, Judge Persky presided over the trial of a nineteen-year-old Stanford swimmer, a White male, charged with three counts of felony sexual assault (digital penetration) on the Stanford campus, stemming from one incident. The victim was a biracial (Asian American/Caucasian) twenty-two-year-old woman. The two met at a fraternity party where they became highly intoxicated. After the student was convicted by the jury, Judge Persky followed the probation department's recommendation and ordered the now-expelled student to serve a six-month jail sentence.

Then all hell broke loose. Judge Persky became the target of a recall campaign initiated by a female Stanford law professor, outraged that the judge had not imposed a harsher period of incarceration. Before the recall campaign was over, the name "Persky" would become infamous throughout the country and beyond.

In June 2016, when he imposed the six-month sentence, Aaron Persky, White male spouse of an Asian American woman and the father of two biracial young sons, was in his midfifties and had served without controversy on the Santa Clara County Superior Court for thirteen years. Well respected in the legal community, he was a Stanford graduate who earned his law degree from the University of California–Berkeley School of Law. Before joining the bench, Persky had, for seven years, been a county prosecutor with a caseload that included the prosecution of sex crimes.

The recall campaign insisted that the six-month jail sentence was "out of line." It wasn't. Judges almost always follow the sentencing recommendations of probation officers who evaluate the circumstances of the crimes, the background of the defendants, and the concerns of the victims. What was "out of line" was the recall campaign's demand that the young man serve two years in prison. The incarceration imposed by Judge Persky and recommended by the probation department more than fit the crimes of which this young man was convicted. No reasonable judge who considered the mitigating and aggravating circumstances of the crime would have sentenced him to state prison. I certainly would not have done so. And no reasonable probation officer would have recommended a prison sentence. The female probation officer assigned to the case did not do so, either.

The young man had no prior criminal history, was highly intoxicated when he interacted with the even more highly intoxicated victim, did not plan or lie in wait for her, and expressed remorse for his actions. Additionally, his expulsion from Stanford University ended a probable Olympic swimming career. Most saliently, Judge Persky branded him with a scarlet letter by ordering him to register as sex offender for the rest of his life—a punishment that was entirely ignored by the recall campaign.

Sex offender registration is the most punitive of punishments because it forever restricts where the registrant can live, work, and attend school. Moreover, failure of a sex offender to annually register with a local law enforcement agency can result in a felony conviction and is punishable by up to three years in state prison. Convicted murderers fare far better; they have no such restrictions. Once their debts to society are paid, felons convicted of taking the lives of others are free to return to the community, secure employment, and live anonymously among us. For murderers, there is the hope of redemption; for defendants like the ex–Stanford student sentenced by Judge Persky, there is no such hope.

The recall campaign also attacked Judge Persky for his alleged track record of imposing lenient sentences on male defendants convicted of sex offenses, citing five instances to support their claims. Once again, his sentencing decisions in those cases had been deliberately misconstrued and distorted. In fact, he had no such track record.

The California Constitution, Article 2, Section 13, provides: "Recall is the power of electors to remove elective officers." Nineteen states and the District of Columbia permit recalls of elective officers. Ten of the nineteen states include judges in the category of elective officers. Seven of those ten states do not require any legal grounds to recall judges. All that is needed is to collect the required number of signatures of registered voters to place the recall on the ballot. The signature numbers vary from state to state and county to county. Simply put, disagree with a judge's ruling in any of those seven states and you can target her for a recall, even when her ruling is entirely lawful.

Georgia, Minnesota, and Montana require that recall petitions state specific grounds, such as malfeasance, misconduct, failure to perform duties of the office, or conviction of a serious crime while in office. More importantly, Georgia and Montana specifically exclude a judge's discretionary performance of a lawful act or mandatory duty as the basis for a recall. In those two states, when judges make rulings that are mandated by law (such as when a judge is required to impose a life sentence) or when they make decisions in which they are permitted to use their discretion (such as when a judge can choose to impose a jail sentence or a prison sentence), recalls are not permitted, no matter how unpopular the decisions. When judges follow the law, they cannot be the subjects of recalls. If the Montana and Georgia recall standards had been in effect in California when Judge Persky lawfully exercised his discretion, there would have been no basis for a recall, and he would still be on the bench. Judges engaged in the discretionary performance of lawful acts must be protected from the slings and arrows of the mob. It is my hope that ultimately all states will follow the lead of Georgia and Montana by amending their constitutions to include this limitation on judicial recalls.

Recalls of judges are unique to the states. Federal judges, be they trial court judges or appellate judges all the way up to the U.S. Supreme Court, cannot be recalled, no matter how controversial their decisions.

The inclusion of judges in recall elections is a controversial one. As far back as 1911, President William H. Taft vetoed a resolution authorizing statehood for Arizona because he objected to that state's constitutional provision allowing the recall of judges. He labeled the recall of judges "pernicious and destructive," adding that it is "a mistake to suppose such a powerful lever for influencing judicial decisions and such an opportunity for vengeance because of adverse ones will be allowed to remain unused." In 1912, Arizona's constitutional convention backed off and Taft signed the resolution making Arizona our forty-eighth state. (That same year, a reconvened Arizona constitutional convention reinstated the recall of judges in its constitution; no Arizona judge has ever been the subject of a recall—yet.) In California, recalls of judges are rare. Since 1911, when recalls were adopted by the state, there have been twenty-seven attempts to recall individual supreme court justices and one attempt to recall all seven of the justices in 1966. Because recall supporters failed to gather the required number of signatures to qualify these recalls for the ballot, none have succeeded. The last successful judicial recall in California before the recall of Judge Persky was in 1932, and what a recall it was.

Organized by the Los Angeles County Bar Association, three Los Angeles County Superior Court judges were recalled by the county's voters. Judges John L. Fleming, Dailey Stafford, and Walter Guerin were targeted for appointing receivers as political patronage. (Receivers, frequently individuals with backgrounds in finance, are appointed by judges to temporarily operate businesses whose assets are in danger of being wasted in the aftermath of lawsuits filed by shareholders or employees.) The judges were accused in a forty-seven-page report of engaging in a "pay to play" scheme and conducting themselves "in a manner contrary to judicial ethics and prejudicial to the proper administration of justice." The *Metropolitan News-Enterprise* put it this way: "Men they named as receivers did not necessarily have qualifications for the job. . . . Judges allowed receivers excessive fees and accepted from them petty gifts and loans. Receivers were solicited to deposit funds in a bank in which one judge was interested. Receivers spent lavishly among court attaches and newspapermen. The report found 23 American Mortgage receiverships handled by the same pair of co-receivers." (Back then, there was no governmental entity to investigate complaints of judicial misconduct or to discipline errant jurists. California's Commission on Judicial Performance wasn't established until 1961.) All three judges were sent packing by the voters. Fleming returned to his law practice only to be suspended some twenty years later for persuading an elderly female client to sign over her entire estate to him. Guerin resumed practicing law. And Stafford, in 1934, unsuccessfully ran against a sitting judge who was up for reelection. The blatant acts of malfeasance of the three judges rightfully disqualified them from serving on the bench. They were corrupt—plain and simple.

The case against Judge Persky was neither plain nor simple. Unlike Judges Fleming, Guerin, and Stafford, he had committed no acts of malfeasance that would disqualify him from serving on the bench. So, how did Judge Persky respond to the malicious attacks on his entirely lawful sentencing decisions? How did he answer the false claims that he had a track record of bias? What did the judge have to say about all of this? Nothing, absolutely nothing. He was prohibited from defending himself by the *California Code of Judicial Ethics.*

In 1972, the American Bar Association (ABA), the nation's largest organization of lawyers and judges, adopted the Model Code of Judicial

Conduct, which consists of six canons or principles that regulate what judges can and can't do—on and off the bench. The canons are accompanied by detailed rules and comments that explain them. Today, every state court, as well as the federal judiciary, utilizes its own code of conduct or code of ethics, based on the ABA's Model Code of Judicial Conduct. There is one exception, and it's a big one—the United States Supreme Court. The code of conduct that governs federal judges does *not* apply to our nation's highest court. In March 2019, when asked why the Supreme Court should not be governed by a code of conduct, Associate Justice Samuel Alito told a House appropriations committee that applying such a code to the Supreme Court would be "inconsistent" with the Constitution. At that hearing, Associate Justice Elena Kagan agreed, adding that while the justices conduct themselves properly, Chief Justice John Roberts was studying whether the Supreme Court should create its own conduct code. His studying aside, a proposal is pending in Congress that would apply the federal courts' judicial code of conduct to the high court.

Trial judges make thousands of decisions that usually leave, in their wake, winners and losers. Within the ranks of losers are those who go on the attack against judges whom they believe, right or wrong, ruined their lives. They assert to all, on social media and beyond, that judges are racists, or sexists, otherwise biased, or just plain stupid. Some distribute flyers from courthouse steps proclaiming that judges are incompetent; others picket courthouses with signs denouncing judges as being the spawn of Satan. So, what do these codes of conduct and codes of ethics tell those judges who want to defend their decision-making?

The general rule, adopted by all state and federal courts, is that judges cannot publicly comment about pending cases. Typical is California's Canon 3B (9) that strictly prohibits public comment by judges:

> *A judge shall not make any public comment about a pending or impending proceeding in* any court *and shall not make any nonpublic comment that might substantially interfere with a fair trial or hearing.* [*Emphasis added.*]

If a judge cannot publicly comment while her case is pending, when is it no longer pending? It depends. If an appeal has been filed after a judge has ruled, the case is pending until the appellate courts have finally ruled, which could be weeks, months, and sometimes years down the road. In a criminal case, even when there is no appeal, it is still pending as long as the defendant is on probation; a probation violation would land him in court to again face the judge who sentenced him. Because of California's Canon 3B (9) prohibition on public comment, Judge Persky was muzzled; he was unable to explain to the public the underpinnings of his decisions in each of the cases singled out by the recall campaign because they were all "pending" cases. If he were to speak out, he would be in violation of the canon—for which he would almost certainly be disciplined, with removal from the bench a possibility.

When an accused person remains silent in the face of accusations, suspicions abound, especially, as in this case, when the recall campaign portrays the judge's silence as evidence that the allegations against him must be true—if he doesn't have anything to hide, he would defend himself. Unaware that judges are prohibited from making public comments about their cases, Santa Clara County voters were understandably distrustful of Judge Persky. What kind of man is this who has to rely on surrogates to speak for him? I was the most vocal of the judge's surrogates. When I explained that the *California Code of Judicial Ethics* did not permit Judge Persky to rebut the recall campaign's false allegations, and when I spoke of the importance of respect for the independence of the judiciary, my words fell on deaf ears. At public debates, when I described in detail the facts of each of the cases so distorted by the recallers, and after I recited the rules that Judge Persky had lawfully applied in each case, I received a chilly response. And when I spoke about the sanctity of judicial independence and why the recall threatened that independence, the reception was even chillier. The repeated derision of the very idea of an independent judiciary by the recall campaign's spokespersons, two Stanford law professors, didn't help.

It is one thing to recall a judge for an act of malfeasance; but it is quite another thing to recall a judge for making a *lawful* decision that we don't like. Think about it. Judges take an oath to defend and to bear true faith and allegiance to the Constitution. But today, a judge can lose her job if, in defending the Constitution and bearing true faith and allegiance to it, she renders a decision that happens to be controversial. Putting the judicial finger to the wind to gauge public opinion is fast becoming the standard for judicial decision-making. And when that happens, when the cacophony of the mob determines how judges decide their cases, our *independent* judiciary becomes our *dependent* judiciary.

The importance of an independent judiciary cannot be overstated. This democratic principle was recognized as far back as 1776 in the Declaration of Independence, when the Continental Congress penned its twenty-seven grievances against King George III, one of which was: "He has made Judges dependent on his Will alone, for the Tenure of their Offices, and Amount and Payment of their Salaries." More than 240 years later, legal scholars Bruce Fein and Burt Neuborne eloquently proclaimed the sanctity of an independent judiciary:

> *Judicial independence in the United States strengthens ordered liberty, domestic tranquility, the rule of law, and democratic ideals. At least in our political culture, it has proved superior to any alternative form of discharging the judicial function that has ever been tried or conceived. It would be folly to squander this priceless constitutional gift to placate the clamors of benighted political partisans.*

Sadly, today the principle of judicial independence is ignored, misunderstood, or not understood at all by many Americans. For some, it is code for judges circling the wagons. For others, it means that judges are not being held accountable. Neither is true. State court trial judges *are* held accountable to the public in a number of ways. Their decisions are reviewable by the appellate courts, and if a judge's error deprived a litigant of her constitutional right to a fair trial, the error will be remedied. There are state disciplinary bodies with the authority to investigate complaints when judges are accused of misconduct and, when appropriate, to impose discipline as severe as removal from the bench. When their terms are up and if they choose to stand for reelection, judges can be challenged by individuals who believe they can better serve on the bench. That was not, alas, how things proceeded in *l'af-faire* Persky.

On Tuesday, June 5, 2018, after a grueling campaign in which almost $2 million was expended, the lion's share by the recall side, Judge Persky lost his seat on the bench, along with his pension. The turnout had been low; only 25 percent of the county's electorate bothered to vote on the recall. Of that 25 percent turnout, 60 percent cast their votes in favor of the recall; Judge Persky had been recalled by a mere *15 percent* of the county's electorate. The unfortunate message of the recall? Judges would be well served to make decisions that please the majority of voters, no matter how small that majority, or be prepared to fight for their judicial lives.

The U.S. Constitution guarantees to individuals accused of criminal conduct the right to defend themselves, no matter how heinous their crimes. It is no small irony that an accused murderer can speak out in his defense, but the judge who presides over that case cannot. It is time for the states to revise their judicial codes of conduct and ethics to give to judges the right of self-defense. Fortunately, but too late for Judge Persky (and because of him), the California judiciary has done just that. In July 2020, the *California Code of Judicial Ethics* was revised, allowing judges targeted for a recall or facing a contested election to respond directly to false and biased information concerning an unpopular decision. It also permits other sitting judges to respond to unfair criticism of a colleague. The perils of judging are not limited to recalls; there are also lawyers and litigants who take pleasure in filing contrived and meritless complaints when judges rule against them.

Case in point: In early December 1991, I received an envelope in the mail with the return address "Commission on Judicial Performance." I knew that this couldn't be good news. It wasn't. Inside was a letter from the commission informing me that an anonymous person had filed a complaint alleging that I engaged in misconduct in not one, not two, but three cases in the family court. The commission wrote that I had twenty days to provide a written response.

I read the complaint, and even though the commission had redacted the complainant's name and address at the request of the complainant, I knew who it was—a middle-aged, White male attorney with a reputation for contentiousness and for dragging out cases in order to rack up attorney fees. His identity was obvious because he was the one person common to all three cases and, not coincidentally, on the losing side in all three.

In the family court, one of my goals was to curtail acrimonious family conflicts and, as importantly, to rein in the amount of attorney fees that litigants would have to pay. I tried to settle cases as early as possible in the court process, which is why this lawyer and I frequently bumped heads—the briefer the proceedings, the lower the attorney fees.

And what terrible things had I done? In each case, he accused me of directing a female client to pay court fees without first giving each the opportunity to be heard. According to him, I was a rogue judge who issued orders against his clients and who barred them from contesting my rulings. None of this was true. I spent more than eight hours writing a nine-page response to which I attached copies of the actual court documents that clearly disproved his claims. In early February 1992, a second letter from the Commission on Judicial Performance exonerated me of any wrongdoing. Three years later, I was, again, the subject of a complaint, this time with potentially devastating consequences.

In 1995, a litigant falsely accused me of egregious misconduct. I was stunned. The case found its beginning after Gwen Wilson, an African American mother of three adult children, suffered a stroke in 1984. Over the years, her condition had deteriorated until eventually she displayed symptoms of dementia. Thereafter, her children began fighting among themselves, in and out of court, for control of their mother's personal and real property. The tipping point came in December 1993, when Gwen signed a quitclaim deed that transferred ownership of her residence to Julia, one of her daughters.

There are two types of deeds that are the most commonly used for the sale or exchange of real property (land and buildings). A quitclaim deed is typically used for a nonsale transfer of real property, such as when a residence is transferred from one family member to another. The deed does not carry with it any assurance that the person transferring the property is the legal owner, which means that the new owner assumes the risk. A warranty deed is for the sale of real property. With this deed, the owner "warrants," or guarantees, that she is the actual owner and that no one else has any claim to the property. So, while a quitclaim deed is a quick way to transfer property, it's not as reliable as a warranty deed.

With her quitclaim deed in hand, Julia then refinanced her mother's home, obtaining sufficient cash to pay for repairs to the home, purchase a Mercedes-Benz for herself, and, in her words, "repair my credit status." Unsurprisingly, another of Gwen's daughters retained a lawyer to void the transfer of their mother's home to Julia. It was in December 1994, when I was the supervising judge of the probate court, that the case landed in my courtroom.

At the hearing to void the transfer, Julia testified that she loved her mother and that it was her mother's desire that Julia have the home. However, a physician testified that he had examined Gwen and concluded that due to her deteriorating mental state, she did not have the capacity to execute the quitclaim deed. It became clear to me that Julia had improperly secured her mother's signature on the quitclaim deed. In legal parlance, she had used "undue influence" over her mother. After listening to all of the witnesses, I voided the quitclaim deed and directed everyone to return to court in a few weeks for a settlement conference to see if we could bring an end to the family's discord.

The next month, in January 1995, I met with the family members and their attorneys in my chambers. After much back-and-forth, I hammered out an agreement that included a schedule for Julia to repay to her mother's estate the money that she had improperly obtained. We then went back into the courtroom where, as my court reporter transcribed every word, I recited the terms of the settlement. And to be extra cautious, I asked every one of the family members to state, on the record, if each understood the settlement and if each agreed to abide by its terms. Everyone, including Julia, answered yes to both questions. Done.

Three weeks later, Julia was back, having filed a motion to vacate the settlement, writing:

> *I was under duress and stress while I was in the discussion with the Court in chambers. I was extremely nervous and afraid. I was mentally unable to even participate in discussion of settling the matter without the advice of counsel. I was unable to concentrate or focus on what was really being discussed. I had been under the care of a psychiatrist starting treatment for stress and depression on or about September 1, 1994. . . . I do not possess the knowledge or understanding to be able to reach a settlement in this matter without the assistance of an attorney.*

She included a declaration from a licensed clinical social worker who attested to Julia's depression. As expected, Gwen's children and Gwen's court-appointed attorney, a lawyer with the Office of the Public Guardian, all opposed Julia's request. I agreed with them and denied her motion; there was no merit to her claim. Julia had willingly participated in the settlement conference and stated, on the record in open court, that she agreed with the settlement. Done.

In mid-May 1995, Julia returned. This time, she filed a Statement of Disqualification for Cause of Judge LaDoris H. Cordell. It left me dumbfounded. In this document, Julia claimed that I should be disqualified because I was biased against her:

> *Approximately three weeks after the hearing on January 7, 1994, Judge Cordell started making sexual advances towards me. Said advances took place at the Lucky Store where I am employed. They occurred during the months of January, March, May and June 1994. On occasions she flirted with me. She openly stared at my breats [sic]. On one*

occasion while staring at my breats [sic] she said "Nice," and licked her lips in a sexually suggestive manner; she also reached out and felt my breasts in one occasion, stating "I like that." I rejected her advances, and she has since then become biased, prejudiced and hostile against me. Judge Cordell's subsequent decision in matters related to my mother's conservatorship reflect her bias, prejudice, and hostility.

What?! Things only got worse when, a few days later, I received a phone call from a reporter with the local newspaper. He wanted to interview me about Julia's allegations; she had given him a copy of the disqualification statement. Benita, my bailiff, and Olga, my courtroom clerk, were upset and concerned about me. *I* was upset and concerned about me. I did my best not to show my distress at work and presided over my cases as if everything were fine.

At home, it was another story; I was a mess. My younger daughter was a teenager and aware of what was going on; her older sister was away at college and out of the fray. Thankfully, Florence, my partner of many years, came to the rescue, assured me that we would survive this, and encouraged me to stay focused on what I needed to do.

California Code of Civil Procedure permits a litigant to request that a judge be disqualified from presiding over a case "for cause." It states that if "a person aware of the facts might reasonably entertain a doubt that the judge would be able to be impartial," then the judge can be disqualified. The law requires that the person seeking to remove the judge must provide specific facts, in writing, and must do so "at the earliest practicable opportunity after discovery of the facts constituting the ground for disqualification." After the person files the disqualification papers, the judge can opt to disqualify herself, after which the case is assigned to another judge. But if the judge refuses to disqualify herself, she has ten days to file "a written verified answer admitting or denying any or all of the allegations contained in the party's statement and setting forth any additional facts material or relevant to the question of disqualification." After that, the decision about whether or not to grant the disqualification request is assigned to another judge. The clock was ticking. I had ten days to file my answer.

Five days after I received the disqualification papers, I responded:

We judges are always vulnerable to the slings and arrows of dissatisfied litigants. In every case over which we preside, there are at least two opposing parties, at least one or more of whom will likely feel that his or her interests have been poorly served. Fortunately, the vast majority of disgruntled litigants are constrained from acts of vengeance by a deep and abiding sense of decency. Under the dictates of civilized discourse, which implicitly provide the essential underpinnings of our legal system, there are limits beyond which even the most outraged litigant fears to tread. Julia W., in her Statement of Disqualification, has so exceeded these limits that it is only by dint of extreme self-discipline that I fashion a response to her libelous accusations in a manner that comports with civility. I, therefore, engage in the distasteful task of denying every one of these disgusting accusations, point by point.

I labeled Julia a liar, and I explained the suspicious timing of her disqualification request. According to Julia, I preyed upon her between January 1994 and June 1994. But it was not until May 1995 that she decided to make these accusations. During the entire time that I had presided over the case, some eighteen months, she never once voiced a complaint about me. It was only after I refused her request to set aside the settlement that she complained. Along with my answer, I included a copy of the transcript of Julia's testimony about how she had taken her mother's property and a copy of the transcript of the settlement hearing. I concluded, "This disqualification represents the last gasp of a profoundly vengeful, diabolical, perverse, and deceitful woman."

Since the judges on my court all knew me, it would have been a conflict of interest for any of them to preside over a disqualification hearing. Thomas Black, a superior court judge in Santa Cruz County, about thirty-five miles south of San Jose, was designated to hear it. I didn't know Judge Black and only hoped that after he reviewed all of the pleadings, he would rule in my favor. I felt helpless and vulnerable; my career and my reputation were now in the hands of a stranger in a black robe.

The following month, in June 1995, Judge Black mailed his decision to all of us:

> *I have reviewed the Statement filed by Ms. W., the Verified Answer to Disqualification Statement filed by Judge Cordell and various other pleadings and documents. The allegations presented in these pleadings and documents do not provide a sufficient basis for recusal. The motion is denied.*

Done. Judge Black had ruled in my favor. Julia's disqualification motion was history. But there was still the newspaper reporter who continued to hound me about Julia's lurid allegations. Even though the disqualification request had been dismissed, Julia could still appeal the decision, which meant that matter was still "pending." Under Canon 3B (9), I was prohibited from making any public comment to the reporter or anyone else other than to simply deny the accusations. I knew that if he ran the story, all that anyone would ever remember about my tenure on the bench would be those salacious allegations.

Things came to a head when the reporter, a man in his early thirties, called and told me that the story would go to print that evening. When I asked him if he believed Julia's claims, he said he did not but thought that the allegations would make a good story. My repeated pleas that he not run the story went nowhere. When I got home, desperate and at my wits' end, I called the paper's publisher. While I had never met him, I had heard that he was a serious and thoughtful person. When we spoke, I told him everything—about the court case, the timing of Julia's allegations, the demise of her disqualification attempt, and his reporter's revelation that he didn't believe Julia's claims. He listened, and when I finished he said that he would think about it. I hung up the phone and sat alone in my bedroom, the door closed, watching the clock as the publishing deadline neared. Just minutes before 8:00 P.M., the print deadline, the phone rang. It was the publisher; he told me that the story would not run. I thanked him, hung up, and cried. Done.

Julia kept coming. She filed twice in a California court of appeal; both filings were dismissed. Then she filed a motion in *my* court asking me to reconsider the settlement; I reconsidered and denied her motion. Next, she filed a lawsuit against me in the federal court. (All of her previous filings had been in the state court.) In her federal complaint, she named me and the entire superior court as plaintiffs. The pressure of all of this litigation was wearing me down, just what Julia likely wanted. I was working full-time and still presiding over cases as if nothing were wrong. But inside, I was completely stressed, not knowing what Julia would throw at me next. Finally, I decided to lawyer up.

Santa Clara County's Office of the County Counsel is composed of lawyers who represent a variety of county departments and their staff; they also represent the county's judges. I turned to that office for representation and was assigned a brilliant young female attorney who took care of me. In November 1996, almost two years after Julia started her war of litigation against me, a federal judge dismissed her complaint "with prejudice," which meant that she could never again file a complaint that had anything to do with her mother's estate against me or anyone else in federal court. The judge's dismissal also included a threat of a monetary fine. "The Court sanctions Plaintiff in the amount of $1,000" but suspended the payment "so long as Plaintiff does not file another frivolous claim in federal district court based on the same or similar facts."

Done.

HOT-BUTTON ISSUES

Bacchus Unbound

The Drunk Driving Dilemma

If you drink, don't drive. Don't even putt.

—DEAN MARTIN, SINGER AND COMEDIAN

Gross vehicular manslaughter while intoxicated is the unlawful killing
of a human being without malice aforethought, in the driving of a vehicle,
where the driving was in violation of Section 23152 of the Vehicle Code
[driving under the influence], and the killing was . . . the proximate result
of the commission of an unlawful act . . . and with gross negligence.

—CALIFORNIA PENAL CODE 191.5(A)

O n an August afternoon in 1996, I presided over the sentencing
hearing of Jorge Romero. In the spectator seats, to my left,
sat the family and friends of Carol Klamm, a thirty-seven-
year-old woman whom Mr. Romero killed when, six months earlier, he
drunkenly drove his pickup truck head-on into her car on Highway 85
near San Jose. His blood-alcohol level was .19 percent, the equivalent of
nine or ten beers, more than twice the legal limit. In the spectator seats,
on my right, were Mr. Romero's family and friends. On the advice of his
attorney, Mr. Romero had pled guilty to gross vehicular manslaughter
while intoxicated, a felony.

State legislatures enact laws that define all forms of criminal behavior, and they prescribe the punishments for those crimes. In California,
the legislature made gross vehicular manslaughter while intoxicated

punishable by a state prison term of four, six, or ten years. That Mr. Romero was going to prison was clear; the only question was for how long. To answer that question, I was required to consider aggravating and mitigating circumstances pertaining to the crime. If I determined that the aggravating factors outweighed the mitigating factors, I was obligated to impose the maximum term. Conversely, if the mitigating factors outweighed the aggravating factors, I would impose the minimum term of four years. If, however, the two factors were equally balanced, the mid-term of six years would be the sentence. *The California Rules of Court* lists almost forty aggravating and mitigating factors, among them whether the person used a firearm (an aggravator) or if the defendant was a passive participant who provoked but didn't participate in the crime (a mitigator).

I had received a presentencing report written by a probation officer that summarized the police reports and described Mr. Romero's background. I learned that he had suffered a severe head injury as a result of the accident and had very little memory of what happened. The report concluded with a recommendation that Mr. Romero be sentenced to prison for six years, the mid-term.

Mr. Romero's defense attorney and the prosecutor disagreed. Not surprisingly, his lawyer asked for the minimum sentence, while the prosecutor demanded that I throw the book at Mr. Romero and send him away for the maximum of ten years.

The police reports described the events that transpired that fateful day: Mr. Romero began drinking and driving at 9:00 A.M. A friend who had caught up with him warned him, twice, to stop driving. Mr. Romero, ignoring the advice, continued to drive until he hit a parked car, stopped, stepped out of his truck, then got back behind the wheel. Driving at speeds as high as one hundred miles per hour on Highway 85, he crossed the dirt median strip and crashed head-on into Carol Klamm's car.

The courtroom was packed for the sentencing hearing. Mr. Romero was represented by a seasoned and respected Latino defense attorney. Similarly, the prosecutor was a seasoned and respected member of the

DA's office. She was White, as were all of the spectators sitting behind her. On the other side of the courtroom were the friends and family members of Mr. Romero. All were Latinx.

First to take the witness stand was Mr. Romero, who, assisted by a Spanish-language interpreter, apologized for killing "that person." I believed that Mr. Romero was sincerely remorseful, but given his head injury, his memory lapse, and the language barrier, I could see that his remorse wasn't coming across very well to Carol's family members and supporters, some of whom shook their heads in disgust. When Mr. Romero's mother next testified, again with the assistance of the Spanish-language interpreter, she sobbed and pleaded for mercy for her son. "My son is a good person!" There was more headshaking from Carol's side of the courtroom.

Newspaper and television reporters were seated prominently in the front row of the spectator seats, scribbling in their notebooks and watching my every move. Because the great majority of hearings and trials are open to the public, journalists and reporters don't need a judge's permission to be in the courtroom to observe and report on what happens.

I had been surprised and relieved that there wasn't a request from the media for camera coverage of the hearing. Each state sets its own rules for camera access. In California, whether to allow cameras in the courtroom is left entirely to the judge's discretion but is guided by eighteen factors that include "the security and dignity of the court," "the parties' support of or opposition to the request," and "any other factor the judge deems relevant," whatever that means.

The 1994 double-murder case of O. J. Simpson was the first trial in the country to be televised from beginning to end. At Judge Lance Ito's direction, one camera was installed above the jury box. It captured everything, including, alas, the judge's inability to control the lawyers. In a vain attempt to rein them in, Judge Ito fined them—the highest total ever ordered by a judge against attorneys in a criminal trial in California. That eight-month trial would lead state court judges throughout the country to consider the use of cameras in their courtrooms with great hesitation. No judge in her right mind wanted to end up "Ito'd" by a courtroom camera. In the aftermath of the O.J. trial, state courts enacted rules that have strictly regulated the use of cameras by the media in courtrooms.

Mr. Romero's mother's testimony was followed by the testimonies of Carol's parents, husband, sister, and three best friends. When her husband turned to me and tearfully said that Carol was the love of his life and a wonderful mother of their two teenage children, I almost lost it.

After two hours of testimony, it was the lawyers' turn to persuade me with their closing arguments. The prosecutor went first. Speaking compellingly and passionately, she argued that justice for Carol's family could only be served if Mr. Romero were to serve the maximum time in prison. As I listened, I looked down at the photograph of Carol that had been included in the probation report. Next, Mr. Romero's attorney stood and, speaking from his heart, made a strong argument for why the minimum sentence was appropriate: despite Mr. Romero's poor judgment on that fateful day, he was not a bad person worthy of ten years in prison.

When the lawyers finished speaking, I removed Carol's photograph from the file and handed it to Olga, my courtroom clerk. I told her: "Please take this to Mr. Romero. I want him to see who Ms. Klamm was." Olga got up, walked to the counsel table where Mr. Romero and his attorney were seated, and placed the photo of a smiling Carol Klamm in front of him. He looked at it, then hung his head.

All eyes now turned to me. I had to decide what to do, and I needed to do it quickly. I looked down at the notes that I had taken during the testimony of the witnesses. *You know the rules; just apply the sentencing factors,* I thought. On the one hand, the crime involved great bodily harm. He took a life. That's an aggravator. But on the other hand, he had no prior serious criminal history and hadn't intended to harm Carol—or anyone, for that matter. That's a mitigator. On the one hand, Mr. Romero's level of intoxication was nearly twice the legal limit. No one forced him to drink those beers and get behind the wheel. That's an aggravator. But on the other hand, he admitted his guilt early on, sparing Carol's family the trauma of a trial. That's a mitigator. On the one hand, he had a chance to stop and chose not to. That's an aggravator. But on the other hand, he is sincerely remorseful. I don't see him reoffending. That's a mitigator.

Enough. I took a deep breath, looked up, steadied my voice, and then did what I believed to be was right. Mr. Romero would serve the maximum term of ten years in prison. I felt that the severity of the consequences of Mr. Romero's drunk driving, especially in light of the fact that he had been warned to stop, left me no other choice. I couldn't justify a lesser sentence.

As Mr. Romero was led away in handcuffs, I watched as his lawyer walked across the courtroom and spoke quietly with Carol's father, after which the two shook hands. And as I stepped down from the bench and headed to my chambers, Carol's parents, her husband, and her sister walked across the courtroom, extended their arms, and hugged me. Her husband sighed and whispered that he didn't know how he was going to make it. Carol's sister held my hand for a moment, turned, and slowly walked away.

Until that time, state law required barriers only where the median strips on highways were less than forty-five feet wide. Because the Highway 85 median strip was forty-six to fifty feet wide, no barrier had been erected. In the twelve months after Carol Klamm's death, six more motorists died as a result of vehicles that crossed the Highway 85 median, ultimately leading the state legislature to revise the law. Today, barriers must be installed on any high-volume freeways with medians up to seventy-five feet wide—nearly double the previous standard.

The damage wrought by drunk drivers in this country is staggering. According to the National Highway Traffic Safety Administration (NHTSA), every day thirty Americans die in drunk driving crashes. The NHTSA also reports that 1.5 million people are arrested for driving under the influence of alcohol and/or drugs in any given year, and one-third of them are repeat offenders. Over the last decade, California saw an average of more than 130,000 drunk driving arrests and more than 25,000 victims of alcohol-involved crash injuries. In 1984, I became one of those statistics.

Heading home on Highway 101 after a long day at the San Jose courthouse, I was rear-ended by a drunk driver who totaled my car and left me with bruises and a hairline fracture of my lower spine. My one little bit of satisfaction in this painful ordeal was the driver's look of horror when the California Highway Patrol officer told him that he had just plowed into a judge's car.

But judge or not, the punishment he received was little more than a slap on the wrist. The sixtysomething-year-old man who wreaked havoc in my life pled guilty to misdemeanor drunk driving, for which he received a fine and a sentence that had him picking up trash along the roadways for three weekends. He kept his license.

With an aching back that plagues me to this day, I returned to work eight weeks later with a far different perspective on the crime of drunk driving. Before the accident, I had mindlessly bought into the system at our court: "You've seen one DUI, you've seen 'em all." Since there were so many of these cases, the objective was to dispose of them quickly, which, in practice, meant getting as many defendants as possible to plead guilty early in the court process. After that, sentencing them was easy because we had a playbook of sorts: A first offense meant probation for three years, a fine, no jail, DUI classes, and no license suspension. A second offense, almost the same as the first. A repeat offender received three years' probation, a fine, a few weekends picking up trash, more DUI classes, and no loss of the license. The process worked just fine, at least for us.

Becoming the victim of a drunk driver forced me to realize that while the system we had created might be efficient, it did little to keep travelers safe from drunk drivers. I needed to do something. But what? How could I make the system deal more effectively with the problem of drunk driving? I struggled with this issue for months until I read about the ignition interlock device.

This device was designed to prevent individuals from driving their cars when they had imbibed alcohol. Installed into the ignition system of the vehicle, it resembled a cell phone with a small mouthpiece attached to it. In order to start the car, the driver blew into a mouthpiece, after which his blood-alcohol level was registered and displayed on the device.

It is illegal in all fifty states for anyone over twenty-one years of age to drive with a blood-alcohol concentration (BAC) of .08 percent or higher. Under the age of twenty-one, the legal threshold is lower, but how much lower varies from state to state. (Blood-alcohol concentration is the percentage of alcohol in a person's bloodstream. A .08 percent BAC means that for every one thousand parts of a person's blood, eighty parts are alcohol—generally, the equivalent of four beers or four shots of hard liquor.) If *any* alcohol was detected in the driver's body, the ignition interlock device blocked the car's ignition system; just one drink would activate the device.

Because it was preventive not reactive, the ignition interlock device was a sentencing option that resonated with me. Now I might be able to keep drunk drivers off the road. This possibility excited me; I spent several hours meeting with the manufacturer's representative to learn all that I could about how the device functioned. It would cost a defendant $50 per month to lease it, along with a onetime $150 installation fee.

On May 28, 1987, I began sentencing first-time convicted drunk drivers to install breath devices in their cars but not before giving them the option of choosing thirty days in jail if they didn't want the device. Interestingly, most opted for the device. I was the first judge in California to offer this option. My hope was that other judges on my court would follow suit. As defendant after defendant chose the ignition interlock device, things went smoothly inside my courtroom. But outside, a storm was brewing.

The first indication that something was amiss came when the presiding judge (PJ) paid me a noontime visit in my chambers. He got right to the point and told me that he was concerned that I had not conferred with my fellow judges before sentencing defendants to use the ignition interlock devices. (The presiding judge, the court's leader and spokesperson, is chosen every two years by a majority vote of the judges.) He informed me that the four judges who, along with me, presided over DUI cases complained that what I was doing wasn't appropriate and that they weren't going to use the devices in their drunk driving cases. I told him that I didn't understand why the manner in which I handled the DUI cases in my own courtroom was of concern to them. My courtroom was just that—*my* courtroom. The PJ was clearly unhappy with me. I had a feeling that this was not the end of the matter.

By early June, I had sentenced over forty first-time offenders to install ignition interlock devices. It was then that one of the supervising attorneys in the district attorney's office stopped by my chambers. He lost no time advising me that I was breaking the law. The man had my attention.

Convicted drunk drivers are required to pay state-mandated fines. To ensure that the defendants in my court could afford to pay the monthly costs of the devices, I had been suspending a portion of their fines. The supervising DA informed me that when I did so, the defendants' fines fell below the mandatory minimum by $50. *Really?* I thought. *This was a quibble over $50?* Poker-faced, I listened and then told him that it was within a judge's discretion to suspend fines and that in my view, ensuring the safety of drivers on the highways far outweighed a $50 loss to the state's coffers. He was unimpressed. He told me that I needed to stop suspending the fines. I declined to do so.

By October, after I had sentenced more than seventy convicted drunk drivers to install ignition interlock devices in their cars, I was served with a lawsuit seeking a court order to stop me from suspending the fines. The district attorney was taking me to court. I needed a lawyer.

On Thursday, October 22, 1987, I headed to court represented by an attorney with the Office of the County Counsel. The lawyers in that office represent the county on all manner of legal issues, including judges who find themselves in hot water. The lawyer assigned to me was a smart woman who, more than twenty years later, would become a well-respected judge on our court. In the superior court, the district attorney argued that this case was open-and-shut. The fines that I had been imposing were below the state-mandated minimum and therefore illegal. My lawyer countered that judges have the discretion to lower fines and that protecting society from drunk drivers justified my suspension of the fines. It was strange sitting at the counsel table, a defendant in a lawsuit, and looking up at a judge who would shortly determine if I had violated the law. It didn't take long for me to get the answer. Right after the lawyers finished their arguments, the judge made his ruling: "Judge Cordell's fine suspensions are unlawful. I direct her to stop suspending the fines. Although I appreciate her motivation for doing so, no matter how noble her cause, the defendants in her court who are ordered to install the breath devices must be ordered to pay the full amount of the fines."

So, that was the end of my ignition interlock sentencings. No way was I going to require defendants to bear the burden of the large fines along with the monthly costs to lease the devices. Things went back to the way they were. I was frustrated and ready to move on.

The local press had a field day reporting on every twist and turn of this saga: "Alco-Lock: Judge Sentences 39 to Breath-Test Devices," "Every Breath They Take," "Drunken-Driving Sentences Under Fire," "Head 'Em Off at the Wheel," "The D.A.'s $50 Quibble," ending with "DUI Crusade Sidetracked."

Almost a year later, in August 1988, things took a dramatic shift. Byron Sher, my Stanford contracts professor many years earlier, who was also a member of the California State Assembly, had been following the ignition interlock story. He now intended to introduce a bill in the state assembly that would allow judges to do what I had been forbidden to do—suspend fines so that defendants could, once again, afford to pay for the interlock devices. I was happily stunned.

True to his word, in just a few months, Assemblyman Sher introduced

Assembly Bill 2889. At his request, I traveled to the state capitol in Sacramento and testified in support of the legislation. Under Sher's guidance, the bill moved through the assembly and senate with very little opposition. Most disheartening to me, though, was the reluctance of the local chapter of Mothers Against Drunk Driving to support the bill. Their feeling was that even if ignition interlock devices were effective, convicted drunk drivers should be punished, and those devices weren't sufficiently punitive. But even without MADD's support, AB 2889 landed on the desk of the then-governor Deukmejian for his signature.

Mind you, during this time, I had to stop imposing the devices as a sentencing option. As a consequence, the old system picked up where it had left off; nothing had changed. So, when the bill reached the governor's desk, I was ready to get back to business. But, as I was learning, systems resist change; this time the resistance was in the form of a terse letter from my judicial colleagues to the governor:

September 2, 1988
Dear Governor Deukmejian:

This is to advise you that the Santa Clara County Municipal Court, at a meeting of the court, elected not to take a position regarding AB 2889 authored by Assemblyman Byron Sher. We leave it for you to take whatever action you deem appropriate.

Very truly yours,
Rene Navarro, Presiding Judge

The judges' letter feigning neutrality was a travesty. If they were "neutral," why write anything at all? It was patently clear that the real import of their message to the governor was that they opposed the legislation. The local newspapers got it, weighing in with "San Jose Judges Ask Governor to Wait on Bill," "Judge Denies Vote Was Anti-Cordell," and an editorial supporting me: "Money's Not Everything."

Eighteen days later, the judges on my court got what they wanted:

September 20, 1988

I am returning bill No. 2889 without my signature. This bill would authorize courts in Santa Clara County to implement an ignition interlock device program. Under current law, the Office of Traffic Safety is required to implement a pilot program in four counties for the use of ignition interlock devices. . . . If evaluation of the program is positive, it would be appropriate to extend it at that time. Until then, expansion is premature.

Cordially,

George Deukmejian

"Deukmejian Vetoes Cordell-Inspired Bill" was the final newspaper article on the subject. My effort to prevent people from driving while drunk had been stymied, once again. This system just wasn't going to change, even with the help of a state assemblyman.

The courts, no less than the rest of us, resist change. All of the players—the judges, the lawyers, the probation officers, the courtroom clerks, the bailiffs—get into a rhythm, a way of doing things. Get through the day as uneventfully as possible, go home, and get paid. We become so comfortable doing things one way that we fail to notice when things are not working. Routine, you see, can blind us to systemic problems.

Fast-forward four years to 1992. Sher, now a state senator, was back. He had quietly reintroduced the ignition interlock bill in the senate, and to my delight, the newly elected governor, Pete Wilson, had signed it into law. It was now legal for judges to suspend the fines of convicted drunk drivers so that they could lease the ignition interlock devices that, by this time, had been fondly nicknamed "Blow-and-Go." Success, finally!

Today, almost all fifty states have some form of ignition interlock laws. Thirty-four states and the District of Columbia have "all-offender" laws where every convicted drunk driver—first timer and repeat offender alike—must utilize the device. Unfortunately, while California law requires all repeat drunk driving offenders to install the devices, only those first-time offenders who cause injury must do so.

According to the *American Journal of Preventive Medicine,* five out of six studies found that participants in the interlock programs were 15 percent to 69 percent less likely than other offenders to be rearrested for drunk driving. A 2017 study that found ignition interlock devices reduced alcohol-involved fatal crashes concluded that the devices were a "significant public health benefit."

What started as my attempt to alter the way that the courts do business succeeded, albeit not without setbacks. As the only African American judge on our bench and one of just a handful of women, perhaps any proposal for change that I might have made at the time would have been viewed as suspect by many of my colleagues. That being said, what I learned from that experience is that irrespective of race or sex, the greater the buy-in by everyone involved, the more likely that change in our legal system can happen. Since what a judge does in her courtroom is her own business, I had no obligation to confer with my colleagues. But, at the very least, had I let my colleagues know that I intended to utilize ignition interlock devices, perhaps the road to change would have been an easier one. I learned in dramatic fashion that judicial egos, no less than other egos, need occasional stroking and that attention must be paid.

It's All in Your Head

Mental Health Cases

Upon reflection, I marvel that no one saw through me enough
to bundle me off to the nearest mental institution.

—MAYA ANGELOU, *GATHER TOGETHER IN MY NAME*

She was Latinx, in her forties, attractive, intelligent, and nervous. It was January 1994 when, seated at the witness stand, Isabel E. was doing her best to convince me that she had the mental capacity to refuse to consent to electroconvulsive therapy (ECT). Concerned about her ever-deepening depression, a family member had brought her to a psychiatric hospital, where she had been involuntarily committed for treatment.

The Greek physician Hippocrates (460–370 BCE) may have been the first to recognize the need for involuntary civil commitment of individuals with mental illness when he suggested that these patients "be confined in the wholesome atmosphere of a comfortable, sanitary, well-lighted place." That he proposed humane surroundings for those so confined demonstrated his understanding that mental illness is a natural phenomenon and that those with mental illness are deserving of compassionate treatment.

Over the centuries, mental health practitioners lost sight of that Hippocratic principle. In the early 1400s, Bethlem Royal Hospital became England's first mental institution when it began accepting residential patients. Dubbed "Bedlam," it was so notorious for its inhumane treatment of patients with mental illnesses and developmental disabilities that its very name became synonymous with chaos and madness.

In the United States, until the late 1700s, those with serious mental illnesses were relegated to jails, prison, and poorhouses. When mental institutions were established in the United States in the early 1800s, the harsh treatments inflicted on patients discouraged commitments. Case in point was Patrick Henry, one of this nation's Founding Fathers, whose first wife Sarah suffered from major depression that was frequently accompanied by violent outbursts, necessitating that she be restrained in a straitjacket. Patrick refused to commit her to Eastern State Hospital, Virginia's first mental institution, where patients were typically bled, blistered, dunked in water, and restrained. Instead, with the assistance of one of his slaves, he opted to care for his wife at home until her death at the age of thirty-seven.

Things began to change when, in the mid-1800s, Dorothea Dix brought national attention to the abusive treatment of persons with mental illness. Traveling for two years throughout her home state of Massachusetts, Dix documented the inhumane treatment of patients committed to mental institutions. In 1834, after she had submitted a detailed report of her findings to the state legislature, Massachusetts enacted a law that dramatically improved the care provided by its Worcester Insane Asylum. According to the *Encyclopedia Britannica*, "In the next 40 years Dix inspired legislators in 15 U.S. states and in Canada to establish state hospitals for the mentally ill. Her unflagging efforts directly affected the building of 32 institutions in the United States."

As early as 1845, the right to challenge an involuntary confinement and treatment was put to the test in the courtroom in the landmark case of *Matter of Josiah Oakes*. Mr. Oakes, deemed to be a "lunatic" and forcibly confined to a mental institution, petitioned the Massachusetts Supreme Judicial Court for his release. Following a two-day hearing, Chief Justice Lemuel Shaw denied Mr. Oakes's request to be released and ordered him returned to the asylum, reasoning that Oakes needed to be confined for his own good:

The right to restrain an insane person of his liberty, is found in that great law of humanity, which makes it necessary to confine those whose going at large would be dangerous to themselves or others. In the delirium of a fever, or in the case of a person seized with a fit, unless this were the law, no one could be restrained against his will. . . . The question must then arise, in each particular case, whether a person's own safety or that of others requires that he should be restrained for a certain time, and whether restraint is necessary for his restoration, or will be conducive thereto. The restraint can continue as long as the necessity continues.

The fact that a person with mental illness contested his involuntary confinement in a court of law in the 1800s was highly unusual; that the court gave thoughtful consideration to his argument was remarkable.

Today, every state and the federal government have involuntary civil commitment laws with specific rules that govern when a person, such as Isabel E., is temporarily detained or in some cases confined or "conserved" for lengthy stays in locked psychiatric facilities. California led the way in 1967, when Governor Ronald Reagan signed into law the Lanterman-Petris-Short (LPS) Act, named for the three California legislators who coauthored the bill. The LPS Act, sometimes referred to as the "Magna Carta of the mentally ill," was groundbreaking legislation that revolutionized California's involuntary civil commitment laws by balancing patients' civil liberties with their need for treatment. To that end, the act requires judicial oversight of a series of steps that must be followed whenever a person is held for an evaluation and confined for treatment.

Specifically, when a person such as Isabel is involuntarily brought to a hospital, she can be and, in fact, was held there for seventy-two hours, during which time she was evaluated by mental health professionals. Her evaluation concluded that she was "an imminent danger to self or others" because of her mental illness. As a consequence, the hospital was allowed to hold her another fourteen days. However, within four days, she had the right to a hearing at the county hospital, presided over by a mental health hearing officer where she was represented by a deputy public defender. After that hearing, her confinement was upheld. She then had the right to appeal the decision to a superior court judge. That's where I came in.

Isabel wasn't challenging her commitment to the hospital; given her disabling depression, she recognized that hospitalization was appropriate. It was the *condition* of her hospitalization, the ECT, that she feared. When Isabel refused to consent to ECT treatments, the prescribing physician was obliged to obtain an order from a judge—me—declaring that Isabel lacked the capacity to withhold her consent. If I were to make that finding, Isabel would be administered a course of ECT against her will.

In 1938, Ugo Cerletti developed the first ECT device. According to *Psychology Today*, "Psychiatric legend holds that Cerletti was shopping at a butcher shop one day in Italy and noticed that the butcher would deliver an electrical shock to the heads of pigs before slaughtering them. The electricity caused the animal to enter an anesthetized coma-like state. Cerletti wondered whether electricity applied to the heads of human patients would similarly produce anesthesia before provoking convulsions." Before this, insulin was utilized to produce the convulsions that were perceived to alleviate many of the debilitating symptoms of psychiatric illness. The downside of this insulin therapy, however, was that it had the unfortunate property of occasionally killing a patient.

The first person Cerletti treated was a patient diagnosed with schizophrenia who experienced delusions, hallucinations, and confusion whose symptoms, as a result of the electrical shock, decreased dramatically. The apparent efficacy of ECT was so great and so popular that Cerletti was nominated for a Nobel Prize in Physiology or Medicine.

In the 1960s and 1970s, ECT was perceived as barbaric and fell out of favor. With some technical improvements, however, it made a comeback in the 1980s. Today, it is estimated that one million people a year worldwide receive ECT treatments. Still, it remains a controversial treatment for people with serious major depression. Some believe it is an effective treatment, and some don't. And there is always the uncomfortable question about the ethics of forcibly administering such treatment.

At the time of Isabel's hearing, all I knew about electroconvulsive treatment was what I had learned from watching *One Flew Over the Cuckoo's Nest*, a 1975 feature film starring Jack Nicholson, who played the character Randle McMurphy. Confined in a locked psychiatric hospital, he was strapped down and forcibly administered electrical shocks. The repeated treatments eventually rendered him a vegetable. Alas, Mr. McMurphy, unlike Isabel, had no access to a mental health judge to whom he could plead his case.

In mental health hearings, there are no juries; judges are the sole arbiters. The first witness at Isabel's court hearing was the hospital's psychiatrist. He testified that ECT was the only appropriate course of treatment for her. The doctor, an avuncular White male in his seventies, testified that Isabel's unremitting major depression had resisted a litany of medications. Questioned by the attorney for the hospital to which Isabel had been committed, the doctor testified that in his view ECT was the only remaining option for his patient. He insisted that given the severity of her depression, Isabel was unable to appreciate the therapeutic benefits of the ECT; she didn't have the capacity to consent to the treatment.

I asked the psychiatrist to describe the therapy. He explained that ECT had come a long way over the years and that recent studies had confirmed its effectiveness in treating depression. Then he described how the treatment is administered. "The patient is given a general anesthesia and a muscle relaxant. Then electrodes are attached to the patient's scalp and an electric current is applied that causes a brief seizure or convulsion. A few minutes later, the patient wakes up and has no memory of the treatment." He assured me that he would be the one to perform the ECT treatments on Isabel, the number of which would depend on how quickly and how well she responded, but they would, in all likelihood, be administered two to three times a week for one month. He also noted that a possible side effect of the ECT was some memory loss, but he quickly added that this was a small price to pay for alleviating Isabel's major depression.

That day, there were a few visitors in the courtroom. My partner, Florence, a clinical psychologist who for twenty years had plied her trade at the county's inpatient and outpatient psychiatric units, had brought five Ph.D. student interns with her to observe the goings-on in the mental health court. The students, in their late twenties and early thirties, were in the process of completing their internships, which included neuropsychological testing of patients in the county's locked psychiatric unit, leading group therapy sessions there, and spending one-on-one therapeutic time with some of the patients. The previous day, Florence had asked me if it would be okay to bring her students to watch the mental health hearings. I told her no, absolutely not. Undeterred, she explained that exposing her students to the dynamic of the mental health court and acquainting them with how the law dealt with patients in our mental health system surely outweighed any discomfort I might have in being observed. She had it wrong. I didn't mind being watched. What I minded was being watched when I had no idea of what I was doing. There was no training, no classes, no anything to prepare judges for the mental health assignment. And was I ever unprepared. Still, Florence was right; if her students were willing to work at the county's inpatient psychiatric unit, they needed to see how the courts handled these cases, warts and all. Reluctantly, I relented. So, there they were, seated in the jury box, taking it all in.

During the psychiatrist's testimony, I occasionally glanced at Florence and noticed that she had a worried look on her face. I didn't give it too much thought and chalked it up to her concern that I do well at this, my first mental health hearing. When the doctor finished his testimony, I thought, *He was clear and to the point. It seems like she doesn't have the capacity to give her consent. After all, he's the expert.* As he left the witness stand and walked to his seat in the rear of the courtroom, I noticed that Florence was writing something. *Must be taking lots of notes for her students,* I thought. The psychiatrist folded his arms and gave me a confident nod.

The only other witness was Isabel. Patients who contest their confinement or treatment are typically represented by court-appointed deputy public defenders, lawyers who specialize in this area of the law. They care deeply about their clients and zealously advocate for them. Representing the county's psychiatric facilities and the treating physicians are lawyers with the county counsel's office, competent and professional in their questioning of the doctors and the patients.

Isabel's attorney, a seasoned deputy public defender, was a very tall, lanky man in his early forties; he represented Isabel with patience and compassion. Under his gentle questioning, she recounted, in eloquent fashion, the history of her depression: Fifteen years earlier, she had her first bout with depression; it was deep and so long-lasting that out of desperation she consented to electroshock therapy. After the treatment, her depression did lift, but the side effects proved devastating. She testified that at the time, she had been a librarian who worked for a large governmental agency where she was highly respected and frequently consulted by researchers on all manner of subjects. What distinguished her from her colleagues was her extraordinary memory; it allowed her to quickly direct customers to the exact journals, books, or research papers they were seeking on a variety of subjects. However, in the wake of the ECT, Isabel's memory was so disrupted that she felt she had no choice but to leave her job. It was years before she deemed herself capable of returning to work.

Now, years later, Isabel had secured a job as a librarian at a prominent Silicon Valley company; she did not want to risk losing it to another course of ECT. What she wanted was more time to allow her depression to lift, even if it meant subjecting herself to an experimental drug. When her attorney asked her, "Is there anything else you want to tell the judge?" she turned, looked me in the eye, and pleaded: "Please just give me a little more time. Please." With that she looked down, hands clasped in her lap, and sighed.

The deputy county counsel, who represented the hospital, wisely chose not to cross-examine her, since Isabel was unlikely to provide any additional information that would assist me in making my decision. Unlike the many criminal proceedings over which I had presided, here there was no need for the adversarial and contentious questioning of witnesses by the attorneys. I thanked Isabel and told her that she could return to sit next to her lawyer. As she stepped down and walked to the counsel table, I saw that the psychiatrist was shaking his head, as if to let me know that I shouldn't take Isabel's concerns seriously.

During the two years that I was to spend in the mental health court, I became fascinated by these hearings. From the testimony of the treating physicians, I learned about medications and the various diagnoses of mental illness. I marveled at how psychiatric symptoms manifested themselves in patients' testimony.

At one hearing, a fifty-nine-year-old woman with schizophrenia who had a fixed delusion rode the buses in San Jose all day and night, looking for "Bob," a man who had no last name and for whom she gave no description. Finally, she was placed in a board-and-care home by a public guardian, the person designated by the county to oversee the welfare of people with severe mental disabilities who have no family members willing or able to care for them. When I asked the woman why she wanted to leave the board-and-care home, she told me it was because she should be living with Bob in an apartment. I had no choice but to deny her request to leave.

At another hearing, a twenty-eight-year-old man testified that he wanted to leave the psychiatric hospital and live on his own. After hitting himself in the head with a hammer right in front of his mother—which left him with a steel plate permanently implanted in his skull—he had been involuntarily hospitalized. His mother's testimony did little to aid his quest for freedom; she didn't believe in mental illness or medications and testified that what her son needed was to not think about his problems and become a Christian.

And there was the forty-five-year-old woman from Mississippi with five children, who was 5'1" and weighed more than two hundred pounds.

For three weeks, she stopped eating, refused to take her diabetes medication, and began giving away her clothing and household furniture. In his concern for his mother's mental state, her adult son brought her to a psychiatric hospital for commitment. In my courtroom, she testified that she was now ready to go home. When I asked her why she had refused to take her medicine, she told me: "Your Honor, I don't need it anymore." I pressed her further. "Who told you to stop taking your medication?" "God." When she finished testifying and returned to sit with her attorney, I told her that she would have to stay in the hospital for a while longer. She cried and pleaded with me to let her go home. So, I gave it one more try and said, "If you start eating and take your diabetes medicine, you can go home." "But Your Honor, I don't need to." I sighed and reiterated my order denying her release.

Some of what I heard at these hearings broke my heart. A young man in his early thirties had been sentenced to three years in prison for committing a burglary, in which he had taken nothing. Burglary is the unlawful entry into a home or commercial building with the *intent* to commit a crime. In other words, one doesn't have to steal anything to be convicted of burglary; it is the *unlawful entry* plus the *criminal intent* that matter. Convicted of burglary, he served time at San Quentin and Folsom prisons where, after being repeatedly raped, he became highly unstable and unable to function on his own. He now resided in a locked psychiatric unit, likely for the rest of his life. His testimony was confused, but I understood his message: he wanted to go home. However, it was clear from the testimony of his treating physician that the man's delusional thinking rendered him unable to care for his basic needs. I denied his request.

Another heartbreaker was the twelve-year-old girl whose sexual molestation by a family member had left her suffering from major depression and behavior disturbance. She had been placed in a group home for troubled adolescents, where she was prescribed antidepressants and received counseling. However, after she went into a rage in which she destroyed her dorm room and threatened suicide, her treating physician recommended that she be committed to a psychiatric hospital for fourteen days. She refused to go; she wanted me to allow her to remain in the group home. By this time, I knew what questions to ask of her treating psychiatrist: What medications was she taking and for what purpose? What would be her daily routine at the hospital? What improvement did he want to see? His answers were clear, credible, and concise. I was satisfied that a two-week stay at the hospital was appropriate.

But I digress. The afternoon of my first mental health hearing with Isabel, as I sat at the bench pondering ECT or no ECT, Benita walked across the courtroom to the jury box where she was handed a note by Florence, which she then handed to me. I read it and immediately announced, "Let's take a short recess. I'll resume in about fifteen minutes." With that, I walked into my chambers, sat down, and read it again. "Look up the medications that the doctor has been prescribing before you do anything! None of them are for depression!!!—Florence." At the bottom of the note, she had scribbled the names of several drugs. Florence rarely, if ever, used exclamation points; she had my attention.

I reached for the *Physicians' Desk Reference (PDR)*, the one book passed from judge to judge when they rotate into the mental health assignment. An unprepossessing tome with dark blue covers and filled with pages and pages of words in tiny font, the *PDR* contains information about every drug imaginable. I looked up each of the nine medications listed in Florence's note, all of which the psychiatrist had testified that he prescribed for Isabel. According to the *PDR*, none of them were antidepressants, even though he had stated, under oath, that Isabel suffered from major depression. Rather, the medications that she had been prescribed were for anxiety, sleep, psychosis (delusional thinking), and obsessive thoughts. I took a deep breath, sat back in my chair and thought, *Unbelievable! They didn't teach us this in law school! Time to make this right.*

I got up and returned to the bench, turned to Isabel, and said, "After listening to all of the testimony, I looked up the medications that your doctor has been prescribing for you. None of them appear to address your depression. I have no idea why your physician has not treated your major depression with antidepressants. It makes me wary of his eagerness to subject you to ECT."

At this point, the psychiatrist stood and stormed out of the courtroom. I continued, "I will *not* require that you undergo ECT at this time because I believe that you understand what ECT is and how it may affect you. In other words, I find that you have the capacity to withhold your consent to the treatment. It is my belief that you should be given the opportunity to take antidepressants, especially in light of the dire effect that the previous ECT treatment had on you." With that, Isabel's eyes brightened, and her lawyer smiled. I wished her well and told her the hearing was concluded. If Florence hadn't been there, what would I have done? Ignorant and uninformed, I had no business presiding over this case. I needed to up my game and figure out what the hell I was doing.

Many tutorials with Florence were to follow, the first of which was my introduction to the *Diagnostic and Statistical Manual of Mental Disorders (DSM)*. Now in its fifth edition, the *DSM-5* is *the* authoritative guide to the diagnoses of mental disorders. It lists, among other things, the criteria used in determining mental disorders. First published in 1952, the *DSM* has evolved over the years in significant ways, most obviously growing from 132 pages to 947 pages in the most recent edition. Today, the *DSM* has been translated into over twenty languages and is utilized as a mental health resource in Europe and Asia as well as in the United States. Throughout my time on the mental health court, the *DSM* was always on my bench, right next to the *PDR*. As for Isabel's psychiatrist, I later learned that the hospital staff quietly referred to him as Sparky.

In 1995, my second year in the mental health court, the rate of tuberculosis cases in Santa Clara County had increased 27 percent over the previous two years, ranking our county fifth among California's largest counties in the number of reported cases per population. Fifty-nine-year-old Ella P., a resident of our county who had been diagnosed with infectious tuberculosis, hadn't been following her prescribed medical protocol for treatment. After her eviction by an angry roommate who feared infection, the police brought Ella to a hospital where the county's public health officer ordered her forcibly quarantined under the California Tuberculosis Control Law.

The earliest isolation of individuals with contagious diseases dates back to biblical days. As noted in verses one and two of the fifth chapter of the Bible's book of Numbers, people afflicted with leprosy were quarantined: "And the Lord spake unto Moses, saying, Command the children of Israel, that they put out of the camp every leper, and every one that hath an issue, and whosoever is defiled by the dead." In the Middle Ages, when the bubonic plague took an estimated twenty million lives across Europe, the city of Venice quarantined sailors on plague-infested ships for forty days on a nearby island. In 1792, seventy Russian Jewish immigrants suspected of having typhus were forcibly removed from their homes in New York City's Lower East Side and quarantined in tents on an island in the East River. And in 1917, nearly thirty thousand American women known to frequent military camps were forcibly quarantined, pursuant to a federal order that allowed for their incarceration until mandatory testing deemed them free of sexually transmitted diseases.

The authority of the states (and the federal government) to impose quarantines is derived from their inherent "police power," a mandate to protect, preserve, and promote public health, safety, and welfare. When the governors of California and New York issued shelter-in-place orders during the 2020 coronavirus pandemic, they did so under their inherent police power to protect the public. Similarly, since police power is frequently delegated to local governments, city mayors and county public health officials can impose requirements on residents by restricting their movement, closing businesses, and directing the wearing of protective masks in public.

But the exercise of police power is not unlimited; it is always subordinate to state constitutions and to the U.S. Constitution and can never be used to deprive an individual of life, liberty, or property without due process of law. Ella was the first person in our county to contest the California Tuberculosis Control Law; however, there were people who, years earlier, turned to the courts to challenge confinements linked to contagious diseases.

In 1900, the San Francisco Department of Public Health did not permit Chinese residents to leave the city unless they submitted to a bubonic plague vaccination, whether or not they had been exposed to the disease. Wong Wai, one of twenty-five thousand Chinese San Franciscans targeted by the quarantine, filed a federal lawsuit and won. A unanimous panel of three federal judges found the quarantine to be racist, writing that it was "boldly directed against Asiatic or Mongolian race, as a class, without regard to the previous condition, habits, exposure to disease, or residence of the individual; and the only justification offered for this discrimination was . . . this particular race is more liable to the plague than any other. No evidence has been offered to support this claim, and it is not known to be a fact."

In 1980, the state of West Virginia filed a petition asking that William Arthur Greene be involuntarily confined in Pinecrest Hospital under the state's Tuberculosis Control Act. At his hearing on the petition, the trial judge appointed an attorney to represent Mr. Greene, who was indigent, and then immediately proceeded to take evidence, depriving Greene's lawyer of an opportunity to prepare. At the end of the hearing, the judge granted the state's petition and ordered Mr. Greene's commitment.

Shortly thereafter, Mr. Greene filed a petition with the West Virginia Supreme Court of Appeals, requesting his immediate release. The court concluded that involuntary commitments of those with communicable diseases were no different from involuntary commitments of persons with mental illness in that both impinged on the rights of individuals to "liberty, full and complete liberty." The justices ended Mr. Greene's commitment and ordered the trial judge to conduct another hearing at which Mr. Greene would be provided the same due process rights as those afforded to people facing involuntary commitments to mental hospitals.

Returning now to the highly infectious Ella, there was no way that I could conduct her hearing at the courthouse. Benita; Olga Olivas, my clerk; the court reporter; and I piled into my car and headed to the hospital. Once there, I donned my robe and took a seat at the head of a large table in one of the hospital's conference rooms. A few minutes later, in walked Ella, wearing a hospital gown and a surgical mask, accompanied by the county's public health officer. Seated next to her was her attorney, and next to them was the deputy county counsel representing the hospital.

Ella nodded as I began: "Good afternoon. I am Judge Cordell. I'm here to rule on a petition by the county seeking your confinement in the hospital to treat your tuberculosis." I asked the two attorneys to state their names, then asked Olga to swear in the witnesses, of whom there were two—Ella and the public health officer. With all of us seated at the table, I asked the deputy county counsel to proceed.

Her one and only witness was the public health officer, a slightly built, intelligent-looking man in his forties, who testified that Ella was diagnosed with infectious tuberculosis. He described the disease and its weeks-long treatment, and he further explained that a failure to adhere strictly to the regimen of medications could result in a real epidemic in the county. Adding that county health officials had to be aggressive in dealing with TB to avoid an outbreak, he concluded, "The cost of keeping Ella here runs about $956 a day, but the social cost of allowing her to walk free is potentially higher. It's not great being confined, but our bottom line is to make sure that she is treated and made well. We have to protect those people on the street who aren't wearing masks. We have to protect people from getting coughed on."

Ella's attorney had no cross-examination of the county health officer; I had no questions of my own to ask him. With that, Ella was questioned by her lawyer.

Ella's Lawyer: Why do you oppose the hospital's petition?
Ella: I feel like I'm in prison. I'm not a criminal. I'm a human being. I haven't done anything wrong. I just want to go home to write, listen to music, and crochet.
Ella's Lawyer: How do you spend your time at the hospital?

Ella: I go out on the patio and smoke. I stay on the phone a lot. Everything's closing in on me. I like being outside. I feel like I'll go stir-crazy if I don't get out.

Ella's Lawyer: Will you take your medication if the judge lets you go home?

Ella: Of course! Whatever I have to do, I'll do it!

Ella's Lawyer: No further questions, Your Honor.

On cross-examination by the county hospital's lawyer, Ella grew defensive.

County Counsel: Do you agree that you have infectious tuberculosis?

Ella: Well, that's what they say, but I don't know. I feel just fine. I have asthma and I'm a smoker, but I don't feel that I have TB.

County Counsel: Isn't it true that you have not taken your medications on a regular basis, as the doctor told you?

Ella: I do the best that I can. I will tell you that if I can get out of here, you better believe that I'll take the medicine.

County Counsel: Isn't it true that you have been drifting from home to home for years and don't have a stable place to live?

Ella: Well, I'd stay with my son and my sister, and this person and that person.

County Counsel: No further questions, Judge.

Then Ella's attorney had one last question: "Is there anything else that you want Judge Cordell to know?" Ella leaned toward me and said, "Yes. I assure you, Judge Cordell, that I will take my TB medication and follow the doctor's orders, all of them, if you will let me out of here."

I was ready to rule:

I believe that the law allowing a person to be quarantined is one that should be applied only when the risk of harm to the public outweighs the deprivation of an individual's freedom. It is clear that you have infectious TB and that you don't appreciate that you have the disease. It is also clear that you don't seem to understand the serious risk that you pose to others. I believe that if released, you will not follow your prescribed regimen of medication. Therefore, I have no choice but to grant the county's petition and order that you be detained at this hospital for treatment for a period of time not to exceed ninety days.

She didn't argue with me; she had been heard. Before exiting the conference room, Ella thanked me. The four of us headed back to the courthouse.

By May 1995, nearly eighteen months into the mental health assignment, my competence and knowledge about mental health law had improved significantly. So, when twenty-one-year-old Dan M.'s case was called, I settled in to listen to the testimony and consider his request to be released from the psychiatric unit of a local hospital. I noticed that there were approximately twenty spectators in the courtroom, including five or six paramedics who had transported Dan, along with three other patients waiting for their hearings that afternoon.

During the testimony of his treating psychiatrist, I noticed Dan constantly fidgeting in his seat, repeatedly clenching and unclenching his fists. I assumed that he was nervous, understandable given that his freedom was at stake. His attorney, a likable deputy public defender who sat next to him, didn't seem concerned. I was. Something was a little off.

With Dan now seated to my left at the witness stand, I leaned over and watched him closely as he answered his lawyer's questions.

Dan's Lawyer: If you are released today, where are you going to live?

Dan: Well, I have many opportunities. I can do whatever I want. It's a free country.

Dan's Lawyer: What are you going to do?

Dan: Well, I might go see the white buffalo. I might go to Mexico. I might go up to Alaska. It's pretty nice up there this time of year. Might go to Florida. That looks pretty nice. I could stay with friends in town. I am not limited to any one person or thing.

. . .

Dan's Lawyer: Why don't you tell me about these episodes of going in bathrooms or disrobing.

Dan: That's a weird one. I am not saying I am completely sane like a normal person. . . . The closest thing you can call it is a reenactment of Jesus. . . . It's because I am looping in this lifetime. This isn't where I wanted to go. I am looping. As I loop, I know I have experienced this before. . . . That's like manifest destiny. It became manifest destiny for me in disrobing. I never stole anybody's property. I was calling 911. I went in one house asking for water, to use their bathroom. Then I saw the pig, and I broke that. I mean, that's not my fault. One house I did make a mistake. There was a twenty-dollar bill sitting right out there, and I grabbed it because that's my number. I picked up a jar of Jelly Bellies, but they were hot, so I threw those down and gave them the twenty dollars back.

Dan's Lawyer: You are taking medication now?

Dan: Yes.

Dan's Lawyer: Do you want to keep taking it?

Dan: About the medication, what I want to say, I came to the doctor as a homeopathist and not a doctor-doctor. . . . I am taking cannabis indicia. Indicus is high, and sativa is low, and they counteract. I was going to pick up my sativa, but the FBI picked me up. The FBI followed me, thinking that I was a threat to them, like an activator, grower, something like that.

At this point, I had heard more than enough. It was pretty clear that Dan's delusional thinking necessitated further treatment at the hospital.

I interrupted and asked if his attorney had any further questions. He said no, whereupon Dan turned toward me and yelled, "Am I free to go?" Given how agitated he was, I thought it best that I put some distance between the two of us before announcing my ruling. I directed him to return to his seat. Dan stood, hesitated for a moment, then slowly walked back to the counsel table and sat next to his attorney.

Me: I find that you have a mental disorder that renders you currently disabled and—

Dan: What?! You denied my hospital—No way! This is fucking outrageous!

With that, he jumped up and ran toward me. I quickly stood up and backed up against a wall behind my bench. At the same time, Harrison Taylor, a deputy county counsel, a stocky Black man in his thirties, ran after Dan, who had abruptly changed direction and darted into the jury deliberation room, directly to my left. Benita was right on his heels and followed Dan into the room. As Taylor joined in the chase, he tripped and fell headfirst against the side of the jury box. Amazingly, he managed to get back up and run into the jury room. Once inside, Dan jumped onto the long conference table that ran the length of the room and sprinted in the direction of the room's open window. Just as he was about to leap through the window, Benita and Mr. Taylor reached up and pulled him to the floor. Then Benita placed him in an armlock and with the assistance of Mr. Taylor, dragged Dan, kicking and screaming, back into the courtroom. At that point, one of the paramedics held Dan as Benita quickly placed him in handcuffs.

While I had had my share of disrespectful and angry defendants, one of whom sent me a death threat in a *signed* letter from prison, this was my first encounter with violence in the courtroom. According to *Trends in State Courts,* a project of the National Center for State Courts, "Violent acts surrounding court cases have been steadily rising despite the presence of increased courthouse security," such that "all court proceedings have an associated inherent risk and potential for violence escalation."

And then there is *Court Cam,* a popular television show that debuted on network television in 2019 (renewed in 2020 for another season) that shamelessly promotes itself as "a behind-the-scenes look into some of the most wild, unruly and dramatic moments caught on tape in courtrooms across the country; witnesses, judges and victims share their perspectives of the emotional outbursts and chaotic moments." Violence in the courts is now fodder for entertainment.

The paramedics removed Dan from the courtroom and transported him back to the psychiatric unit. Mr. Taylor, bleeding from his lip, his hand, and the right side of his face, went to the hospital for treatment. Benita opted for an ice pack to treat her bruised and sprained right hand and wrist. Thanks to them, I emerged unscathed, albeit shaken up. And I was furious—not with Dan who was ill and in need of treatment. I was upset because immediately after the incident, a paramedic, one of the first responders who ordinarily deported themselves in a professional manner, pulled me aside and told me that Dan should have been placed in restraints during the hearing. The paramedics, he informed me, were aware of Dan's history of violent outbursts and yet hadn't bothered to alert Benita or me. Even more upsetting was the fact that Dan had been seated only a few feet away from me when he testified, while the paramedics casually sat in the rear of the courtroom. Had Dan lunged at me then, I would have been an easy target.

My time on the mental health court concluded as it began, with a hearing involving another deeply depressed middle-aged woman who refused to take her medication. The psychiatrist testified that she was not competent to consent to her treatment and that the medication he had prescribed was for her own good. She testified that the prescribed medications caused her awful side effects—nausea, drowsiness, and headaches. Like Isabel before her, she didn't deny that she had a mental illness and needed help. And, like Isabel before her, she insisted that the medications were doing her more harm than good. Finding that she had the capacity to consent and that her refusal to take the medication was a choice she had the right to make, I ruled in her favor. Even though it had taken me two years and Florence's mentoring to get me to this place, I was confident about my decision. And I was also confident that psychiatric patients seeking justice in our courts must never be subjected to a judge's on-the-job training.

For judges without a Florence in their lives, there are alternatives. Courts can create mental health primers that include definitions of major diagnoses and their basic treatments, descriptions of medications and their uses, a list of local psychologists and psychiatrists with whom judges might consult, and a compilation of all applicable mental health laws and procedures. Also, before undertaking mental health assignments, judges can get clearance to visit inpatient units at locked psychiatric hospitals where they can observe the conditions under which patients are held and treated.

Parsing Sentences

Judicial Discretion

My object all sublime, I shall achieve in time—
To let the punishment fit the crime.
—W. S. GILBERT, *THE MIKADO*

A member of San Jose's Hmong community, thirty-year-old Mr. Fau was charged with misdemeanor statutory rape—sex with a minor, even with the minor's consent. In this case, the minor, a twelve-year-old girl, had been married in a Hmong ceremony to Mr. Fau. Shortly thereafter, she was pregnant. When she delivered the baby, hospital personnel promptly notified the police, and Mr. Fau was arrested.

Hmong villagers in Laos and Vietnam worked with the CIA against the North Vietnamese during the Vietnam War. Then, in the 1970s and 1980s, assisted by the enactment of the Indochina Migration and Refugee Assistance Act of 1975, thousands of Hmong immigrated to this country. Today, the largest Hmong urban population in the world, some sixty thousand, resides in the Minneapolis–Saint Paul area. In San Jose, they are a small and tightly knit community with their own unique customs, one of which is to permit the marriage of girls when they attain puberty, usually at age twelve, thirteen, or fourteen.

On the advice of his attorney, Mr. Fau pled guilty to the statutory rape charge and was now before me for sentencing. What was I to do with this man? His attorney explained to me that in the Hmong community his client had done nothing wrong; these marriages are a tradition. He continued, "It isn't like the girl was forced, Your Honor." Incredulous, the female prosecutor stood and countered: "Judge, how in the world can a twelve-year-old consent to marriage and to having sex with a man more than twice her age?!" She wanted me to send Mr. Fau to jail; his attorney wanted me to send him home.

Jails are county-run facilities that house individuals who, unable to post bail or denied the opportunity to do so, await trial. Jails also house inmates who have been convicted of crimes and are serving sentences of no more than one year, usually for misdemeanor convictions. In California, on any given day, approximately seventy thousand women and men reside in the state's 110 jails. Jails and prisons are not the same, although many people think that they are. Prisons are state-run institutions, deliberately situated in remote areas where inmates convicted of felonies are housed for terms ranging from more than one year to life.

Annually, our nation's jails and prisons—1,719 state prisons, 109 federal prisons, 3,263 jails, 1,772 juvenile correctional facilities, and 80 Indian Country jails—are filled with more than two million men, women, and children. (Native Americans are both U.S. citizens and tribal nationals. Their tribal courts have authority to prosecute crimes committed on Indian lands and to sentence those convicted to serve up to one year in Indian Country jails. More serious crimes with longer terms of incarceration are handled in the federal courts.)

In many states, including California, there are crimes known as "wobblers" that prosecutors can charge as felonies or misdemeanors, depending on the circumstances of the crimes. Statutory rape is a wobbler. The prosecutor in Mr. Fau's case could have chosen to file the statutory rape charge as a felony. In light of the fact that the victim was just twelve years of age, I was baffled why the prosecutor decided not to. Having pled guilty to the misdemeanor, the maximum punishment that Mr. Fau faced was one year in the county jail. With a felony conviction, he would have faced a maximum of four years in state prison. But it wasn't my call. Prosecutors alone choose the charges; judges alone choose the sentences.

So, what was I to do with Mr. Fau? Several members of the Hmong community showed up in support of Mr. Fau that afternoon, among them, his "wife," her parents, and the couple's baby. His attorney, a deputy public defender, argued that sending Mr. Fau to jail would do far more harm than good for his young family. He was, after all, the breadwinner; without him, how would his now thirteen-year-old wife and their infant survive? Social services would undoubtedly swoop in to place the girl in a children's shelter and her child in foster care. Send him to jail and break up the family? Don't do it, Judge. *Good points,* I thought.

The prosecutor contended that if I didn't send Mr. Fau to jail, what message would be sent to the Hmong community? That it's okay for grown men to impregnate young girls? Culture or not, marrying off twelve-year-olds to grown men is not permitted in America. She concluded by telling me that Hmong's cultural practice was yet another form of female oppression. *Makes sense,* I thought.

So, now what? Should I send Mr. Fau to jail? If so, for how long? I had the discretion to choose, which is why this decision was so hard.

What exactly is judicial discretion? Consider the guidance provided by California Penal Code section 1170(b) when judges must decide the lengths of incarceration in considering the imposition of prison sentences: "When a judgment of imprisonment is to be imposed and the statute specifies three possible terms [minimum, mid, and maximum], the choice of the appropriate term shall rest within the *sound discretion* of the court. . . . The court shall select the term which, in *the court's discretion,* best serves the interests of justice." (Emphasis added.) What does it mean to use discretion that "best serves the interests of justice?" At best, it's a directive to judges to consider and weigh every single aggravating and mitigating circumstance. At worst, it's carte blanche to do whatever we want.

For any given crime, other than capital murder where the punishment is death, sentencing options available to a judge can range from no jail time, a few months on probation, and a small fine to several years in prison, large fines, and even court-ordered castration. I usually landed somewhere in between.

The exercise of judicial discretion makes a judge's life especially difficult when there are several lawful options from which to choose and when, as was the case with Mr. Fau, all the parties—the defense attorney, her client and his many family members, and the prosecutor—are staring at you, waiting for you to do their bidding.

Since Mr. Fau now had a criminal record, I believed that the message had been sent to the Hmong community that their cultural tradition notwithstanding, marrying and impregnating young girls was a violation of the law for which they would be prosecuted. So, I suspended his one-year jail sentence and sent him home. Should he again violate the law, then off to jail he would go. Did I abuse my discretion? Definitely not—my decision was a lawful one. Did I do the right thing? I believe so; reasonable minds could differ.

With the passage of California's Three Strikes and You're Out law, judicial discretion went the way of the dinosaur. Born of grief and public outrage, the law was enacted after the 1992 brutal murder of eighteen-year-old Kimber Reynolds and the abduction, rape, and murder of twelve-year-old Polly Klaas in 1993. Polly was kidnapped from a slumber party. Kimber was brazenly shot in the head during a purse snatch. Their killers were repeat offenders with criminal histories that included violent assaults, kidnapping, and robbery. Ironically, their killers had the same last name—Davis. Polly Klaas and Kimber Reynolds were to become the poster children for California's three-strikes law, a mandatory minimum sentencing scheme that would lock up thousands of repeat offenders for a minimum of twenty-five years to life.

Mandatory minimum sentencing laws paint all defendants with the same brush. It doesn't matter who the defendants are, what trauma they may have experienced, or what circumstances gave rise to their conduct. Under these laws, all offenders are deemed menaces to society who need to be locked up for long periods of time. With mandatory minimums, there's no need for judges to trouble themselves with aggravating or mitigating circumstances. Instead, judges are rendered little more than rubber stamps for prosecutors who choose which defendants they will charge with strikes.

Initially, under California's Three Strikes and You're Out law, *all* felonies qualified as third strikes; it didn't matter if the crimes were serious or nonserious, violent or nonviolent. (In the other twenty-six states that subsequently enacted three-strikes laws, only violent and serious offenses can qualify as third strikes.) Over 80 percent of defendants who are serving twenty-five-years-to-life sentences in California prisons were convicted of nonviolent and nonserious third strikes, such as stealing a pack of batteries, possession of marijuana, and bouncing checks. Even juveniles could be convicted of strikes under this law.

In 2012, California voters brought the three-strikes law more in line with similar laws in other states by eliminating a majority of the nonserious and nonviolent crimes that could qualify as third strikes. But before 2012, California's mandatory minimum law worked like this: Let's say that you were convicted of a residential burglary (a serious felony) for which you served time in prison. When you were released, you were convicted of assault with a deadly weapon (a violent felony) for which you served yet another term in prison. Now, you have two strikes—one serious felony conviction and one violent felony conviction. A few months later, you were arrested and subsequently convicted of possession of cocaine. Because the prosecutor had the discretion to classify that drug charge as your third strike, the judge had no choice but to sentence you to a minimum of twenty-five years to life in prison.

Most Californians who voted for the three-strikes law were not aware that it included a two-strike provision that automatically doubled the prison term for a second violent or serious felony conviction. So, for example, a person convicted of strong-arm robbery (theft by force), a violent felony, and who, twenty years later, is convicted of felony drunk driving (causing injury to someone while driving intoxicated), a serious felony, now has two strikes. Felony drunk driving normally carries a prison term of three years, but since it is a second strike, the mandatory sentence is doubled to six years.

A rationale for mandatory minimum sentences is that they protect the public from violent criminals, certainly the case for serial killers and sexual predators. The problem, though, is that only a minority of inmates convicted of strikes are violent offenders; the majority of Americans incarcerated for strike crimes are in prison for *nonviolent* drug offenses and property crimes, such as burglary, car theft, vandalism, and shoplifting.

In the late 1990s, when the harsher version of California's three-strikes law was in its heyday, prosecutors up and down the state went wild, exercising their discretion to charge all manner of crimes as strikes. It seemed that every time I looked up, there was another Latinx or African American defendant standing before me facing two, three, or more strikes. My perception wasn't far from the truth. Only two years after Californians voted for the three-strikes law, African Americans made up 43 percent of third-strike defendants, imprisoned at more than thirteen times the rate of Whites—a huge disparity when you consider that African Americans were just 7 percent of California's population. At the time, Vincent Schiraldi, a well-known criminal justice reformer, said, "If one were writing a law to deliberately target blacks, one could scarcely have done it more effectively than 'three strikes.' It can truly be said that 'three strikes' is California's apartheid."

In 2006, Santa Clara University political science professor Elsa Chen conducted a study to determine the extent that racial disparities existed in the implementation of California's three-strikes law. After examining 171,000 individual data records on inmates in the California prison system, she concluded that African American offenders were significantly more likely than Whites and Latinx offenders to receive third-strike sentences, regardless of the nature of their offenses.

Santa Clara County, where I presided, was no exception. Indeed, its use of the three-strikes law was the toughest among the San Francisco Bay Area's nine counties. And among the state's twelve largest populated counties, Santa Clara had the greatest overrepresentation of African American and Latino second and third strikers. Even after I retired from the bench in 2001, the racial disparities occasioned by the three-strikes law in Santa Clara County lingered on. A 2004 report concluded: "While 2.7% of the county was African American, 27% of its striker population was African American or 10 times greater." Prosecutors charged a disproportionate number of defendants of color with strikes, and judges were powerless to stop them.

As the number of third-strike defendants grew, so did my frustration. Here I was, a Black woman at the helm of our legal system with no choice but to enforce a law that I knew was inflicting far more harm than good. I was a participant, albeit a reluctant one, in creating what had become the mass incarceration of people of color.

For several months, Mr. Boddie had been writing weekly letters to me from jail, begging me to preside over his case. I had no idea who he was. Only after his public defender was able to have his case assigned to me for pretrial discussions did he end up in my courtroom. Mr. Boddie was Black, thirty-four, and facing sixty-one years to life as a three striker. His two prior strike convictions occurred in 1990 when, loaded on crack, he stabbed two people whom he believed owed him money for drugs, with each stabbing charged as a separate strike by the prosecutor. Six years later, in 1996, Mr. Boddie stood accused of using a gun to rob a man at an ATM to fuel his drug habit. If convicted, this robbery would be his third strike. Mr. Boddie's attorney wanted me to dismiss one of his earlier strikes so that he would no longer be a three striker, thereby avoiding a twenty-five-year-to-life sentence. Apparently, word had circulated throughout the jail that Judge Cordell might be willing to dismiss strikes when other judges wouldn't even consider doing so. Defendants awaiting trial, some with two or three strikes, were lining up, willing to plead guilty in the hopes that at their sentencing hearings I would dispose of their strikes.

Prosecutors are accustomed to having their way in the courtroom; after all, they represent the people. As a consequence, there is a lot of pressure on trial judges to rule in their favor. I quietly fumed that my colleagues were consistently acceding to prosecutors when dismissing strikes in certain cases was an option. The judges' unwillingness to even consider removing strikes left me squarely in the crosshairs of the district attorney's office, who went on the offensive against me.

The DA's weapon of choice is the affidavit of disqualification that allows a lawyer to switch to another judge by alleging, under penalty of perjury, that the judge cannot be fair. That's it. There's no requirement to explain *why* the judge can't be fair; simply asserting it in an affidavit makes it so. Once the affidavit is filed, the judge has to step aside, no questions asked. Both sides can "affidavit" a judge—once. When the prosecutor files her affidavit, that's all she gets. Then the judge who replaces her is fair game for the other side. And should the defense attorney file an affidavit, removing the second judge, both sides are stuck with the third judge, whoever she or he may be.

Disqualifications of judges are rare, so when prosecutors began filing affidavits against me, word quickly spread throughout the courthouse that I was being targeted in strikes cases. In one instance, a prosecutor apologized to me when filing an affidavit, saying, "I really have no problem with you hearing this case, but I've got my marching orders." Interestingly, none of my decisions dismissing strikes had ever been reversed by an appellate court, clear proof that I was following the law.

Unwilling to plead guilty only to be sentenced by judges who would not even consider dismissing their strikes, three-strike defendants were left with no choice but to take their chances at trial. With not enough courtrooms in which to try them, the number of three-strike cases awaiting trial piled up, and judges angrily pointed accusatory fingers at the DA's office. Then, as abruptly as the disqualifications of me began, they stopped. Prosecutors had called off their dogs. I was back presiding over three-strikes sentencing hearings.

Mr. Boddie's parents were seated in the courtroom when their son, dressed in jail garb and handcuffed, was brought in by the sheriff's deputies. They were distraught but grateful for the time that I allowed them to tell me about their son. "He's a good person but it's the drugs that have ruined his life." "He's an addict but he doesn't deserve to die in prison." I

was moved by their concern, but it was the interaction between the prosecutor and Mr. Boddie that really moved me—and not in a good way.

Mr. Boddie was seated in the empty jury box; I stepped down from
the bench and stood near him, next to his female public defender. Standing to my right was the tall and heavyset prosecutor. And to his right
were Mr. Boddie's parents, both African Americans in their late sixties,
seated in the front row of the spectator seats. I told Mr. Boddie that he
could say whatever he wanted to all of us and that we had all agreed that
whatever he said would not be used against him, should his case proceed
to trial.

Mr. Boddie begged and pleaded with the prosecutor to dismiss one of
his strikes but to no avail. "My job is to protect society, and I think that
you are a very dangerous person who should be locked up for life." The
prosecutor continued, "Actually, Mr. Boddie, I think that you are not a
bad person. I think that you were doing fine until you got hooked on
crack. Then you started breaking the law. I hope that when you get out
in twenty-five years or so, you'll have learned your lesson. If you plead
guilty now, I'll lower your sentence of sixty-one years to life to twenty-
five years to life. That's the best that I can do."

I looked at his parents, then to Benita, and then to Mr. Boddie, all
of whom, grim faced, shook their heads. I glanced at the prosecutor and
thought, *What a patronizing, condescending, self-righteous, clueless person
you are. Didn't you just acknowledge that it was Mr. Boddie's drug addiction
that brought him into the criminal justice system? Hadn't you just said that
Mr. Boddie was not a bad person? So, what would locking him up for the rest
of his life accomplish?*

Then everyone turned to me. The law was clear—I could not lawfully
dismiss any of Mr. Boddie's prior strikes because they were too recent
and because they involved violence. But in case I might be leaning in
that direction, the prosecutor told me: "Judge, if you dismiss any of Mr.
Boddie's strikes, our office will immediately file an appeal!" I looked him
straight in the eyes and said, "This isn't a life case, and you know it. Everyone agrees that Mr. Boddie has a serious drug problem and that he

should do time in prison but not as a three striker. I may not be able to dismiss any of his strikes, but *you* can. You have the discretion to charge strikes and you have the discretion to make them go away. Agree to dismiss one of his strikes and let's discuss how much time he should serve."

My words went nowhere; we ended in a stalemate. The prosecutor had his instructions and wouldn't budge; I was powerless to do anything. As he was being taken out of the courtroom, Mr. Boddie turned to me and said, "I prayed to God that my case would be sent to you and my prayers were answered. I know that you tried to help, but I can't agree to a life sentence. I'll just have to go to trial." His parents were sobbing. *This three-strikes law*, I thought, *is no good, and neither is this prosecutor.*

With California leading the way, mandatory minimum sentencing laws enabled prosecutors and judges across the nation to fill our prisons to overflowing, resulting in America's mass-incarceration mess and the rise of the prison-industrial complex. Today, twenty-nine states and the federal government have these laws.

Between 1994 and 1998, as a direct result of California's harsh three-strikes law, the Golden State led the pack with a whopping *40,511* strike convictions. Georgia was next with 942, followed by South Carolina at 825, and Nevada at 304. Three states (New Mexico, Connecticut, and Alaska) had 1, and three (Montana, Utah, and Virginia) had none at all.

One rationale promoted by supporters of mandatory minimum sentencing is deterrence. The theory is that really long sentences make potential offenders and would-be reoffenders think twice before committing crimes. But does that theory hold water? Consider the case of Terry Nichols who, along with Timothy McVeigh, bombed the Alfred P. Murrah Federal Building in Oklahoma in 1995, killing 168 people and injuring 500 others. For this horrific act of domestic terrorism, McVeigh was put to death and Nichols received *161 life sentences* with no possibility of parole. The message from the Nichols court could not have been clearer: commit acts of domestic terrorism and either you will be put to death or you will spend the rest of your life locked in a cell. Yet, the following year, Eric Rudolph exploded a bomb during the 1996 Olympics in Atlanta, Georgia, killing one spectator and injuring 110 more. A federal judge sentenced Rudolph to prison for two consecutive life terms. The next year, in 1997, Ali Hassan Abu Kamal shot seven visitors at the Empire State Building, killing one, after which Mr. Abu Kamal fatally shot himself. From 1995 to 2016, there were 620 acts of domestic terrorism in the United States, resulting in 3,393 deaths.

So, what of the deterrent effect of laws like Three Strikes and You're Out? Surely the threat of decades of incarceration and life sentences must have sent crime rates plummeting. In 2001, authors Franklin Zimring, Gordon Hawkins, and Sam Kamin conducted a comprehensive study of the impact of California's three-strikes laws on the state's crime rates and published their findings in *Punishment and Democracy: Three Strikes and You're Out in California (Studies in Crime and Public Policy)*. They found that before California's three-strikes laws, crime rates were already declining and that after the law's enactment, the decline continued at about the same rate. They also determined that third-strike offenders were no more likely to commit violent crimes than those who were charged with nonstrike offenses. Further, they noted that were the three-strikes law the cause of a significant part of the decline, the rate of decline should have increased after its passage. Instead, the rate of decline remained constant.

More recent studies have analyzed the impact of three-strikes laws on crime rates and reached similar conclusions. "States which have implemented three strikes laws have not experienced reductions in violent crime rates to any greater extent than those with no such legislation." The idea that mandatory sentences function as a deterrent is a myth.

Rodney Krueger, a White man in his thirties, had two strike convictions for robbing a bank—the same bank, twice. In 1982 and again in 1984, an unarmed Mr. Krueger walked into the bank, and each time he handed the teller a note demanding money. He chose that particular bank because it had no security guard, thereby presenting no danger of anyone being injured by gunfire. After serving time in prison for the two robberies, he remained crime-free for almost a decade, until 1995, when he tried to cash three checks totaling $230 on a nonexistent bank account. Oddly, the district attorney's office viewed Rodney Krueger as just the sort of person to whom the three-strikes law ought to apply. So, Mr. Krueger's three bad checks became his three bad strikes, leading the prosecutor to seek a sentence of seventy-five years to life—twenty-five years for each check—*to run consecutively*. (Multiple prison terms can run *concurrently*, which means that the defendant serves only one of the terms; or they can run *consecutively*, which means that each term is served one right after the other.) Had Mr. Krueger been convicted of passing those bad checks in any of the other twenty-nine states with three-strikes laws, he never would have faced a life sentence; those states' laws did not have California's draconian "anything-and-everything-goes" definition of a third strike.

The crime of presenting a check with insufficient funds is, like statutory rape, a wobbler. Among the several crimes that fall into the wobbler category is grand theft (stealing something of greater than $400 in value). In very limited circumstances, judges can reduce felony wobblers to misdemeanor wobblers. And when the felonies go away, so go the strikes.

In Mr. Krueger's case, the prosecutor opted to charge the bad checks as felonies. Unsurprisingly, his public defender asked me to reduce them to misdemeanors. This was a no-brainer. Rodney Krueger was not the kind of person that the voters had in mind when they approved the three-strikes law; this man was no menace to society and deserved another chance. Over the prosecutor's vehement objection, I reduced Mr. Krueger's three felonies to three misdemeanors. He was no longer a three striker. On the advice of his lawyer, he promptly pled guilty to bouncing the three checks, misdemeanors, whereupon I sentenced him to serve ninety days in the county jail.

Mr. Lopez and Mr. Saenz were each convicted of serious sex crimes. Fifty-year-old Mr. Saenz had *nine* prior sex crime convictions, including the rape of a seventy-one-year-old woman he committed when he was just seventeen years old. Mr. Lopez, in his forties, had prior convictions for assault with intent to commit rape and for kidnapping. I couldn't understand why these men weren't still in prison. The crime that brought each into my courtroom was a violation of California Penal Code Section 290.

Generally, this law mandates that convicted sex offenders must annually register with their local law enforcement agencies. Even when they relocate to another state, convicted sex offenders must annually notify California law enforcement agencies of their whereabouts. It was that provision of the law that the two were accused of violating. The prosecutor had charged their violations as third strikes so that if convicted, they would serve a mandatory minimum of twenty-five years to life.

All fifty states, as well as the District of Columbia, Guam, Puerto Rico, and the Virgin Islands, require sexually violent predators to register for life. Sex offenders who have committed nonviolent crimes, such as indecent exposure or possession of child pornography, must register for shorter periods of time, ranging anywhere from ten to twenty-five years. There are exceptions, though. In Iowa, no matter how egregious the conduct of the offenders, there is one term of registration—ten years. Missouri, on the other hand, requires lifetime registration for all sex offenders—no exceptions for anyone.

After Mr. Lopez and Mr. Saenz were paroled from state prison in the mid-1990s, Mr. Lopez went to Michigan and Mr. Saenz headed to Texas. Neither man bothered to inform his parole officer that he no longer resided in California. The conditions of their parole prohibited them from leaving the state without the permission of their parole officers. Each had been apprehended and returned to California for their parole violation hearings and I quickly determined that each had violated California Penal Code section 290. But, in the law as in life, sometimes nothing is as it seems.

Three months before Mr. Lopez and Mr. Saenz entered my courtroom, the California Supreme Court decided the case of *People v. Franklin*. In the *Franklin* case, Donald Dwayne Franklin was convicted of child molestation and sodomy in 1985. As a result, he was required, upon completion of his prison sentence, to register as a sex offender. He first registered in 1989 but failed to annually register thereafter. In 1995, Mr. Franklin and his wife moved to Texas but did not notify any California law enforcement agency of his relocation. Later that year, he was arrested and returned to California and eventually convicted of failing to let California authorities know of his move to Texas, a violation section (f) of California Penal Code section 290. Because his earlier child molestation convictions constituted two strikes, this third conviction for violating section 290, a felony, made him a three striker. As a result, the trial judge sentenced him to prison for twenty-five years to life. Mr. Franklin filed an appeal.

In 1999, the California Supreme Court reviewed Mr. Franklin's appeal and determined that section (f) was so poorly written that it failed to make clear to convicted sex offenders that they were obligated to inform California authorities when they moved to another state. As a result, the court threw out Mr. Franklin's conviction, leaving him a free and undoubtedly happy man.

Supreme courts are the states' highest courts. (The exception is New York State, where trial courts are called supreme courts; their highest court is the court of appeals.) Supreme courts don't conduct trials; rather, they review the rulings of trial court judges, and in some instances, when laws are unclear, they issue their own interpretations. Litigants who are dissatisfied with the rulings of trial judges can first appeal to their states' appellate courts (typically called courts of appeal), and, if still unsatisfied, ultimately to their supreme courts. Decisions of courts of appeal and supreme courts have the force and effect of law; when appellate courts speak, you listen. Trial court judges are required to follow those rulings without exception.

After the California Supreme Court issued its *Franklin* decision, the state legislature quickly rewrote section (f) to make it clear to convicted sex offenders that they must notify California authorities when they depart the state. But because both Mr. Lopez and Mr. Saenz left California *before* the law was rewritten by the legislature, their attorneys argued to me that the *Franklin* decision should apply to their clients, which would mean that their third strikes, just like Mr. Franklin's, had to be dismissed.

As expected, the prosecutor forcefully argued that the two men were not in the same category as Mr. Franklin because, unlike Mr. Franklin, they were on parole. It seemed to me to be a difference without a distinction. Parole or not, all three men had been required to notify authorities before leaving the state under the earlier version of section (f).

The problem was that if the *Franklin* case applied to Mr. Lopez and Mr. Saenz, men with horrible records of violent sex crimes, I would have to hand each a get-out-of-jail-free card. And if I were to do that, the district attorney's office would quickly put out the word that Judge Cordell had just freed two sex-offending three strikers, which wouldn't bode well with the county's voters when it was time for me to stand for reelection.

So, I continued the two cases for a couple of days to confer with our court's research attorneys. Maybe, I hoped, they would see the issue differently. Not so—they agreed that the reasoning of the *Franklin* case applied to Mr. Lopez and Mr. Saenz. I dismissed their third strike convictions, and the prosecutor angrily vowed to appeal.

In California, there are six appellate districts presided over by 105 "justices." (In the federal system, the person presiding in the federal appellate courts is a "judge." Only those who sit on the U.S. Supreme Court are "justices.") Appellate court justices don't work solo; they make decisions in groups of three, called panels. If at least two of the three justices on a panel agree, the majority rules. State appellate court justices are busy. In 2018, California's appellate courts ruled on 15,343 civil and criminal appeals. During my time on the bench, I'd been reversed a few times by appellate courts. I wasn't happy being told that I was wrong; and I didn't always agree with their reasoning. But I understood that laws can be interpreted in different ways, which is why judicial review of our decisions comes with the job. Appellate courts serve the important purpose of keeping trial judges in check and holding them accountable.

Amazingly, the DA's office never appealed my decisions in the Saenz and Lopez cases.

Because I considered the three-strikes law to be draconian and more than a little racist, you might think that I tried to avoid the sentencing hearings. I didn't. I took seriously the requests from defense attorneys to dismiss strikes against their clients; and when the law permitted me to dismiss them, I did. But the oath I had taken was to uphold *all* of the laws of the state, not just the ones of which I approved. By the time that I left the bench, I had handed down life sentences to eight defendants under the three-strikes law, all of them repeat offenders convicted of serious crimes. But did they deserve to be put away for the rest of their lives? Yes and no. If you believe that everyone, even the worst of the worst, can be redeemed, then the answer is no. If, however, you believe that there are some people whose history of criminal conduct is so egregious that they are beyond redemption, the answer is yes.

The jury trial of Robert Allen Anderson in May 1996 was my very first three-strikes trial. He was a biker in his forties, whose first two strikes were convictions for robbery and mayhem. The robbery stemmed from an incident where Mr. Anderson stabbed a victim in the face and then robbed him of his leather jacket. The mayhem charge was far worse. Most of us think that mayhem is a kind of destructive chaos, as portrayed by the character in the Allstate Insurance commercial named Mayhem, who wreaks havoc everywhere he goes. The legal definition of mayhem is slightly different: "Every person who unlawfully and maliciously deprives a human being of a member of his body, or disables, disfigures, or renders it useless, or cuts or disables the tongue, or puts out an eye, or slits the nose, ear, or lip, is guilty of mayhem." Think the infamous 1997 boxing match in Las Vegas between Mike Tyson and Evander Holyfield when, in the third round, Tyson bit off a piece of his opponent's ear. Or Lorena Bobbitt's act of mayhem in 1993, when she cut off her husband's penis. Mr. Anderson's mayhem took the offense to a new level—he kidnapped a woman, held her in a motel room, and tortured her by, among other things, tattooing her vagina with the words "This is mine."

Mr. Anderson's third strikes, the crimes that brought him into my courtroom, involved yet another woman whom he dragged into his car. Once inside the car, he pushed her head under the steering wheel, telling her, between beatings and biting her on the face and hand, that he was going to take her somewhere, slit her throat, and kill her slowly. She somehow managed to jump out of the car and run to a nearby house to call the police. After Mr. Anderson's unsuccessful attempts to break into the house, he took off in his car and was arrested shortly thereafter.

When I entered the courtroom for the start of the jury trial, I was taken aback by what I saw—a thin, long-haired White man whose arms and neck were covered with swastika tattoos. Mr. Anderson was a White supremacist. He was likely just as shocked and unnerved upon seeing me. I glanced over at Benita, who shook her head. There I sat, staring at an avowed racist to whom I was obligated to be fair and impartial. Could I? Did I even want to?

Several years earlier, in 1983, having been on the bench for about a year, I had presided over the case of two young men, twenty-year-old Donald Ferraro and his eighteen-year-old friend Romulo Alvarez. Both were charged with vandalism. I opened the court file and quickly skimmed the police report. I looked up at them, whereupon they quickly averted their eyes and looked to the floor; and well they should have. The report revealed that they had gotten the bright idea to burn a cross on the lawn of the home of a Black family and to paint "KKK" on the family's garage. I'm sure that they were thinking, *Of all of the judges on this court, we land in front of the one and only Black judge?* Yes, I was offended by what they had done; but more importantly, I wanted to know what exactly would possess two clean-cut White and Latinx boys in Silicon Valley to do this.

Judges are required to preside in an impartial and unbiased fashion. In California, the *California Code of Judicial Ethics* establishes standards for ethical conduct of judges on and off the bench, as well as for candidates for judicial office. The code consists of six canons, or key principles:

Canon 1. A judge shall uphold the integrity and independence of the judiciary.

Canon 2. A judge shall avoid impropriety and the appearance of impropriety in all of the judge's activities.

Canon 3. A judge shall perform the duties of judicial office impartially, competently, and diligently.

Canon 4. A judge shall so conduct the judge's quasi-judicial and extrajudicial activities as to minimize the risk of conflict with judicial obligations.

Canon 5. A judge or candidate for judicial office shall not engage in political or campaign activity that is inconsistent with the independence, integrity, or impartiality of the judiciary.

Canon 6. Compliance with the Code of Judicial Ethics.

It was canon 3 that gave me pause. Would I be able to perform my judicial duties "impartially"? Could I deal objectively with two young men who had committed racist acts against a Black family? Could I put aside my own experiences with racism and deal with them fairly? If I couldn't, the canon required me to say so in open court and then request that the case be assigned to another judge.

That morning, I had a courtroom full of people whose cases I had yet to hear, so I needed to decide what to do—right then. The very fact that I briefly wrestled with this issue signaled that I was aware of the possible bias I might be harboring. That was a good thing. My gut feeling was that the two were salvageable. I looked up from the file and told them that if they chose to plead guilty in my court, I would keep an open mind when it was time to sentence them, their racist conduct notwithstanding. After briefly conferring with their lawyers, each pled guilty to misdemeanor vandalism. I ordered them to return in a few weeks to learn their fate.

According to the police report, neither of them had a criminal record. After arguing with a young Black man, they decided to pull their cross-burning KKK stunt at his home. I believed that their conduct, while certainly hurtful to the Black family and offensive to me, was motivated less by racial hatred than by stupidity and immaturity. So, what does a judge do with two immature vandals? You send them to school.

Third World Cultures was a class offered at a nearby local community college. I tracked down the instructor and obtained his permission to allow them to attend the semester-long class. Five weeks later, when they stood before me to be sentenced, I told them that if they passed the course and wrote an essay for me on a subject relevant to the class, I would give them their get-out-of-jail-free cards. But if they failed the course, I would sentence them to serve thirty days in the county jail. I also ordered them to write letters of apology to the victims.

Even though the law permitted me to sentence them to up to one year in jail for the vandalism, it made no sense to me to incarcerate them. What good would come of cooling their heels in a jail cell for a month? Rather than lock up their bodies, I thought it better to unlock their minds. Because of judicial discretion, I could tailor the punishment to fit the crime

A few months later, at their final court appearance, they presented me with handwritten essays (both about Martin Luther King Jr., of course), along with a letter from the instructor stating that each had earned a passing grade of C. I didn't get the feeling that they were going to run out and become card-carrying members of the NAACP, and that wasn't my purpose. But, after reading what Mr. Ferraro said to a local newspaper reporter in an article about creative sentencing, I got the sense that choosing school over jail had been the right thing to do. "If I had gone to jail," he said, "I'd be more mad. It wouldn't have changed me the way the class did."

I could impartially deal with two cross burners; now I had to do the same with a swastika-tattooed White supremacist. Benita learned from her fellow bailiffs that Mr. Anderson had a history of acting out in court, yelling and banging his head on the table and walls. So, right off the bat, before jury selection began, I said to him: "I have one rule. When you are in *my* house, you show me respect and I, in return, will show you the utmost respect. Do we have an understanding?" He nodded and stared at me. I knew that it might be a different story when the victim took the witness stand.

The prosecutor announced that he might have to issue a "material witness warrant" to arrest and jail the victim, a key prosecution witness, who was in hiding out of fear of Mr. Anderson. She was terrified, and for good reason, given how savagely he had attacked her. Material witness warrants allow prosecutors to arrest and temporarily incarcerate reluctant witnesses, including victims. Leon Cannizzaro, New Orleans's district attorney, used these warrants so frequently that he became the subject of a 2017 lawsuit brought by victims of rape and child sex trafficking, who, on his orders, had been held in jail. One of the women, a mother of three, he jailed for five days to force her to testify against her abusive ex-boyfriend. Hands and feet shackled, the victim was brought into the courtroom wearing a jail-issued orange jumpsuit; her abuser was dressed in street clothes. After pleading guilty, he walked out of the courtroom, having received no jail time.

Mr. Anderson behaved throughout the weeklong trial. He kept his mouth shut, even through the compelling testimony of the terrified victim who had summoned the courage to show up voluntarily. On the advice of his attorney, Mr. Anderson exercised his Fifth Amendment right not to testify. After deliberating a tad longer than did the jurors in the O. J. Simpson trial, the jury found him guilty of everything—attempted kidnapping, making a terrorist threat, and assault with force likely to produce great bodily injury. When the verdict was read, Mr. Anderson returned to his ways, cursing out everyone in the courtroom, including me.

In late June, Mr. Anderson was back to be sentenced. Under the three-strikes law, I was mandated to impose a sentence of fifty-five years to life. *Yes, this was a very bad man who should be locked up for a long, long time,* I thought, *but for fifty-five years?* Twenty years, even thirty, would have been plenty. When I asked him if he wanted to say anything, he shook his head and said no. However, his wife had a lot to say. (Yes, throughout all of this, she remained with him.) She stood and told me that her husband was not a bad person, that she liked being tied up and whipped by him, as it was their way of showing affection to one another. She even handed me a letter of support that she had written on his behalf.

Their true love notwithstanding, I did what the three-strikes law required and imposed on Robert Allen Anderson the longest sentence that I had ever handed down. It took my breath away as I uttered, "I order you to serve fifty-five years to life in state prison." Escorted by two sheriff's deputies, Mr. Anderson slowly walked out of the courtroom; I stood and walked slowly to my chambers.

It has been famously written that "discretion is the better part of valor." Amid mounting criticism of judges by the public and by government leaders, the judicial exercise of discretion *is* valor. When judges consider legally acceptable alternatives and choose sentences that ensure that the punishment fits the crime and that the public is protected, they exhibit courage and hone true to the constitutional principle of judicial independence.

The Art of the Plea Deal

The Plea Bargain Dilemma

Necessity never made a good bargain.
—BENJAMIN FRANKLIN, AMERICAN STATESMAN

Crystal and Nathaniel, both African American, were in custody. She was a twenty-year-old mother of a two-year-old son; he was her twenty-three-year-old live-in boyfriend. In a last-ditch effort to see if both could be persuaded to accept plea bargains, they were in court with their attorneys to discuss the matter with me at a pretrial conference. It was a Tuesday in December 1996; their jury trial was set to begin the following Monday.

The facts of the case were disturbing: While Crystal was meeting with a vocational counselor, Nathaniel waited outside in a nearby park with her son. When she joined them at the park, Crystal noticed that her son's clothing was soiled and asked Nathaniel what happened. He told her that the boy had fallen while they were playing in the park. Later that evening, they rushed the child to the emergency room, where it was discovered that he had a broken arm, described by the physician as a spiral fracture caused by a twisting motion—not from playing in the park.

The hospital personnel called Child Protective Services, and shortly thereafter, Crystal's son was removed from her custody and placed with the biological father. Nathaniel was charged with child abuse for breaking the boy's arm. Crystal was charged with conspiring with Nathaniel to cover up what he had done after telling the police that it was *she* who caused the injury when she was changing the boy's clothes.

This was Nathaniel's second time around the block. Two years earlier, he had been convicted of child endangerment involving another child. In that case, the injury was a fractured skull. The mother (not Crystal) told investigators a story eerily similar to the one spun by Crystal—while changing her son's clothes, she had caused him to fall and hit his head. However, a medical examination concluded that the type of fracture the boy sustained—on the left side of his head with force coming from the right—meant that the injury could not have occurred from a fall. Rather, the diagnosis was that the skull fracture resulted from a right-handed fist that had connected to the left side of the child's head.

I was one of the few judges on our court who, with the agreement of the attorneys, engaged defendants in plea bargain discussions. Gaining permission from the lawyers was never a problem because both sides had the same objective—get the defendants to plead guilty so that they could move on to their next cases, of which there were dozens. The prosecutor and the defense attorneys were eager for me to work my plea bargain magic with Nathaniel and Crystal.

Plea bargaining has been a part of America's criminal justice system since the mid-1800s when, according to George Fisher in his book *Plea Bargaining's Triumph*:

> *Overworked prosecutors of the first three-quarters of the [nineteenth] century [plea] bargained in liquor and murder cases because rigid penalty schemes gave them the leverage they needed. So, too, overworked judges of the last quarter of the century turned to plea bargaining for relief from their out-of-control civil caseloads, because they had far greater power to coerce pleas on the criminal side than to induce settlements on the civil side.*

But it was not until 1970, in the case of *Brady v. United States,* that the U.S. Supreme Court officially sanctioned the practice. In order to avoid the possibility of facing the death penalty, Mr. Brady had pled guilty to a charge of kidnapping. The trial judge then sentenced him to fifty years in prison, a sentence that was subsequently reduced to thirty years. On appeal, he argued that his guilty plea was not voluntary since it was induced by the prosecutor's offer to remove the death penalty from consideration. The U.S. Supreme Court ruled against Brady, giving prosecutors and judges across the country the official go-ahead to have their way with plea bargains:

> *We would have serious doubts about this case if the encouragement of guilty pleas by offers of leniency substantially increased the likelihood that defendants, advised by competent counsel, would falsely condemn themselves. But our view is to the contrary, and is based on our expectations that courts will satisfy themselves that pleas of guilty are* voluntarily and intelligently made *by competent defendants with adequate advice of counsel, and that there is nothing to question the accuracy and reliability of the defendants' admissions that they committed the crimes with which they are charged. In the case before us, nothing in the record impeaches Brady's plea or suggests that his admissions in open court were anything but the truth.*

Today, defendants accept plea bargains and plead guilty in nearly *98 percent* of criminal cases in federal and state courts, leaving just 2 percent of defendants whose fates are determined by jury verdicts. Thanks to plea bargains, criminal jury trials, guaranteed by the Sixth Amendment's mandate that the accused "shall enjoy the right to a speedy and public trial, by an impartial jury," have gone the way of the wind.

The court's stamp of approval on plea bargaining was contingent upon the *voluntariness* of the guilty pleas. Today, prosecutors routinely pile on charges—many of them repetitive and unnecessary, increasing the potential time of incarceration—only to offer to dismiss them in return for guilty pleas that carry less prison time. Are those pleas voluntary? Of course not; they are coerced. And when this widespread practice of prosecutorial overcharging leaves *innocent* defendants with little choice but to accept plea deals, what then? In 1970, the Supreme Court gave us its answer in the case of *North Carolina v. Alford.*

Henry Alford was indicted for first-degree murder in 1963. On the advice of his attorney, he agreed to a plea bargain offered by the prosecutor wherein he would plead guilty to second-degree murder, thereby avoiding the death penalty. At the time of entry of his plea, the prosecutor summarized the evidence against him for the trial judge. Then Alford took the stand and testified that he had not committed the murder but instead that he was pleading guilty because he faced a threat of the death penalty if he did not do so. The judge accepted his guilty plea and sentenced him to thirty years in prison, the maximum for second-degree murder. Thereafter, Alford filed an appeal, claiming that his guilty plea was invalid because it wasn't voluntary but rather the product of fear and coercion.

In 1970, his appeal landed before the U.S. Supreme Court. A majority of the justices upheld Alford's plea of guilty, finding that "an individual accused of crime may voluntarily, knowingly, and understandingly consent to the imposition of a prison sentence *even if he is unwilling or unable to admit his participation in the acts constituting the crime.*" (Emphasis added.) In other words, it's perfectly legal to plead guilty in a plea bargain while simultaneously proclaiming your innocence. With its decision in *Alford,* the high court gave a green light to prosecutors to offer plea deals to defendants who maintain their innocence.

Throughout the country, so-called *Alford* pleas have become a staple of plea bargaining. Only Indiana, Michigan, New Jersey, and the federal courts prohibit their use. The U.S. Department of Justice, in 2000, noted that 17 percent of the 1.3 million women and men in our state prisons are there because of *Alford* pleas—that's 221,000 people serving time for crimes they say they did not commit.

Of course, there are those who maintain that they are innocent but, in fact, aren't. There are also many who profess their innocence and, in fact, they are. According to the National Registry of Exonerations, since 1989 there have been two thousand exonerations of defendants wrongfully convicted of serious crimes, including murder; *three hundred (15 percent) of them pled guilty to crimes they did not commit.* Some criminologists estimate that the overall rate of innocent defendants who plead guilty, whether by *Alford* pleas or not, is between 2 percent and 8 percent. But even if the percentage were just one percent of the 2.3 million inmates in state and federal prisons, that would mean more than twenty thousand defendants pled guilty when they were factually innocent. Alas, plea bargaining operates on the assumption that some innocent defendants will be wrongfully convicted.

Still, as recently as 2012, Associate Justice Anthony Kennedy lauded the practice, writing for the court: "To note the prevalence of plea bargaining is not to criticize it. The potential to conserve valuable prosecutorial resources and for defendants to admit their crimes and receive more favorable terms at sentencing means that a plea agreement can benefit both parties."

The U.S. Supreme Court's imprimatur notwithstanding, legal scholars continue to disagree about whether plea bargaining is beneficial or detrimental to the criminal justice system. Some see plea bargaining as a relief valve for our backlogged courts. I can't argue with that; prosecutors file so many cases (in my view, too many cases) that there are not enough judges and courtrooms in which to try them. Others view plea bargaining as coercive of the indigent and people of color, most of whom do not have the wherewithal to retain high-priced attorneys who, unlike overworked public defenders, have the time and resources to go toe-to-toe with prosecutors. I can't argue with that, either. But what is not in dispute is that for better or worse, "plea bargaining has not merely endured, but has grown to be the dominant institution of American criminal justice." And now, I was about to put my plea bargaining skills to the test, yet again.

Nathaniel's grandmother, in court to support her grandson, was in her early fifties. She had raised him and was clearly concerned about his welfare. I was glad that she was there because I hoped that she would be supportive of what I had to say to him. Clad in my robe and standing next to the jury box, I introduced myself and asked her to sit near me at the counsel table. Seated in the otherwise empty jury box were Crystal and Nathaniel, each in jail garb and handcuffed; their public defenders sat behind them with the prosecutor standing close by.

I presented the prosecutor's plea bargain to them: he was willing to offer Crystal misdemeanor child endangerment and a county jail sentence if Nathaniel were to plead guilty to felony child abuse and serve a maximum of four years in prison. (The minimum term of incarceration for felony child abuse is two years; the maximum is six. Four years is the midrange.) It was a package deal: both had to accept or no deal and they could go to trial. Crystal stuck to her story that she accidentally broke her son's arm, while Nathaniel continued to maintain his innocence. I didn't believe either of them; the medical facts just didn't fit their stories. So, I told Crystal that if she accepted the prosecutor's offer, I would sentence her to no more than six months in jail, even though the maximum time that I could impose was one year. Given that she had already been in jail for three months awaiting trial, in just ninety days she would be out of custody.

Then I told Nathaniel that if he pled guilty to the felony, I would sentence him to prison for either two years or four years, depending on what I learned at his sentencing hearing. I advised him that even though I would not be the judge to preside over his trial, it was a certainty that if he chose to testify, the prosecutor would question him about his prior conviction for child abuse, and if that were to happen, he could forget it. No jury would believe him. Then I told him: "Look, it is a real possibility, Nathaniel, that if you are convicted at trial, the prosecutor will argue for maximum time, and, knowing the judges who might be assigned to preside at your trial, a sentence of six years is a very real possibility." I waited a moment to let my words sink in. Then I said, "I believe that you injured Crystal's son. Don't you think it is time to fess up and deal with what you've done?" His lawyers sat silently, nodding their heads in agreement; Nathaniel's grandmother looked at me, then directly at her grandson.

Visibly shaken, Nathaniel stared at me for a few seconds; then he asked to speak to me alone, with only his attorney present. With everyone's agreement, the three of us moved away to the opposite end of the jury box, putting us a few feet from everyone. With Nathaniel's attorney now sitting next to him, I leaned over the edge of the jury box and quietly asked, "What is it you want to say to me?" Silence. It was a full minute before he softly uttered, "I want to say . . . I want to tell you . . ." At this point, tears streaming down his face, he said, "I want to say, I did it. I did it." He hung his head and sobbed; his attorney was ashen faced. Because I needed to understand just what he was admitting to, I asked, "What exactly did you do, Nathaniel?" More silence and then: "I guess I lost it. He wouldn't get off the swing when I told him to, so I grabbed his arm and I guess I twisted it too hard. . . . I'm so sorry."

I walked over to Nathaniel's grandmother and sat in the chair next to her. When I told her that Nathaniel had admitted breaking the child's arm, she shook her head and then asked if she could talk to him. As we walked over to Nathaniel, I prayed that she would continue to be supportive of him. What he didn't need right now was a tongue-lashing. My prayer was answered. She stood in front of her grandson and said simply, "I love you, Nathaniel, no matter what."

After a few more minutes of discussion to firm up the terms of the plea bargain with the attorneys, I sat at the bench and began the process of closing the deal. Following the standard questioning by me to ensure that Crystal's guilty plea was voluntary and that she understood that she would have another ninety days to serve in jail, she quickly pled guilty to the misdemeanor. Nathaniel was next. Because he cried so hard that he could barely speak, it took me nearly twenty minutes to question him about his guilty plea. At one point, I asked him if he really wanted to go forward and plead guilty; he insisted that he did. The moment finally came when I asked, "Nathaniel, what is your plea to one count of child abuse, a felony?" He looked at me and said, "Guilty."

There are many instances when plea bargains are lawful and fair—not just for the defendants but, as importantly, for their victims. That was the case when I set out to persuade Kenny Jackson to accept a plea bargain. Mr. Jackson, a handsome thirty-one-year-old Black man, was born with profound hearing loss. In August 1996, after sitting in jail awaiting trial for over a year, Mr. Jackson was in my court, facing fifteen counts of molesting his young stepdaughter. The molestation charges included fondling and digital penetration over a period of two years, beginning when the child was eight years old. The supervising judge assigned me this case with the urgent directive to secure a guilty plea; should the case proceed to trial, he didn't want the court to incur the expense of providing a special monitor and recording system to accommodate Mr. Jackson's hearing disability. I, however, was far less concerned about our court's budget than I was about ensuring that the now twelve-year-old girl would not be forced to describe to fourteen strangers in a jury box (twelve jurors and two alternates) what Mr. Jackson had done to her because, according to the prosecutor, she was acutely depressed and understandably terrified of testifying.

If convicted of all of the charges, Mr. Jackson would face a maximum of 120 years in prison. After some prodding by me, the prosecutor was willing to offer him, in return for his guilty plea, fourteen years and lifetime registration as a sex offender. So, I went to work. At my request, Mr. Jackson's mother was in the courtroom; I wanted her there should her son want to talk to her. We started discussions at 9:30 that morning, and five hours later, after lots of tears from his mother and my explanations (all in writing) to Mr. Jackson about why he should accept the plea bargain, he did. His twelve-year-old victim would not have to testify and could rest assured that her stepfather no longer posed a threat.

It was no coincidence that defendants of color and their attorneys wanted to appear before me, the only Black judge among a sea of White jurists in a criminal court system overflowing with African American and Latinx defendants. *Judge Cordell will make this racist system operate fairly. She can be trusted. She's a sister. She gets who I am.* The power of that racial connection is enormous.

I knew from experience the importance of connecting to someone in authority who looked like me, especially at those times in my life when I was feeling most vulnerable. When I first arrived at Stanford Law School in 1971, one of just a handful of Black law students, I was overwhelmed by the prestige of the institution and by the reputations of its brilliant professors, not one of who was female or African American or any color other than White. My comfort level, on a scale of one to ten, hovered just above minus twenty. I felt entirely isolated. Would my White classmates see my presence here as legitimate? Would I pass muster? Had the school erred by admitting me? More importantly, had I just made the biggest mistake of my life by coming to Stanford?

My fears were dispelled at least in part when, shortly after I arrived, I knocked on the door of the law school's assistant dean, Thelton Henderson. There he was, this African American lawyer and Stanford administrator, later to become a celebrated federal court judge, who smiled and welcomed me into his office. It was then that I knew that I was going to be okay. I was no longer alone; I had a protector. Thelton assured me that I would do fine, and I believed him. I trusted this man who told me without hesitation that I belonged there. Throughout my Stanford stay, Thelton Henderson was always there for me. And during my judicial career—and to this day—it has been Judge Henderson to whom I have turned when I have needed counsel and guidance. From the halls of academia to the halls of justice and beyond, race matters.

My tenure on the criminal court bench was a conflicted one. By simply donning my robe, I knew that I lent legitimacy to a system that disproportionately targeted people of color. The majority of cases over which I presided involved defendants who looked like me. My presence on the bench gave defendants of color hope that they would be seen not as a bunch of gangbangers, thugs, and drug addicts but as human beings; and it would allow for the possibility that many, perhaps most, were better than the worst crimes they had ever committed. One of my life's sad recognitions is that it is far easier to understand the humanity of even the most egregious of offenders when that person resembles you—less so when she does not.

It was October 1998 when I first laid eyes on Leo Hill, a three striker facing a mandatory life sentence. He had been brought from the jail to my courtroom for pretrial discussions with the prosecutor, his defense attorney, and me. The judge before whom a defendant pleads guilty is always the sentencing judge. Mr. Hill's public defender, aware of my reputation for judicial independence, wanted him to plead guilty in my court in the hope that I would dismiss one of Mr. Hill's strikes, thereby taking a life sentence off the table.

Leo Hill was African American, forty-four years old, about 5'9" with a stocky build and a shaved head. He earned his first two strikes in 1981 when he stabbed a woman to death and assaulted her brother. The three had spent the day drinking heavily when an argument among them escalated into a physical altercation. The woman attacked Mr. Hill with a pole, whereupon he grabbed a knife and stabbed her in the heart, killing her. The woman's brother then fought with Mr. Hill, knocking him unconscious. Mr. Hill was convicted of two felonies—involuntary manslaughter in the death of the woman and assault of her brother. He was sentenced to seven years in prison. After serving three years of his sentence, he was released on parole.

Seventeen years later, in 1998, Leo Hill was back; it appeared that little had changed. Mr. Hill and the new woman in his life engaged in a drunken argument. After he punched her several times, she grabbed a screwdriver to defend herself. He fled but shortly thereafter was captured by the police. As he was being transported to jail, Mr. Hill yelled from the patrol car: "I should have killed the bitch! I've done it before!" *Scary guy,* I thought as I read the police reports.

In the pretrial discussions with his defense attorney and the prosecutor, I learned that after Mr. Hill's release from prison in 1982, he had married a stable and upstanding woman. When he returned to his violent drinking episodes, she divorced him. Then he began a rocky relationship with the woman he assaulted in the case now before me. That relationship had deteriorated to the point where Mr. Hill, after experiencing suicidal thoughts, checked himself into a psychiatric hospital.

Following his arrest for the third strike, Mr. Hill resided in the county jail for over a year. During that time, he was a model inmate, obtained his G.E.D., and successfully completed every educational and rehabilitation program that the jail had to offer (anger management, alcohol and drug recovery). And he found God, a fairly common discovery among inmates. Still, I entertained the possibility that Mr. Hill had, in fact, undergone a genuine transformation. Perhaps his long stint in jail had done the trick. I didn't know; more information was needed. But before I could worry about sentencing him, Mr. Hill had to agree to plead guilty. It was time for a pretrial conference.

Mr. Hill and I went back and forth at his pretrial conference that afternoon. He was terrified of pleading guilty to a third strike and just as terrified of going to trial. He repeatedly implored me to guarantee that if he were to plead guilty, I wouldn't impose a life sentence. I repeatedly told him that I couldn't do that because I did not have all the facts and because each side had the right to weigh in at the time of sentencing. I told him:

> *I can't guarantee you anything other than that I will seriously and objectively look at your case. Yes, I have dismissed strikes in the past, but there are also cases in which I haven't. Should you plead guilty, your attorney will have the opportunity to present evidence to me at a hearing to demonstrate why I should dismiss your strikes. And the prosecutor will have the chance to argue to me that I shouldn't do so. Your case is a difficult one, for sure. I know that you have made strides while in the jail, but at the same time, your strikes are serious ones, as is your current offense. So, I don't know what I'll do. But you need to know that if you are convicted at trial, it is the trial judge who must sentence you, and it won't be me. Most judges on our court will not consider dismissing strikes, so you will likely face a mandatory life sentence. At least with me, you have a chance. But, in the end, it's your call.*

His strikes involved violence of the worst sort—murder and a violent assault. I couldn't yet say what impact, if any, the seventeen-year gap between his crimes would have on his sentencing. Nor did I yet have the facts to assess if his professed transformation was genuine.

My pretrial discussions with Mr. Hill went on for several weeks until there was nothing left to say. At pretrial conference number four, I told Mr. Hill that the discussions were over. Now he had to choose—plead guilty in my court or go to trial in another judge's courtroom. I retreated to my chambers and waited. A few minutes later, Benita told me that everyone was ready. I returned to the courtroom. With his attorney by his side, Leo Hill told me that he had decided to plead guilty and roll the dice with me at his sentencing. The man looked absolutely petrified, while the attorneys looked relieved. They could now cross this trial off their lists of things to do. I knew that the judges on my court would be pleased that one more case had been deleted from our overloaded criminal trial docket. Benita nodded her approval. And Olga, my courtroom clerk, proudly placed yet another call to the clerk's office to report that her judge had just settled her umpteenth criminal case. The Queen of Pleas had done it again.

It was the week before Thanksgiving, 1999, when Mr. Hill returned to my courtroom. I had earlier ordered that he undergo a psychiatric evaluation. Before I could read the evaluation, Mr. Hill changed his mind and told me that he wanted to go to trial. He asked to withdraw his guilty plea.

Motions to withdraw guilty pleas are frequently used as stalling tactics by defendants. I don't hold it against them; I'd do the same thing if I were looking at the possibility of a life sentence. When I asked him why he had changed his mind, Mr. Hill told me that he had relied on the advice of his attorney to plead guilty and now believed that he had been provided incompetent representation. I can't tell you how many times I've heard that one. Because he had called his lawyer's competence into question, I was required to hold a separate hearing to consider this claim, and I was required to appoint a different lawyer to represent Mr. Hill for this inquiry. So, I postponed his sentencing.

Mr. Hill's newly appointed attorney went right into action by filing a formal motion to withdraw Mr. Hill's guilty plea. But this time the reason wasn't because of a malfunctioning lawyer; this time it was *my* fault. The lawyer claimed that I had promised Mr. Hill that if he pled guilty, I would not impose a life sentence; and he wanted me to honor that promise or allow his client to have a trial. All of my pretrial discussions were held in open court at which both lawyers were present. Since all guilty pleas must be recited in open court and on the record, a simple review of the transcript of the proceeding would establish that I made no such guarantee.

But before I could rule on that request, the attorney filed yet another motion. This one was to disqualify me from ruling on Mr. Hill's request to withdraw the guilty plea! His reasoning went like this: Because I had personal knowledge about the circumstances of Mr. Hill's guilty plea, I should not be the one to decide if he should be allowed to withdraw that plea. In other words, I knew too much. Of course I had personal knowledge about Mr. Hill; I was the one who talked to him about his plea, and I was the one before whom he had pled guilty in open court. That is precisely why the law requires that the judge who takes the guilty plea is the same judge who must rule on a request to withdraw that plea. The attorney then requested a continuance to prepare for the hearing. I sighed and, preferring to err on the side of caution, gave him his continuance. The stalling continued. There were more continuance requests that I reluctantly granted. It was not until early April 2000, a year and a half after his first appearance in my court, that I finally held the hearing on Mr. Hill's motion to disqualify me; I denied it.

With that decision, I was now ready to rule on Mr. Hill's motion to withdraw his guilty plea based on the claim of incompetent counsel. His lawyer asked me for yet another continuance, explaining that he had just hired an expert witness to testify about how incompetent Mr. Hill's first attorney had been. However, the expert was presently unavailable, thus the need for a continuance. I had to hand it to this lawyer for coming up with every imaginable way to delay the case. I gave him the continuance, this time to early May. God, I wanted this case to be over. In May 2000, I finally held the hearing on the incompetency of Mr. Hill's first attorney. I denied his motion, ruling that Mr. Hill's first attorney was competent;

Mr. Hill could not withdraw his guilty plea. Then I set Leo Hill's sentencing hearing for September 2000.

Under the three-strikes law, Mr. Hill faced a mandatory sentence of fifty-five years to life. By including some of Mr. Hill's felony convictions dating back to 1978, the district attorney's office had found a way to add thirty years to the minimum three-strikes sentence of twenty-five years to life. So, with a fifty-five-year-to-life sentence, Mr. Hill, now forty-six years of age, would most certainly die in prison. If, however, I were to dismiss one of the strikes, I could fashion a sentence of, say, twenty or twenty-five years—time enough for his crimes. Leo Hill would walk out of prison a senior citizen and no longer a menace to society. But there was one obstacle. I had to have a legal basis to dismiss Mr. Hill's prior strike convictions. Leo's attorney argued that there was; the prosecutor argued that there wasn't.

On September 7, 2000, just one month shy of two years after Mr. Hill first pled guilty before me, the day of reckoning finally arrived. There was nothing left for me to do but to proceed with the sentencing hearing. I cannot remember being more upset about a case than I was that afternoon. Actually, my distress began the night before. Having reluctantly come to the conclusion that the narrow constraints of the three-strikes law likely didn't permit me to dismiss one of Mr. Hill's strike convictions, I hadn't slept. There was the extreme violence of his two prior strikes and his lengthy alcohol- and drug-induced criminal history, all of which argued against the dismissal of his strikes. At times like this, I hated my job. I dreaded enforcing a draconian law that stopped me from imposing a fair and just sentence on Mr. Hill. Twenty years in prison was sufficient punishment for a man who had done what very few inmates do—undertake genuine rehabilitative work involving anger management and alcohol and drug treatment during a two-year stay in the county jail.

The responsibility for filing charges rests exclusively with prosecutors; judges have no say in those decisions. And prosecutors have unfettered discretion to dismiss charges; they do it all the time when they make plea bargains. Judges, too, can dismiss charges. However, their ability to do so is strictly limited to a narrow set of circumstances defined by decisions of the California Supreme Court. Since I had concluded that none of those circumstances existed in Mr. Hill's case, I couldn't legally dismiss one of Mr. Hill's strikes; but his prosecutor could. I had one final card to play.

In contrast to the rabid law-and-order types I frequently encountered in the DA's office, this prosecutor was compassionate and thoughtful. If I had to, I'd get down on my knees and beg her to dismiss one of Mr. Hill's strike convictions.

I met with the attorneys in my chambers shortly before the sentencing hearing on September 7, 2000, and explained that I did not believe that I had the legal authority to dismiss a strike, but that if I could do so, I would. I explained that a twenty-year or even twenty-five-year sentence was appropriate, and that, considering Mr. Hill's positive work over the preceding two years, the fifty-five-year-to-life sentence demanded by the DA's office was egregiously disproportionate. I gave it everything I had, but the prosecutor had her marching orders—no deal for Mr. Hill. My hands were tied; I had nowhere to turn.

When we entered the courtroom, Mr. Hill was handcuffed and, under Benita's careful watch, seated at the counsel table next to his public defender. I had spoken to Benita frequently about this case; she understood how deeply I had agonized over this decision. As I took my seat at the bench, I looked at her and shook my head, signaling that I had failed. She knew what was coming, should his reaction require her attention, Benita quietly walked over to Mr. Hill and stood directly behind him. I watched as he sat silently during the final arguments of the attorneys. His public defender presented the testimony of a psychiatrist who, after evaluating Mr. Hill, testified that he was a man who had issues with women, had low self-esteem, and when on drugs, could be violent. Not much there that I didn't already know. But he also confirmed Mr. Hill's transformation in the jail as being genuine. Leo Hill was a model prisoner who appeared to be a new person. The prosecutor was unmoved. She forcefully maintained that since I had no authority to dismiss his strikes, and since she wasn't going to, either, I had no choice but to sentence him according to the three-strikes law.

Finally, it was my turn. My voice cracked as I slowly pronounced the sentence:

> *I believe that a sentence of fifty-six or fifty-five years to life is a dispro-portionately harsh one, given the facts of this case and the positive steps that Mr. Hill has undertaken while in custody to turn his life around. I have asked and the prosecutor has declined to reduce or dismiss either of the charges. I respectfully and strongly disagree with the prosecutor's decision. I am required as long as I wear this robe to abide by my oath of office to faithfully uphold and apply the law even when that appli-cation is not to my liking. I will, therefore, reluctantly impose upon Mr. Hill the sentence required by law.*

When I handed down the fifty-five-years-to-life sentence, Mr. Hill, to my relief and to his credit, said not a word. As Benita walked him back to the holding cell, I sat there and thought, *The law is an ass and I am its rider.*

As was my habit, on my hour-long drive home from the courthouse, I used the time to wind down, scroll through the day's events, and then let everything go. That day, I didn't wind down and I couldn't let go. Pulling into my driveway, I realized that I couldn't do this anymore. The Queen of Pleas was done. Five months later, after nearly twenty years, I left the bench for good.

Fast-forward to 2014, fourteen years after Mr. Hill's sentencing and more than a decade after I had retired from the bench, when I received a phone call from a man named David Martin, Leo Hill's appellate attorney. I was stunned by what he told me. In June 1999, fifteen months *before* I sentenced Mr. Hill, the California Supreme Court had ruled in the case of *People v. Garcia* that a trial judge lawfully dismissed a strike in a case that was eerily similar to the facts of Mr. Hill's case. In *Garcia*, the sentencing judge had dismissed the defendant's strike for a prior criminal conviction and then sentenced him to thirty-one years and four months to life in prison. The supreme court ruled that the judge did not abuse his discretion by doing so.

Had I been aware of the decision in the *Garcia* case, perhaps I could have dismissed one of Mr. Hill's strike convictions and imposed a twenty-five-year-to-life sentence, which would have made him eligible for release in twenty-five years instead of fifty-five. But there was a problem. The law presumes that the sentencing judge knows the law; this sentencing judge didn't. I was completely unaware of the *Garcia* decision. Neither the prosecutor nor the public defender had brought the case to my attention. Since the case would have benefitted his client, surely his lawyer would have told me had he been aware of it. Did the prosecutor know of the *Garcia* case? If she did, was she legally obligated to tell us? Probably not.

Federal trial court judges have their own law clerks to research legal issues that arise over the course of trials and hearings and to keep them current on decisions handed down by the appellate courts. Due to budgetary constraints, most state trial judges don't have that luxury; they are pretty much on their own. Their court calendars are packed with cases and there is little time for them to read up on recent appellate court decisions or to peruse legal periodicals. So, what they are left with are annual and semiannual judicial gatherings sponsored by state judges' associations where there is frequently more schmoozing than educating.

The only assistance I could rely on was from my legal interns, students at nearby law schools who were permitted to spend a semester observing court proceedings and occasionally assisting me with research. However, my ability to secure law school interns on a regular basis was hit-or-miss. When I presided over Mr. Hill's case, it was a miss.

No matter, I had blown it. I felt terrible and told Mr. Martin so. To my relief, he believed that there was still some hope because his appeal hinged on two things: (1) the ineffective assistance of counsel by Mr. Hill's public defender's failure to raise the *Garcia* case at the sentencing and (2) the ignorance of the trial judge, aka me. Mr. Martin intended to argue to the appellate court that if I had known about the *Garcia* case, I would have relied on it to impose the lesser sentence. In other words, I needed to admit my ignorance—in writing. This wasn't about ego; I had messed up and now I had the opportunity to make it right. Mr. Martin asked me to write a declaration under penalty of perjury admitting my error and asserting that had I known about the decision, I would have dismissed one of Mr. Hill's strike convictions and imposed a lesser sentence. On April 15, 2014, I sent my declaration to Mr. Martin.

Two years later, in 2016, I learned that the appellate court had reduced Leo Hill's fifty-five-year sentence to thirty-six years. He will be eligible for release in 2037, when he is eighty-three years old.

Since 1989, 2,507 men and women who served a combined twenty-two thousand years in prison have been exonerated. One hundred fifty-six of those exonerees were sentenced to death. As quickly as the criminal justice system churns out wrongful convictions, the wronged churn out lawsuits, and the wrongdoers churn out multimillion-dollar settlements. To date, municipalities have forked out $2.5 billion to settle claims brought by the wrongfully convicted, forcing some to consider bankruptcy.

But in a startling and disheartening twist, municipalities are now using plea bargains to force the wrongfully convicted to relinquish their rights to sue. For example, in 1997, four Indigenous Alaskan men, dubbed the Fairbanks Four, were convicted of the murder of a White teenager. Eighteen years later, when evidence of police misconduct surfaced, prosecutors offered them a plea bargain—dismissal of all charges and immediate release from prison in return for their agreement not to file a lawsuit against the state. Reluctantly, the Fairbanks Four took the deal. In an email, a former prosecutor wrote that if all four did not accept the plea bargain, the state could "face exposure of tens of millions of dollars."

And there was Jimmy Dennis who spent twenty-five years in solitary confinement on death row for a 1991 murder he did not commit. After decades of appeals, in 2013 a federal court judge found that the Philadelphia prosecutor's office concealed evidence that supported Mr.

Dennis's alibi. The judge in that case was clear: Mr. Dennis "was wrongly convicted of murder and sentenced to die for a crime in all probability he did not commit." In 2016, a federal appeals court directed prosecutors to give Mr. Dennis a new trial or set him free. They did neither. Instead, prosecutors offered him a plea bargain: plead "no contest" to third-degree murder and walk out of prison a free man or remain in prison to await a retrial that would likely not begin for years. (A no contest plea means that even though the person is not contesting the charge, the plea is still considered to be a guilty plea.) Understandably, Mr. Dennis chose to accept the plea deal. After his release, he still filed a civil lawsuit seeking compensation for his twenty-five years of confinement. However, in response, the city of Philadelphia successfully argued that because the plea bargain included a no contest plea, there was no affirmative finding of Mr. Dennis's innocence, and without that finding, his lawsuit could not proceed. A Hobson's choice if ever there was one—heads, the prosecutors wins; tails, Mr. Dennis loses. Freedom for the wrongfully convicted and their right to seek compensation must never be plea bargained away.

CONCLUSION

The Fix

Ten Suggestions for Reform

If the system is broken, my inclination is
to fix it rather than to fight it.
—SONIA SOTOMAYOR, UNITED STATES SUPREME
COURT ASSOCIATE JUSTICE, *MY BELOVED WORLD*

Over the course of writing this book, the country was disrupted by two major events—the Covid-19 pandemic and the police murder of George Floyd. The emergence of Covid-19, and with it California's shelter-in-place requirement, served to buttress the discipline I needed to complete my writing. The murder of George Floyd, on the other hand, had no such upside. While I have been blessed with the capacity to focus on whatever matter is at hand, there are times that national events derail my self-discipline. The nine-minute twenty-nine-second killing of George Floyd was one such event. I allowed myself the time to mourn his and so many other senseless deaths and to focus more intensely on the need not just to reform but also to reimagine our legal system—a system created by the founders of this nation, White men, some of them slave owners, who demanded equality and justice for all who looked like them. Unsurprisingly, then, the administration of justice in America has, for years, fallen short of its promise of equal justice under the law. Bad lawyers, bad jurors, bad judges, uninformed and indifferent voters, opportunistic legislators, and the unconsciously biased all conspire to produce a legal system that way too often does more harm than good for people of color and poor people of any color.

In writing about my experiences as a Black woman jurist, I have described decisions that I rendered, some of which I regret. But judges must take an oath to uphold all of the laws, even those laws with which they disagree. I dutifully adhered to that oath; as a consequence, I was obligated to impose sentences under California's three-strikes law and the state's felony murder rule, laws that I believed were draconian and unjust. With this book, I acknowledge my role in this legal system—the good, the bad, and the ugly. In so doing, I encourage all of us—legal and non-legal people alike—to call out the inequities in our system, be they in our criminal courts, our juvenile courts, our family courts, our traffic courts, or our small-claims courts. To that end, I offer ten suggestions to restore or replace some of our legal system's broken parts.

1. Broken: Law School Training

The standard law school curriculum includes courses on criminal law, civil and criminal procedure, torts, wills and estates, constitutional law, as well as a growing number of clinical programs where students, under the guidance and supervision of their professors, represent clients or write appellate briefs. When I was a law student at Stanford, I had the opportunity to take a clinical course in juvenile law. Under the supervision of Professor Michael Wald, a pioneer in the field, I represented minors in court proceedings. As a result of appearing in court and actually winning a few cases, I knew that I wanted to be a litigator. I loved the adrenaline rush of cross-examination and the challenge of thinking on my feet. Today, clinical education programs are offered at many of the nation's law schools on subjects as varied as international human rights, environmental law, and immigrant rights. Yet, not one law school offers a clinic on judging, even though law school graduates compose the exclusive pool from which judges are chosen.

The Fix: Clinical Education Courses for Judging

Small-claims cases are civil lawsuits where plaintiffs sue defendants for money. In California, the highest amount that can be awarded in small-claims court is $10,000. (When I presided, the upper limit was $5,000.) Importantly, no attorneys are allowed—think *Judge Judy*. It's mano a mano in small-claims court—the perfect venue to involve student judges. So, in February 2001, I created the nation's first clinical program for judging (possibly still the only one) by inviting six second-year law students from a local law school into my courtroom and onto the bench to preside over small-claims trials.

After I assured the litigants that while the students would conduct the trials, I alone would be the decider, they signed waivers allowing the students to hear their cases; not one litigant declined. It helped that the then-presiding judge was supportive and appreciative of the benefits of the program, telling a local reporter: "It's a great experience for the students, and I would imagine that the litigants will get a more thorough review of these cases. These cases are very important to the parties who bring them, and it helps us to get some of our work done with no cost to the court."

Since it was left to the students to conduct the trials, I provided them copies of the court files in advance, giving them ample time to prepare. I sat "second chair," right next to the student-judge who took my seat at the bench. When I felt that an issue had not been sufficiently covered in their questioning of the litigants, I'd pass the student a note or whisper some advice. At the conclusion of each trial, I brought the students into my chambers for a group discussion about the applicable law and the facts established by the evidence. I also critiqued how they handled each trial. For example, reflecting society's gender stereotypes, I found it necessary to encourage some of the female students, who tended to be soft-spoken and a bit timid, to be more forceful when addressing the litigants. Conversely, I cautioned some of the male students about being too cocky and aggressive in their questioning of the parties. As the students presided over the trials, their transformations were amazing. The women became more assertive and the men less arrogant.

With input from the students, I ruled in each case and then assigned to each student-judge the task of writing an opinion that explained the rationale for the decision in each of her or his trials. I reviewed and then signed the rulings, which were then filed with the court, with copies mailed to the litigants.

As revealed by their comments to a local reporter, for the law students—three females and three males—judging was an eye-opener. A student who presided over a dispute between two neighbors about who should pay for the damage caused by a toppled willow tree noted, "I just got really caught up in what the defendant and the plaintiff were saying because this is really meaningful to them." Another said, "I was really impressed with the amount of flexibility you have here from the bench. In law school, we only read about court settings most of the time and they all seem very regimented." And a third student who heard a dispute about the refund of a rent deposit, commented, "Even though my case was really easy because of the terms of the contract, it was still kind of like getting on a roller coaster because things started coming fast and furious. The experience was a once-in-a-lifetime opportunity." And the best part—this life-changing experience came at no cost to the court.

One month after we started this clinical program, I retired from the bench. Unfortunately, if not surprisingly, neither the court nor the law school was interested in continuing it. Systems are resistant to change and innovation; the legal system is no exception.

2. Broken: The Selection and Retention of Judges

When their terms expire, all state court judges must face the voters—in contested or retention elections. In either scenario, money rules. According to Alicia Bannon of the Brennan Center for Justice at New York University School of Law, "As of January 2017, 20 states had at least one justice on their supreme courts who had been involved in a

$1 million election. And during the 2015–16 election cycle, more justices were elected in $1 million-plus elections than ever before. Outside spending by special interest groups—most of which do not disclose their donors—also shattered previous records."

Politicians seek office by promising to do the voters' bidding. Judges are not politicians; the only promise they make is to uphold the Constitution. However, the influx of millions of dollars into judicial races has blurred the line between the two. The influence of campaign cash has seriously jeopardized fair and independent decision-making in the judiciary; contested elections and retention elections of judges must end.

The Fix: Replace Judicial Elections with Independent Nominating Commissions

I was lucky. California governor Jerry Brown opened the door to my judicial career with an appointment to the municipal court. Six years later, as recounted in "Judges for Sale," I won a contested election for a seat on the superior court. While the election process worked for me, it is not ideal. Having experienced both selection systems—gubernatorial appointments and contested elections—I believe that the recommendation of the Brennan Center for Justice for nominating commissions is a good one. The center has proposed utilizing governors to choose judges from a short list of nominees put forward by state nominating commissions or boards. According to the center, "Nominating commissions should be bipartisan, appointed by diverse stakeholders, include non-lawyers, and have clear criteria for vetting candidates. The nominating process should be open and transparent, with publicly available data about the diversity of applicants and nominees." Sixteen states already utilize this approach, so we know that it works. However, in two of those sixteen states—Maryland and California—their governors can ignore their commissions' recommendations and choose someone not on the lists of nominees. That practice should end. Governors should stick to the nominee lists; otherwise, these commissions are simply window dressing.

If contested elections and retention elections are eliminated, an argument can be made that voters will no longer be able to hold judges accountable. After all, if a judge makes a decision that voters don't like, they should have the opportunity to weigh in and express their dissatisfaction by voting for the judge's challenger in a contested election or by voting no when the issue on the ballot is whether the judge should be retained.

But, in fact, with a nominating commission process, voters are able to hold judges accountable. Under this system, when their terms expire, judges who desire to be reappointed are reevaluated by the commissions in a forum that is open and transparent. A significant part of those reevaluations involves feedback from litigants, lawyers, jurors, and other members of the public who have observed the judges' courtroom demeanor and their decision-making. The fact that governors who appoint these judges are, themselves, elected officials provides another level of accountability. If voters are unhappy with their judicial appointments, governors will hear about it at the ballot box.

While a transparent nominating process isn't perfect, when compared with the obscene spending on judicial campaigns with their misleading and inflammatory attack ads on radio, television, and social media, nominating commissions are a far better option. And because they eliminate the exorbitant costs to states and counties of running contested elections, these commissions may end up saving taxpayer dollars.

But as long as states and local governments insist on conducting contested and retention elections, they must do a better job of educating voters. Voter guides should include detailed profiles of the judicial candidates; and in those jurisdictions where judges are evaluated by attorneys, the results of those evaluations should be posted online for all to see.

Temperament, legal acumen, fairness, demeanor, decision-making ability—characteristics so important in judging—must be a vital part of the judicial vetting process. For this reason, in addition to the letters of recommendation, character references, background checks, and in-person interviews that compose the standard evaluation procedures, I believe that lawyers seeking an appointment to the bench should be required to audition for the job. By serving as judges pro tem (judges for a day) in small-claims trials, they can be evaluated by nominating commission members.

As I wrote in "Bitten by the Judge Bug," the idea of becoming a judge first came to me after I volunteered to preside over a small-claims trial as a judge pro tem, an experience that gave me a modest but realistic view of what judging involved. I came away from the experience convinced that the bench was for me. An on-the-job audition for aspiring judges should be required in the judicial evaluation process; it would provide a forum to evaluate the candidate in action.

3. Broken: The Recall of Judges

Independence is the hallmark of the judiciary. It ensures that decision-making adheres strictly to the law, free of the influence of public whim, political pressure, and monied special interest groups. Indeed, every judge—state and federal—takes an oath to uphold the law and to bear true faith and allegiance to the Constitution. As demonstrated by the removal of California judge Aaron Persky in 2018 (described in "J'Accuse!"), the recalls of state court judges have frequently veered from their intended purpose; today, recalls are a direct threat to judicial independence.

Recall is a mechanism by which voters hold accountable state court judges who engage in misconduct, and that's a good thing. But when recalls target judges for engaging in *lawful*, albeit controversial decision-making, as was the case with Judge Persky, suddenly judges start looking over their shoulders rather than at the evidence. The consequences of frivolous recalls are disastrous not only for the judiciary but also for our democracy.

The Fix: Limit Judicial Recalls to Specific Grounds

As I noted earlier in "J'Accuse!" Georgia and Montana strictly limit judicial recalls to instances of judicial malfeasance or failure to perform duties of the office, or to a judge who has been convicted of a serious crime. Significantly, recalls in these two states can never be based on a judge's lawful decision, be it discretionary or mandated by the law, no matter how controversial. With this commonsense approach, misbehaving judges are held accountable and the independence of lawful judicial decision-making is preserved. The states that allow the recalls of judges should model their laws on Georgia's and Montana's recall legislation. And if state legislators are unwilling to do so, voters can enact such laws on their own through the initiative process. Utilized in twenty-four states and the District of Columbia, initiatives allow citizens to place legislation and/or amendments to state constitutions on the ballot, allowing them to vote directly for their passage.

4. Broken: Judicial Disciplinary System

Bad judges, who compose but a tiny minority of the nation's more than thirty thousand state court judges, are a fact of life. Each state has a judicial disciplinary system in which judges accused of misconduct are investigated, given opportunities to be heard, and, if found to have misbehaved, punished. But because there is little to no transparency, members of the public don't know much about their respective states' disciplinary systems, and they know even less about who these bad judges are and what it is they have done. As I noted in "Bad Judges," in the thirty-five states that close all or a portion of their disciplinary proceedings to the public, 97 percent to 99 percent of the complaints against judges are dismissed. The secrecy surrounding these proceedings breeds mistrust, leading inevitably to diminished faith in the judiciary.

The Fix: Bring Transparency to Disciplinary Proceedings

Judges are public servants whose salaries are paid by taxpayers; when they are brought before disciplinary boards for misbehaving, the public has a right to know. Every state should open its judicial disciplinary hearings to the public by allowing in-person attendance at the proceedings and providing video streaming. Additionally, annual reports of all sustained complaints against judges should be issued in a timely fashion and posted online for public viewing. The reports should include the judge's name, a detailed description of the misconduct, the discipline imposed, and a clear rationale for the chosen punishment. You can't build trust in the dark; lifting the shades on judicial discipline is a good place to start.

5. Broken: Juror Compensation

Jury duty is an important civic responsibility, so why is juror compensation so meager? As I noted in "Thank You for Your Service," juror pay, ranging from nothing to $50 per day, is given short shrift by state courts and legislatures. Individuals who give of their time, energy, and attention to serve as jurors in courtrooms across the country deserve better.

The Fix: Establish State Jury Funds to Compensate Jurors

In only a handful of states are employers required to pay the salaries of their employees who serve on juries; and when they pay, it is only for a limited amount of time—usually no more than three days. Thereafter, employee-jurors are on their own.

When businesses can afford to do so, full-time and part-time employees who are called for jury duty should continue to receive their salaries and benefits. Multimillion-dollar companies such as Apple, Facebook, Google, and Uber, all of which spend extraordinary amounts of court time and money resolving disputes, can well afford to pay the salaries of those employees who are on jury duty; I would require them to do so. Conversely, small- and medium-sized businesses that cannot compensate their absent employees without suffering substantial financial hardship should be absolved from having to provide this compensation. Instead, their employees, along with unemployed and retired jurors, could be compensated from a state jury fund that would pay these jurors their state's minimum hourly wage. Funded, in part, by court fees and contributions from corporations, a state jury fund would send the important message that jurors matter.

6. Broken: Juvenile Trials

In the 1971 case of *McKeiver v. Pennsylvania*, the United States Supreme Court held that the Sixth Amendment's guarantee of a jury trial in criminal proceedings does not apply to juveniles; only adults have this right. This means that an eighteen-year-old charged with a serious crime is entitled to a jury to decide his fate, but a fifteen-year-old facing the identical charge is not. In both instances, their felony conviction records follow them for the rest of their lives, including lifetime sex offender registration for certain sex crimes. Juveniles accused of crimes, felonies, or misdemeanors have but one option—a court trial where the judge is the jury. The rationale offered by the U.S. Supreme Court in *McKeiver v. Pennsylvania* that judges are better fact finders than jurors is magical thinking.

The Fix: Mandate Jury Trials in Felony Prosecutions of Juveniles

Because felony convictions, unlike misdemeanors, can result in lengthy periods of incarcerations, a good place to start is by requiring that juveniles charged with felonies be given the right to trial by jury. Judges and prosecutors, those most likely to oppose this approach, will argue that there is neither sufficient time nor resources—courtrooms, judges, staff—to handle an onslaught of juvenile jury trials. But at least eighteen states would disagree. As I noted in "Making a Murderer," these eighteen states already require or allow jury trials for juveniles. When the state expends its time and resources to file felony charges against a juvenile, it is morally obliged to expend its time and resources to convince a jury that those charges are true. One day the United States Supreme Court will revisit its decision in the *McKeiver* case; until then, the states should take the lead and allow juveniles accused of felonies the option of jury trials.

7. Broken: The Felony Murder Rule

The felony murder rule, utilized in forty-five of the fifty states, makes murderers of people who have killed no one. It is invoked by prosecutors when a death results during the commission of certain felonies, even if that death is unforeseeable. In "Making a Murderer," I explained why the felony murder rule required me to convict sixteen-year-old Jessica T. of murder, even though she wasn't present when the crime was committed and had no idea that a murder would even occur. In no other country is this nonsensical felony murder rule practiced.

Murder is a specific intent crime, which means that the perpetrator must intend to kill the victim. However, under the felony murder rule, prosecutors are relieved of the burden of proving intent to kill. The felony murder rule is an antiquated legal doctrine that perpetuates injustice because it mandates that those who did *not* commit the crime do the time.

The Fix: Abolish the Felony Murder Rule

Five states—California, Michigan, Massachusetts, Hawaii, and Kentucky— have abolished the felony murder rule because it holds unequally involved parties equally accountable and punishable. This unjust law should be abolished nationwide. If state legislatures won't do it, then voters can make it happen by utilizing the initiative process.

8. Broken: Life Sentences for Juveniles

In "Les Enfants Terribles," I described the United States Supreme Court decisions that abolished life sentences without the possibility of parole for juveniles convicted of *nonhomicide* crimes and banned mandatory life sentences without parole for juveniles who were convicted of murder. However, in twenty-nine states trial judges still have the discretion to impose sentences of life without the possibility of parole on juvenile killers. I believe that condemning adolescents to life in prison is immoral.

It has been documented that the expense of housing juveniles serving life sentences without parole is prohibitive. According to The Sentencing Project, "a 50-year sentence for a 16-year-old will cost approximately $2.25 million."

As is the case throughout the criminal justice system, racial disparities in imposing life sentences are glaring. Again, according to The Sentencing Project, "While 23.2% of juvenile arrests for murder involve an African American suspected of killing a white person, 42.4% of JLWOP [juvenile life without parole] sentences are for an African American convicted of this crime. White juvenile offenders with African American victims are only half as likely (3.6%) to receive a JLWOP sentence as their proportion of arrests for killing an African American (6.4%)."

The Fix: Abolish Life Without the Possibility of Parole for All Juvenile Offenders

Trial judges should not be allowed to use their discretion to impose sentences of life without the possibility of parole on juveniles convicted of homicides. Banning judicial discretion in these cases does not mean that those who committed murder when they were juveniles will be, willy-nilly, let loose from prison. Quite the opposite; it simply means that after serving considerable time in prison, they will have the opportunity to petition parole boards for their release. For example, in California, inmates who were incarcerated as juveniles must serve fifteen to twenty-five years before they have the opportunity to argue before parole boards for their release. As U.S. Supreme Court associate justice Kennedy acknowledged in 2016, "allowing those offenders to be considered for parole ensures that juveniles whose crimes reflected only transient immaturity—and who have since matured—will not be forced to serve a disproportionate sentence in violation of the 8th Amendment." The discretion to sentence juvenile offenders to life without the possibility of parole, whatever their crimes, is discretion that judges should not be permitted to exercise.

9. Broken: Peremptory Challenges

As I mentioned in "Thank You for Your Service," peremptory challenges allow lawyers to dismiss a certain number of potential jurors without stating why. If their peremptory challenges are suspected of being racially motivated, lawyers must offer race-neutral reasons to explain why they dismissed the jurors. In 1989, Associate Justice Thurgood Marshall decried racial bias in peremptory challenges, writing that peremptories are "perhaps the greatest embarrassment in the administration of our criminal justice system." I agree.

In my view, there are three ways to approach the dilemma posed by peremptory challenges: (1) leave the system of peremptory challenges as it is, (2) abolish peremptory challenges, or (3) enact legislation that will uncover racial bias in peremptory challenges.

The Fix: Enact Legislation to Uncover Racial
Bias in Peremptory Challenges

Peremptory challenges provide incentives for lawyers to lie—to judges and to themselves—about their real motives for dismissing jurors. In 2001, district attorneys in North Carolina were offered a seminar about how to create race-neutral explanations to use in the event that their peremptory challenges of potential Black jurors were contested. Included in the seminar materials was a startling handout titled "Batson Justifications: Articulating Juror Negatives" that instructed prosecutors how to portray behaviors stereotypically associated with African Americans as antiprosecution. (*Batson v. Kentucky* was the 1986 landmark case in which the United States Supreme Court ruled that peremptory challenges must not be based on race.) Among the list of "race-neutral" excuses on which prosecutors could base their racially motivated peremptory challenges were "attire may show lack of respect for the system; rebelliousness," "hairstyle may mean resistance to authority," and "arms folded, air of defiance, lack of eye contact with Prosecutor, and obvious boredom." A legal system that purports to stand for justice and fairness is incompatible with peremptory challenges that too frequently encourage racial discrimination. The status quo is not an option.

Eliminating peremptory challenges entirely isn't a good option, either. As a criminal defense attorney, when I had a bad feeling about a potential juror but couldn't put my finger on exactly why, I used a peremptory challenge to excuse him. If prosecutors and defense attorneys are to effectively represent their clients, they must have some latitude when selecting juries and some comfort with jurors they have selected.

In 2009, North Carolina's legislature passed the Racial Justice Act that allowed inmates on death row to seek life sentences without the possibility of parole—if they could prove that their jury trials were tainted by racial bias. The improper use of racially based peremptory challenges was fair game. However, in 2013, the state's Republican-controlled legislature revoked the law; shortly thereafter, the four death row inmates whose sentences had been converted to life without parole under North Carolina's Racial Justice Act were returned to death row—but, perhaps, not for long. In June 2020, the Supreme Court of North Carolina unanimously ruled that because one hundred death row inmates had filed their claims for review of their sentences *before* the act had been repealed, they can have their day in court to demonstrate why they should be resentenced to life without the possibility of parole.

California assemblyman Ash Kalra authored a proposal for a Racial Justice Act (AB 2542) that "prohibits the State from seeking or obtaining a criminal conviction, or from imposing a sentence, based upon race, ethnicity or national origin." His bill would require trial judges to hold evidentiary hearings when it is claimed that racial bias was a factor in a criminal trial or in sentencing. The act also makes it a violation if "race, ethnicity or national origin was a factor in the exercise of peremptory challenges, whether or not purposeful." As importantly, the legislation gives to judges the ability to remedy the influence of racial bias. So, for example, when peremptory challenges are proven to be racially motivated, judges can reinstate the wrongly excluded juror, declare a mistrial, order a new trial, or continue jury selection with a new jury pool. Will judges and prosecutors find the evidentiary hearings required by AB 2542 to be time-consuming? Yes. But the pursuit of justice takes time. Will some judges fail to see racial bias, even when it is proven at these evidentiary hearings? Sure. But that's why there are appellate justices to review and, when appropriate, correct improper rulings. Racial justice acts, like that one authored by Assemblyman Kalra and signed into law by California's governor on September 30, 2020, have a chance to restore the peremptory challenge to a legitimate place in our criminal justice system. May other states soon follow California's lead.

10. Broken: Plea Bargaining

The Sixth Amendment to the U.S. Constitution guarantees that "in all criminal prosecutions, the accused shall enjoy the right to a speedy and public trial, by an impartial jury." Yet, as a consequence of defendants agreeing to prosecutor-initiated plea deals, where they admit guilt to charges that offer less time in jail or prison, 97 percent of all criminal prosecutions in the United States end without trials. In "The Art of the Plea Deal," I make it clear that plea bargaining is a fact of life in America's legal system. In the words of U.S. Supreme Court Associate Justice Anthony Kennedy, "Horse trading [between prosecutor and defense counsel] determines who goes to jail and for how long. That is what plea bargaining is. It is not some adjunct to the criminal justice system; it is the criminal justice system." Judges, prosecutors, and defense attorneys are all in on it. With too many cases and too few courtrooms in which to try them, plea bargains are the criminal justice system's relief valves; without them, our criminal justice system would implode.

There are benefits to plea bargaining: For defendants, it removes the uncertainty of a trial verdict. For the courts, it frees up courtrooms and staff for trials where plea bargains have been rejected. For prosecutors, it is a powerful negotiating tool that allows them to dismiss some charges as a way to induce defendants to plead guilty.

But there are serious downsides to plea bargaining: Defendants who accept plea deals don't get their day in court. Defendants who reject plea bargains and instead opt to go to trial frequently face harsh punishment from judges, angry that they refused offers to plead guilty. And then, there's the innocence dilemma.

In "The Art of the Plea Deal," I wrote of the case of Henry Alford who, in order to avoid the death penalty, accepted a plea bargain and pled guilty to second-degree murder, all the while insisting on his innocence. The U.S. Supreme Court ruled that the Mr. Alford's plea bargain was proper because there was overwhelming evidence of his guilt and because he benefitted by avoiding the death penalty. But, as importantly, the court gave this warning: if it became evident that plea bargaining was being used more broadly to create incentives for questionably guilty defendants to "falsely condemn themselves," the entire institution of plea bargaining and its constitutionality would require reexamination.

The time has come to reexamine the entire institution of plea bargaining and its constitutionality. Today, *Alford* pleas—utilized in every state, with the exceptions of Indiana, Michigan, and New Jersey—play a major role in plea bargains. They allow defendants to plead guilty while, at the same time, declaring their innocence. I accepted many an *Alford* plea during my time on the bench. Typically, when a plea bargain was worked out, the defendant, in response to my question "How do you plead to the charge," answered, "Your honor, I plead guilty pursuant to *Alford* because I do not want to take the risk of being convicted at trial." I had no choice but to accept the plea, find him guilty, impose a sentence, and move on to the next plea bargain.

A compelling study suggests that the *Alford* plea has created a serious innocence problem for plea bargaining. Professors Lucian Dervan and Vanessa Edkins re-created the "innocent defendant's dilemma" by presenting two difficult choices to students who had to make decisions in the same "mentally anguishing way" that defendants in the criminal justice system make. The participants in the study, seventy-six American college students at a small technical university in the Southeast, were accused of cheating on an exam in a special class for which each had signed up. In fact, only two of the students had cheated. However, all were told that they had two options: admit that they had cheated or argue their innocence before a faculty review board. If they were to take the "deal" and plead to cheating, they would lose the compensation that had been promised to them for their participation in the class. If, however, they insisted on their innocence, each would be required to present the case to a faculty review board. Should the board find the student guilty of cheating, the punishment would include not only the loss of the promised compensation but also notification to the student's faculty adviser and enrollment in a semester-long ethics course that required completion of a paper and a final exam. Finally, the students were told that the faculty review board found 80–90 percent of the students guilty.

The study revealed that *56 percent* of the *innocent students* accepted the plea deal over facing the faculty review board, leading the researchers to conclude: "The study participants' actions appear to be directly mimicking a phenomenon that has drawn much debate and concern in recent years: the students appear to have been selecting 'probation' and immediate release rather than risking further 'incarceration' through forced participation in a trial and, if found guilty, 'confinement' in an ethics course or seminar. In essence, the study participants simply wanted to go home." This study, published in 2013, strongly suggests that plea bargaining's innocence problem is not an exaggeration.

The Fix: End Coercive Plea Bargains

Plea bargains are manipulated by prosecutors. They charge unnecessary and redundant offenses only to offer to dismiss them in exchange for guilty pleas. District attorney offices must cease this coercive practice; it is antithetical to the Sixth Amendment's guarantee that all defendants have the right to trial by jury. If they won't, then voters should hold elected district attorneys accountable at the ballot box.

In the meantime, there are things that judges can do to counter this abusive policy. As recounted in "Judicial Discretion," when prosecutors were being unduly heavy-handed, I pushed back by reducing felonies (wobblers) to misdemeanors, something that judges can do when the circumstances warrant. And because sentencing is the exclusive province of judges, when prosecutors overcharge and demand harsh sentences, judges can, when appropriate and legally permissible, offer defendants more lenient ones.

Prosecutors expect judges to do their bidding—and many judges do. When judges don't, prosecutors aren't pleased. I know firsthand that being on the receiving end of a prosecutor's anger is anything but pleasant. It takes courage for judges to stand up to them. But given their oaths to uphold the sacred principle of equal justice for all, if not judges, then who?

In My End Is My Beginning

Progress is measured not by how far we have come,
but by how far we have yet to go.

—UNKNOWN

I was always a sucker for clarity. Nuance and subtlety always felt like luxuries to me. Perhaps this is a legacy of being Black in America: too many struggles to overcome to spend time obsessing about procedure. Or maybe it was just in my nature to be a pragmatist who worried more about getting things done than about the elegance of the process. Whichever it was, I tended to see the world as black or white. I think that was part of what attracted me to the law: things were right, or they were wrong. So, when I went off to law school, I knew that my path would lead to my being the defender of all things righteous. By the end of my first year at Stanford, I had hints that my plan might not be so clear-cut. In law school, students are assigned to argue both sides of any given position, suggesting that the law might be more complex than my naive construct had allowed for. This became painfully clear when, as a third-year law student, I was in a small seminar taught by Barbara Babcock—the school's first and at the time only female professor. (Barbara was a brilliant lawyer and professor who, until her death in 2020, was my dear, dear friend and mentor.) In one of the classes, she gave us a hypothetical: Two college students witnessed a classmate cheating on an exam. They confronted her and the classmate, a Black female, admitted that she had, in fact, copied another student's answers. She told them that because she worked two part-time jobs, she hadn't been able to keep up with all of the classwork. Professor Babcock asked us if the students should report her to the college administration.

To a person, my White classmates said that the woman should be given a break and the college students shouldn't report her. As I sat and listened to them, I thought, *What is wrong with these people?! Are they serious?* Finally, I couldn't contain myself. "There's nothing to discuss here. She broke the rules and that's it. She was wrong, and she should face the consequences." At that, Barbara chuckled and gave me her you've-got-a-lot-to-learn-kiddo look. She was right, of course. But back then, I had neither the time nor the patience for such talk. Besides, academia seemed to always concern itself with arcane matters that had little to do with the real world.

For six years I practiced criminal law with but one goal—to represent my clients to the best of my abilities, which I did with a modicum of success. But once I ascended to the bench, my notion of the law's blackness and whiteness quickly faded to grayish. Determining what was legal or illegal wasn't the end but the beginning; I was also required to consider what was just and fair.

I quickly learned that judging is as much a test of one's character and courage as it is a test of one's command of the law. Not long into my judging career, I presided over a criminal case in which, following a routine traffic stop, a police officer searched the defendant's car and found a kilo of cocaine in the trunk. The defendant's public defender contested the search, claiming that the officer should have obtained a search warrant before looking in the trunk of the car. Moreover, the defendant had not consented to the search, and the officer had no inkling that the defendant was engaged in any criminal activity. The officer's suspicion that something might be amiss was based solely on the defendant's black skin. He was right about the drugs; but I knew that if I granted his motion and suppressed the evidence—a kilo of cocaine—the defendant would waltz out of the courthouse, free as a bird. I also knew that the district attorney's office would pitch a fit and that the media would have a field day—JUDGE GIVES DRUG DEALER A PASS! In the end, I followed the law, ruled that the search violated the defendant's Fourth Amendment right against unreasonable search and seizure, ruled that the kilo of coke could not be used as evidence, and dismissed the case. The blowback that I predicted was fast and furious. I subsequently learned that I had made it on to the district attorney's so-called Unusual Occurrence list, akin to Nixon's Enemies List, where I would remain for the duration of my judicial career.

Did I always demonstrate judicial courage during my time on the bench? I didn't. Two cases that I heard in 1993 haunt me to this day. One involved a Black defendant who had served eight years in federal prison for the theft of several trailer loads of goods. Not long after his release from prison, he was caught committing the same offense and convicted in state court. For his sentencing hearing, the probation department recommended that since he had committed a similar crime shortly after being released from prison, a maximum term of twelve years in state prison was warranted. The second sentencing before me that same day was that of a young White defendant convicted of bank robbery—his sixth in a string of robberies committed over a period of several weeks, five of which he had pulled off in a neighboring county. (He hadn't been armed and instead passed notes to the bank tellers.) For five of the robberies, he had been sentenced to just one year in the county jail and permitted to serve the time in the county's work furlough program, spending nights in jail and days at his job. Our probation department recommended that I similarly sentence him to one year in the county jail for his sixth robbery, the case before me.

I wouldn't have been troubled by the recommended sentences if both defendants had been White or if both had been Black. The serial bank robber was young, had no weapon, and had no prior criminal history, so prison wouldn't have been appropriate for him. Conversely, the thief was an older man who, after eight years in prison, immediately reoffended; a return to prison was appropriate. But they weren't the same race. I was certain that if their crimes had been reversed—had it been a Black man convicted of six bank robberies—in no way would he have received a one-year county jail recommendation from the probation department. To the contrary, a Black serial bank robber, even one with no criminal history, would have almost certainly been looking at a lengthy prison sentence. Did I speak up and let the probation officer know how I felt? Did I say that there appeared to be a double standard in play? Did I direct them to reconsider their recommendations? Nope. I followed the probation department's recommendations and sent the thief to prison for ten years and the bank robber to jail for twelve months.

Race has always been the elephant in the courtroom. I recall suggesting at a court personnel committee meeting in 2000 that the protocol for hiring the court's traffic court and small-claims commissioners include a statement encouraging cultural and gender diversity. One of the judges, a White male, yelled at me: "This is an insult! What's a minority?! We don't need to state anything about that! People know that's what we want!" I was taken aback and responded, "I am insulted that you would even raise this as a problem! If everyone understood that cultural diversity on this court is important, we wouldn't be in the poor shape we're in today!" There was silence, followed by a lot of throat clearing and averting of eyes. I waited for the two judges of color in the room (both Asian American) and the court's only two female judges to speak up and say something like: "You go, girl!" Instead, what I got was silence. As we left the meeting, a judge whispered to me: "Don't give up on this. We need this." I looked at him and asked, "Why are you whispering?"

With the murder of George Floyd in May 2020 and the dramatic rise of the Black Lives Matter movement, racial disparities—long apparent in criminal prosecutions, sentencings, and incarcerations across the country—are finally front and center in the public discourse. The elephant has exited the courtroom and entered the world stage, giving to judges not only permission but also the obligation to call out the legal system's failings. On June 8, 2020, Louisiana Supreme Court justice

Bernette Joshua Johnson, an African American woman, published an open letter, writing:

> *I readily admit our justice system falls far short of the equality it espouses. And I see many of its worst injustices meted out in the criminal legal system. Inequities there range from courts being funded with fines levied on poor, disproportionately African American defendants, to our longtime use of Jim Crow laws to silence African American jurors and make it easier to convict African American defendants. We need only look at the glaring disparities between the rate of arrests, severity of prosecutions and lengths of sentences for drug offenses in poor and African American communities in comparison to those in wealthier White communities, to see how we are part of the problem. Is it any wonder why many people have little faith that our legal system is designed to serve them or protect them from harm? Is it any wonder why they have taken to the streets to demand that it does?*

When I stepped down from the bench in 2001, I had concerns similar to the ones expressed by Louisiana's chief justice.

I love the law. Being a lawyer and then a judge were my callings. But try as I might, in my attempts to address the legal system's failings from within, I remained frustrated. Once I retired, I vowed that if the opportunity were ever to present itself, I'd try to remedy them from without.

It was 2:17 P.M. on September 8, 2009; I had been retired from the bench for eight years. As Judge Peter Espinoza entered his Los Angeles courtroom, I rose and stood next to Kelly Turner, a Black woman in her early forties. The judge took his seat and said, "This is a hearing on a writ of habeas corpus of sorts. I'm in receipt of all the pleadings, obviously. They've been reviewed in preparation for today's hearing."

Three years earlier, I had written an op-ed against California's draconian three-strikes law for a local newspaper that came to the attention of

Montel Williams, host of a popular national television talk show based in New York City. I accepted his invitation to appear on the show and in September 2006 I went there and talked about my view of the law. The other guests on his show were two Black women whose sister, Kelly Turner, was in her eleventh year of a twenty-five-year-to-life sentence for a third strike—possession of a stolen check in the amount of $144.

When I returned to California and to my job as a vice provost at Stanford University, I couldn't get Kelly's situation out of my head. The injustice of Kelly's life sentence for a $144 third strike was exactly why I was so opposed to the three-strikes law. I objected to the law when I was on the bench, but other than trying to soften its blow at sentencing hearings, I hadn't been able to make any meaningful change to it. Now, as a private citizen and no longer muzzled by judicial canons, here was an opportunity for me to do more than write an op-ed. If I couldn't change the law from the inside, I could fight back by getting someone out from under it on the outside. I had no idea that this fight would go on for more than two years.

In January 2007, I made the three-hour drive to the women's prison in Chowchilla, California. Seated in the large and noisy cafeteria-like visitors' room filled with female inmates and their visitors, many of whom were little children, Kelly and I sat together at a small table and spoke for two hours. I learned that she grew up in Los Angeles, the youngest of three sisters, each of whom had a different father. Mr. Turner, the man who ended up being the man known as "Daddy" to all three sisters, was a cocaine addict and a drug dealer; their mother was an alcoholic. The two parents sold stolen property out of the family home in what became a very lucrative fencing operation. Mrs. Turner was an angry woman who focused most of her rage on Kelly, a chubby little girl, whom she had nicknamed "Kelly-fat-belly." Once, when ten-year-old Kelly failed to respond quickly enough to her mother's summons, her mother kicked her out of the house. Later that night, when Kelly's father came home and found her outside, he tied her to a tree in the front yard and thrashed her with several tree limbs. It got worse. Six years later, her mother pointed a loaded gun at sixteen-year-old Kelly and ordered her out of the house. Neighbors called the police who, accompanied by a SWAT team and helicopters, allowed Kelly to gather her clothes and leave. Her mother wasn't arrested nor was she charged with any crime. Not surprisingly, Kelly's life then took a downward spiral into alcohol and thefts. Several arrests and stints in jail were followed by more arrests and even longer stints in prison.

In February 1997, a few months after Kelly was sentenced to life in prison under the three-strikes law, her mother took her own life, overdosing on pills and alcohol, leaving a suicide note in which she wrote that Kelly's life sentence had devastated her. The prison's warden denied Kelly's request to attend the funeral.

Once I confirmed the details about Kelly's upbringing with her two sisters, I began my quest for her freedom. Mind you, I had left the bench six years earlier and hadn't been in a courtroom as a lawyer for twenty-five years. I was a fish out of water—out of breath but ready to fight. First, I enlisted a San Francisco corporate attorney, Roy Bartlett, as my co-counsel, and then I recruited as experts and advisers a forensic psychiatrist, a highly respected retired appellate judge, and an equally respected appellate attorney, all of whom donated their time to this undertaking. Perhaps the most important member of our team was my former law clerk, Kathryn Collier—by then a gifted appellate attorney—who held my hand and guided me through several rewrites of my section of the legal pleadings that we would file. After *eight* attempts, Kathryn finally gave me her approval; I had produced what I consider to be my finest piece of legal writing.

In August 2009, after two years of researching and writing, we completed a petition for a writ of habeas corpus, a request for Kelly's release due to a sentencing error, and lodged it with the Los Angeles County Superior Court. By then, she was in her fourteenth year of incarceration for possessing a stolen check. A few minutes before the hearing started, I walked over to the bailiff, a White man in his late forties, and told him that I was a retired judge and that I would like to speak to Kelly before the start of the hearing. "Of course," he told me, whereupon he directed both Roy and me through two doors to his left. We walked in and there stood Kelly in the small holding cell. I hadn't seen her since my visit to Chowchilla in 2007; this was Roy's first time with her. Kelly wore a jail-issued blue top, pants, socks, and plastic flip-flops; she looked terrified. I placed the palm of my hand against the bars of the cell and asked her to put the palm of her hand against mine and to look at me. Then, speaking calmly, I told her that in just a few minutes, we would sit in front of a judge and that all she had to do was listen to him. Looking at me, she nodded.

When the bailiff brought a handcuffed Kelly into the courtroom, he directed her to sit in the chair next to me at the counsel table. Seated to my right was Roy, and to his right was the prosecutor, Brent Ferreira. Judge Espinoza spoke. "Are you Kelly Turner?" "Yes, sir." "The court calls for the record the matter of the *People v. Kelly Turner*. Counsel, state your appearances." "Brentford Ferreira for the people." "Roy Bartlett with Covington and Burling for petitioner Kelly Turner. Also, with me at the counsel table is retired judge LaDoris Cordell." Judge Espinoza looked at me and the following exchange occurred:

Judge: Have we met?
Me: Pardon?
Judge: Have we met?
Me: We may have.
Judge: Where are you retired from?
Me: Santa Clara County.
Judge: When did you retire?
Me: 2001.
Judge: Okay. Well, welcome to Los Angeles County.
Me: Thank you.

Judge Espinoza looked down at the court file at his bench and firmly uttered the words that for two years Roy and I had worked so hard to hear. "Okay. If it's agreeable with all of the parties, it would be my plan to grant the habeas and resentence the defendant." I nudged Kelly with my arm and whispered, "He's going to rule in your favor." Kelly lowered her head and said nothing. Judge Espinoza continued, "Ms. Turner is to receive credit for time served, and she's ordered released from the custody of the California Department of Corrections and Rehabilitation. Good luck to you." Kelly smiled and said, "Thank you, sir," to which Judge Espinoza responded, "You're welcome." As we sat there in silence, as his ruling sank in, the judge looked at us, smiled, and said, "You can clap if you want." Kelly's two sisters and a handful of Kelly's supporters who were in attendance clapped, hooted, and cried. Kelly turned to them and with tears running down her face, nodded and smiled.

After Roy thanked the judge and the attorneys in his law firm who provided him assistance, I stood and with tears in my eyes told the judge: "Please know that I've devoted my professional life to public service and to the judiciary because of my belief in our system of justice. Your decision granting our habeas petition and your resentencing of Kelly reinforces that belief, and for this I thank you."

It's been more than a decade since Kelly's release from prison and two decades since I left my life on the bench. Writing this book has given me the opportunity to reflect on that life and, as importantly, to examine the legal system that defined my work. Created by propertied, slave-holding White men, the system did not envision women, people of color, LGBTQ individuals, and poor White males as beneficiaries of the principal constitutional guarantees of due process, equal protection, and fair trials. As a result, judges impose sentences that populate our jails and prisons with disproportionate numbers of Black and Brown people; prosecutors use peremptory challenges with abandon to whitewash juries; and our state and federal benches are primarily the province of White males. These are the consequences of a legal system predicated on exclusion.

In "The Fix," I propose ten ways in which judges, law schools, and legislators can begin the work of instilling fairness for all participants in state court proceedings; and I suggest steps we can take to bring transparency and meaningful, diverse representation to our state court benches. Judging has been the most fulfilling of my various careers. For nearly twenty years, I wielded power over the lives of thousands of people. And for nearly twenty years, I did what I believed to be right. While it is up to the next generation of voters, politicians, activists, lawyers, law professors, and judges to continue to clear the path to a more perfect union, I refuse to give up on our legal system, and I will *never* give up on our judiciary—hopefully, neither will you.

Acknowledgments

I am grateful to Stanford professor Arnold Rampersad who, early on, encouraged me to write a memoir. I thank my childhood friend and Stanford professor Paulla Ebron for connecting me to Kathy Chetkovich, who connected me to one of my favorite authors, Jonathan Franzen, who connected me to Susan Golomb, his literary agent.

Susan, thank you for agreeing to take me on as your client, for believing in my story, for guiding me through the proposal process, and for bringing Celadon and my fabulous editor, Jamie Raab, into my life.

Jamie, I so appreciate your wisdom, your wonderful literary sensibilities, and your editing genius that ensured my voice would be heard throughout the book. Thanks, as well, to assistant editor Randi Kramer for your patience and your spot-on editing advice. I am grateful to the Celadon staff for their work promoting *Her Honor*, among them, Anna Belle Hindenlang and Christine Mykityshyn. To Josh Rubins (my favorite literary lawyer) and to Peter Prato (my favorite photographer), thank you both for using your wonderful skills to put the finishing touches on the book.

I am fortunate to have family who were encouraging of me during the year that it took me to write *Her Honor*. To my sister, Roxanna Wright; my niece, Carla Garrison; my older daughter, Cheran Ivery; my cousin, Renee Jenkins; and my grandchildren, Cayla and Jayden Eason, thank you all for being there for me. To my younger daughter, Starr Lopez, your nearly daily heartfelt words of support meant the world to me. To Quetzalsol Lopez (my awesome son-in-law), to Claude Offenbacher (my brother-from-another-mother), to Tobias and Anthony Keller (my faux sons), and to Devoya Mayo (my daughter-from-another-mother)—I treasure your words of love and friendship.

I am surrounded by a circle of friends whose support proved invaluable in the writing of *Her Honor*. Big thanks to Carla Germano (my wonderful yoga teacher), Bobbie Green (my lovely yoga buddy), Jodi Gandolfi (my fabulous piano teacher), Monica Williams (my awesome pickleball partner), and Henry Organ (my wise and compassionate advisor).

I was also lucky to have two successful authors in my corner. Early on, I was guided by biographer and friend Edie Gelles, who sat patiently with me and gave me suggestions about the writing process. And once I had actually embarked on this writing adventure, Susannah Cahalan, the author of two brilliant books, was there for me throughout. She guided me in the proposal-writing process, gave me terrific editing suggestions, and celebrated with me when I completed the manuscript. Susannah, your selflessness, your generosity, and your friendship I shall forever cherish.

Barbara Babcock, the first woman to be tenured at Stanford Law School, was my teacher, mentor, and dear friend. Even as she was losing her battle with cancer, Barbara volunteered to read and edit some of the chapters in *Her Honor*. Several of her editing suggestions I have included in the book. It was a blessing to have Barbara in my life and a gift to have her contribute to *Her Honor*.

To my parents, Clara and Lewis Hazzard, I owe you everything that I am, and everything that I wrote. Had you not saved the weekly letters that I sent to you over my last eight years on the bench, there would be no book. I miss you so much, but I take solace in the belief that you would have gotten a real kick out of reading *Her Honor*.

Finally, to Florence O. Keller, my muse and the love of my life, thank you for taking the time to read and edit the multitude of drafts that made this book a reality. What a team are we. I couldn't have written *Her Honor* without you.

Index

CELADON
BOOKS

Founded in 2017, Celadon Books, a division of
Macmillan Publishers, publishes a highly curated list
of twenty to twenty-five new titles a year. The list of
both fiction and nonfiction is eclectic and focuses
on publishing commercial and literary books and
discovering and nurturing talent.